11617

The Strawberry Hill Set

by the same author

The Strawberry Hill Set

HORACE WALPOLE AND
HIS CIRCLE

❖

Brian Fothergill

faber and faber
LONDON·BOSTON

First published in 1983
by Faber and Faber Limited
3 Queen Square London WC1N 3AU
Phototypeset by Wyvern Typesetting Ltd, Bristol
Printed in Great Britain by
Redwood Burn Ltd, Trowbridge, Wiltshire
All rights reserved

© *Brian Fothergill, 1983*

British Library Cataloguing in Publication Data

Fothergill, Brian
The Strawberry Hill set.
1. Walpole, Horace
I. Title
828'.609   PR3757.W2
ISBN 0-571-10609-9

Library of Congress Data has been applied for.

To
Owen Meijas Gordon

Contents

Illustrations

Plates 1, 2 and 6 are reproduced from photographs copyright of the Paul Mellon Centre for Studies in British Art.

Preface

This book is about Horace Walpole and his friends, or some of his friends to be more exact, for he was a man of many friendships. It does not set out to be a biography of Walpole, but in writing about a person's circle of acquaintances one must, of necessity, write something of that person himself. 'Tell me thy company,' said Cervantes, 'and I will tell thee what thou art.' In the case of Horace Walpole certain of his friends have an unique interest in that they were the recipients of his letters, or they influenced him, or were influenced by him, in his capacity as an acknowledged arbiter of taste. Walpole's correspondence was so vast, and is now available in more complete editions than ever before, that the need to know something of the people to whom his letters were addressed becomes a matter of increasing concern. What sort of men and women were they, and what was the nature of their various relationships with him? The people whose lives are recorded in this study all reflect one or other aspect of Walpole's multifarious interests, and therefore by implication throw some special light on different facets of his character, illuminating his personality as well as their own. They have been chosen to demonstrate his interests in art and architecture, in court and political intrigue, in literature and connoisseurship, in antiquity, in the social life of his time and in the fortunes of the Whig party to which he always remained attached. They also show his emotional involvements, such as they were. Nearly all the people who appear in these pages knew each other socially, some were his relatives; most (though not all) of the men had been at school with him; and almost all of them belonged to the narrow world of the Whig establishment. In this rather general sense they could all be said to belong to the same set, and in so far as their friendship with Walpole was concerned its centre was Strawberry Hill, his gothic villa or 'castle' by the Thames at Twickenham.

The following gallery of pictures (it claims to be no more than that) makes no pretentions to be a work of original scholarship; it is based upon printed sources, most of which are well known and readily available, and which are listed in the bibliography. For this reason I have dispensed with footnotes, but in quoting from Walpole's letters I have tried wherever possible without disturbing the flow of the narrative to give details of the date as fully as possible so that reference can be made, if desired, to the various editions of Walpole's correspondence. I must thank those who have helped me in writing this book. In particular I should like to mention Mr Sidney Blackmore, Commander Colin Campbell-Johnston, RN, Mr Albert Gallichan and Mr Peter Rose, to all of whom I am especially obliged. I must also express my gratitude to the Historic Buildings Representative of the National Trust and to the Photo Archivist of the Paul Mellon Centre for Studies in British Art. Finally, I am indebted to the Principal of St Mary's College, Twickenham, for kindly allowing me to visit Strawberry Hill, and to Yale University Press for permission to quote from the Yale edition of Horace Walpole's Correspondence, edited by W. S. Lewis.

January 1983   B.F.

I

Horace Walpole
in his Library

On 10 June in the year 1755 a young Swiss artist by the name of
Johann Heinrich Müntz arrived in Twickenham, then a pleasant
rural retreat on the Thames sufficiently remote from the noise and
turmoil of London, to take up an appointment at the villa of Mr
Horace Walpole, the celebrated author, dilettante and arbiter of
taste. Müntz had come to London by way of Jersey where he had
made the acquaintance of Richard Bentley, a fellow artist and
intimate friend of Walpole, and it was through this intermediary that
he had been recommended for his post, but only after his new
employer had received a reassuring answer to the important
question: 'can he paint perspectives, and cathedral-aisles, and holy
glooms?'

Close to the river, just to the west of the village, near a dusty road
that led up a gentle slope, Müntz would soon be able to observe
gothic pinnacles rising above the trees and foliage of a well cultivated
garden. These, however, were no indication of an ancient ruin or
venerable monastic grange; they presented instead every evidence of
the most recent construction. A pointed archway in the high garden
wall led him almost at once to the house, the front door facing him at
the end of a narrow recessed passageway with three cloister-like
arches to the right and a high blank wall to the left. The door opened
and the veritable holy gloom of Strawberry Hill engulfed him.

In the light that filtered through the painted glass windows the
walls of the entrance hall appeared at first sight to be fretted with
gothic traceries, and it was only upon closer inspection that the
delicate medieval-looking lacements were seen to be the effect of
trompe-l'oeil painting on the flat wall surfaces of the hall and
staircase-well. The staircase itself, up which Müntz was conducted,

had a gothic balustrade, and each turn was guarded by a heraldic antelope crouching on the newel post. A gothic lantern was suspended from the vaulted ceiling, while shields, swords, and suits of armour decorated the walls. At the top three arches gave access to a spacious landing hung with more antique weapons as well as swords and scimitars from India and Persia, two ancient muskets and other instruments of destruction. From this formidable armoury another arched doorway admitted the visitor into the library, a single step, as it were, from the spoils of war to the fruits of peace and civilization.

It is nice to think that Müntz first met his employer in the library, for this was the most recent addition to the house and still the pride of its creator and owner, with its bookcases like cathedral choir stalls and its painted ceiling enriched with heraldic shields and representations of armoured knights; it was in this setting, anyway, that he was soon to draw a pen-and-ink picture of his patron, finished in wash and body-colour, a study of elegance, grace, and airiness. We see Walpole sitting in a brocaded chair, one hand resting on the arm, an open book in the other, while more books lie on the floor beside him. He leans slightly forward as though suddenly interrupted in his studies, but it is an agreeable interruption, for he looks pleased, relaxed, and eminently self-possessed. Some few paces away stands a dog as though it, too, had just been disturbed from a pleasant doze. To the right and left are gothic book shelves stacked with heavy folios while between them a mullioned window, its upper lights rich with painted glass, reveals, across a pleasant lawn, a distant view of the Thames. It is summer, the trees are in full leaf, and upon the river a sailing boat makes its way slowly past. Below the window two altar-like fragments in stone proclaim the antiquarian tastes of the still youthful-looking figure who observes us with an intelligent if slightly quizzical regard before returning, as we feel sure he soon will, to the reading from which we have just disturbed him.

In the summer of 1755 Horace Walpole was thirty-seven years old (he was born on 24 September 1717) and had been living at Strawberry Hill for the past eight years, during which time it had undergone a complete transformation, a process of gothic embellishment and enlargement that was to continue for many years to come. He was, as he liked to describe himself, and as all the world knew, 'youngest son of Sir Robert Walpole, Earl of Orford', a form of self-description he would still be using on the title-page of a guide to his villa published over thirty years after Müntz's picture had been painted, when he was almost seventy years old and as well-known in his own right as anyone then living in the literary, social or political world of eighteenth-century England. His relationship to the great minister was a matter of pride and importance to him all his life, and his devotion to the principles of the Whig party was derived from it, though in all other aspects of his personality, in his taste and temperament, even in his physical appearance, he bore hardly any resemblance to Sir Robert at all. This, not unnaturally in a gossip-loving age, was to encourage rumours after his death that he was not his father's son but the offspring of a liaison between his mother and Carr, Lord Hervey, brother to Pope's 'Sporus', a situation which, if true, would have contributed a cruelly ironic note to a mis-placed filial devotion. In fact Walpole bore a very marked physi-cal likeness to his half-sister, Lady Mary Churchill, a daughter of the Prime Minister by his mistress Maria Skerrett, and there can be little doubt that both children derived their existence from the same father, whatever the wayward proclivities of the first Lady Walpole may have been, and the remarkable gap in time (eleven years) between the birth of her youngest son and his next elder brother. Yet was such a lack of similarity between father and son indeed so strange or so unusual? All over England at this time, as Lytton Strachey was later to point out, 'coarse and vigorous fathers were being succeeded by refined and sentimental sons; sceptics were everywhere stepping into the shoes of deists; in France the same movement at the same time brought about the triumph of the Encyclopedia.'

Walpole was devoted to his mother while she lived and to her memory after her death, which occurred in August 1735 while he was still an undergraduate at King's College, Cambridge; and he alone among her descendants thought of raising a monument to her memory. Unlike the Walpoles, Norfolk squires of ancient lineage who had represented their neighbourhood in Parliament for some generations, Lady Walpole came from a background of trade, though also of considerable wealth. Her father was a Baltic timber-merchant, John Shorter of Bybrook in Kent, and her grandfather in his day had been Lord Mayor of London. Her son Horace, who has sometimes been described as a snob, never attempted to hide this unaristocratic connection with commerce; indeed, he took a pride in it. Writing in September 1771 to his friend William Mason on the subject of his printing press, he declared: 'I am neither ashamed of being an author, nor a bookseller. My mother's father was a timber-merchant. I have many reasons for thinking myself a worse man, and none for thinking myself better: consequently I shall never blush at doing anything he did.' Eleven years later he told the same correspondent: 'My grandfather (my mother's father) was a Danish timber-merchant; an honest sensible Whig, and I am very proud of him . . .'

His father, for almost as long as his youngest son could remember, had been the great man of affairs, the chief minister and intimate councillor of the first two Hanoverian kings, the confidential friend of George II's queen. As a boy and youth Horace had had little rapport with his father. He resented the presence of Maria Skerrett as being a slight upon his mother and when, after Lady Walpole's death, the Prime Minister married his mistress, this did not make things any better. The second marriage, however, lasted barely three months, and in the last period of Sir Robert's life he and his son drew closer together and the retired statesman began to appreciate the wit and agreeable flippancy of this last and least characteristic of his off-spring. For all this the bucolic company that frequented Houghton in Norfolk drove the younger Walpole almost to distraction. 'Only imagine', he wrote to a friend from his father's country house in the summer of 1743, 'that I here every day see men, who are mountains of roast beef, and only seem just roughly hewn out into the outlines of human-form, like the giant-rock at Pratolino! I shudder when I see them brandish their knives in act to carve, and look on them as savages that devour one another.'

He was a somewhat effeminate young man, at least in his outward appearance, though this belied a toughness of constitution which despite a fragile exterior and delicate health saw him through eighty years of life. There was, Eliot Warburton declared in his *Memoirs of Horace Walpole*, something feminine in both his manners and in his tastes: 'As a boy, as a youth, and as a man, his character bore but faint traces of masculine impress; owing, no doubt, to that motherly influence to which he often acknowledged his infinite obligations.' On the other hand, Walpole all his life delighted in female company, and much of his best writing was addressed to his women friends in whose society he was always relaxed, intimate and confiding; though somewhat perversely when he himself was a young man he seems to have preferred much older women, those dowagers who 'as plenty as flounders' inhabited the neighbourhood of Strawberry Hill, and only formed attachments to younger women in his old age. This fondness for dowagers, indeed, gave rise to a certain amount of amusement among his friends. When he set off for Northampton-shire in July 1763 to visit Lady Betty Germaine, Gilly Williams (whom we shall meet later) wrote in some glee to George Selwyn: 'Is it not surprising how he moves from old Suffolk on the Thames to another old goody on the Tyne: and does not see the ridicule which he would so strongly paint in any other character?' 'Old Suffolk', the dowager countess and former mistress of George II, was Walpole's friend and neighbour at Marble Hill, Twickenham, and her conversation and reminiscences of the court life of an earlier generation were for him a source of endless fascination.

To posterity, of course, Horace Walpole is known as perhaps the greatest letter-writer in the English language, but to his contem-poraries, only a chosen few of whom knew of his skill and accomplishment in this direction, his fame rested upon his reputation as an antiquary, as the author of a gothic novel and a sombre verse tragedy, as an expert upon the history of the arts in England, as a minor versifier and patron of greater poets, and as a man of wit, position and fashion. Though a Member of Parliament for many years, his political influence, though far from negligible behind the scenes, did not bring him any public acclaim. But most of all, to the curious public, he was known as the creator of Strawberry Hill. This house was to make him famous to posterity, though to a lesser degree than did his fame as a letter-writer, just as he himself made the house famous in his lifetime. It was to become a place of pilgrimage for royalty, for the fashionable world, and for the merely inquisitive. It was visited by people from all over Europe and for better or for worse was to have a profound influence upon taste. Yet the house itself, like its owner, was remarkably fragile and subject to occasional accidents such as falling pinnacles and other minor calamities, the more prone, perhaps, because it was rumoured that much of the gothic embellishment was only constructed of plaster. So it was that Gilly Williams could remark of Walpole himself, while still only in his late fifties, that he had already outlived three sets of battlements.

Horace Walpole was a small man, slim in figure, but described by those who knew him well as compact and neatly formed. John Pinkerton, the Scottish antiquary who met him in later life, wrote:

'His features may be seen in many portraits; but none can express the placid goodness of his eyes, which would often sparkle with sudden rays of wit, or dart forth flashes of the most keen and intuitive intelligence.' His laugh, on the other hand, was described as being 'forced and uncouth'. Forced or not, it often rang out. His sense of humour rarely deserted him and he hated seriousness or pomposity. Of his cousin Henry Seymour Conway, he once wrote: 'Conway says I laugh at all serious characters—so I do—and at myself too, who am far from being of that number', and he confessed: 'I have no dignity.' This was true, certainly, in the sense that he never indulged in false pride or stood upon his rank either in society or in his general dealings with mankind. He made no special claims for himself or for his abilities, but he had a nervous apprehension of ridicule that never deserted him. Satire and ridicule are the special weapons of a highly civilized society; to make a man look foolish in a world that prides itself on being 'polite' and polished is the worst of fates, and it was especially dreaded in the eighteenth century. To avoid ridicule was the constant burthen of Lord Chesterfield's letters to his son, and Voltaire prayed, not without purpose, 'O God, make all my enemies ridiculous.' When he was nearly fifty, Walpole wrote to Madame du Deffand: 'Long before the date of our acquaintance, this fear of ridicule was implanted in my mind, and you should surely remember how greatly it possesses me and how often I have spoken to you of it. Do not seek a later origin for this. From the minute I ceased to be young I have had a horrible fear of being a ridiculous old man.'

Walpole stood in no danger of this, not least because of his refusal to cultivate a dignified public presence. He invariably declined to accept praise when it was offered him, and made a point of disparaging his published works. He wrote to Thomas Gray in February 1768:

You will do me the justice to own that I had always rather have seen your writings than have shown you mine; which you know are the most hasty trifles in the world, and which, though I may be fond of the subject when fresh, I constantly forget in a very short time after they are published. This would sound like affectation to others, but will not to you. It would be affected, even to you, to say, I am indifferent to fame—I certainly am not, but I am indifferent to almost anything I have done to acquire it.

This refreshing lack of humbug was an essential characteristic of his personality; so too was the cheerfulness which he always tried to maintain, even when advancing age brought with it a note of disillusion not eased by the pains of gout and severe rheumatism. 'The world is an old acquaintance that does not improve upon one's hands,' he wrote to Lord Strafford when he was fifty-six and beginning to think himself rather elderly, 'however, one must not give way to the disgusts it creates. My maxim, and practice, too, is to laugh, because I do not like to cry.'

'This world,' as Walpole maintained in his best-known aphorism, 'is a comedy to those that think, a tragedy to those that feel.' To him the world was for the most part a comedy, a scene of human folly and confusion, yet one like those operatic comedies of Mozart in which there is always a haunting note of tragedy in the accompaniment for those who have an ear to hear it. It was a comedy he observed with a shrewd but detached fascination. Fate had placed him, as it were, in a stage box. He had no wish to descend on to the stage and take part in the drama. His privileged position in society offered him an unique vantage point from which to chronicle the age in which he lived. His whole life, even his choice of friends, tended to this end, and his awareness that this would be his destiny began to form, almost unconsciously, from a very early period of his existence.

❧ 2 ❦

It was as though with some prescience of what his life's work was destined to be that at the tender age of nine Walpole managed to persuade his mother into arranging for him to meet King George I. It is the ambition of many children to see the king, but in May 1727 when the young Horace suddenly avowed this 'first vehement inclination' he had ever expressed, he knew that he was perfectly placed to have his desire fulfilled, with his father already for some years the most powerful minister in the land. Sir Robert's 'infinite good nature', we are told, 'never thwarted any of his children', and so on 1 June of that year the curious little boy was taken to St James's Palace and handed over to the care of the king's natural daughter, Lady Walsingham, who led him into an ante-room where they found the king and his mistress, the Duchess of Kendal. Over half a century later Walpole would write: 'The person of the King is as perfect in my memory as if I saw him but yesterday. It was that of an elderly man rather pale, and exactly like his pictures and coins; not tall, of an aspect rather good than august, with a dark tye wig, a plain coat, waistcoat and breeches of snuff-coloured cloth, with stockings of the same colour, and a blue ribband over all.' So concentrated was his attention upon the king that he barely noticed the woman who stood by him beyond the fact of her being a 'very tall, lean, ill-favoured old lady'. The little audience was soon over; the boy knelt to kiss the royal hand, a few words fell from the royal lips, and the child courtier was dismissed. But even in this brief encounter Walpole's luck was with him. Within two days the king had left England for Hanover, and within two weeks he was dead. Horace Walpole must have been one of the last of King George's British subjects to kiss his hand.

When Walpole saw George I he had just started as a schoolboy at Eton. Shortly afterwards he witnessed the proclamation of the new king when he surprised his schoolfellows by suddenly bursting into tears, though, as he later frankly admitted, his tears were induced not so much by memories of this recent meeting with the dead monarch as by the notion that a Prime Minister's son should show more concern than other boys. Perhaps, too, he was aware of the crisis which the king's death had created in his father's career and shared some of the anxiety and insecurity which all his family must have felt until Sir Robert had successfully ingratiated himself with the new ruler.

After leaving Eton Walpole observed: 'I can't say I am sorry I was never quite a school-boy.' It was perhaps because of this that he managed to survive what for many at that period was little more than an ordeal, and even succeeded in enjoying his time at school. An eighteenth-century public school was no place for a physically delicate and highly strung boy. They were for the most part boisterous, brutish and violent places, scenes of rough justice, frequent floggings, and even occasional riots. Eton was no exception. The elder Pitt had been so unhappy there that he refused to submit his own children to the same severe discipline, nor was he alone in thinking that the fights and feuds that formed so large a part of school life were adequately compensated for by the learning imparted by the tutors. Horace Walpole would seem an obvious victim of such a system, but he managed to survive by the force of his very difference from the average product of the place, and also from a toughness of character that lay unexpectedly concealed behind the rather epicene exterior. He quickly formed an alliance with like-minded boys who shared his own dream world, and contrived to keep the rabble at bay largely by ignoring them. In this, it is possible to believe, he was also helped by his position. In the background was the all-powerful minister, and whatever other boys might have thought of this rather odd character in their midst, there were parents to urge them not to molest the son of one in whose hands lay gifts of mitres, coronets, lucrative government posts, snug deaneries and rich canons' stalls.

He had, of course, relations at school: the Conway brothers, Francis and Henry, the elder to end his life Marquis of Hertford, the younger a Secretary of State and Field Marshal and always Walpole's favourite cousin and greatest friend. There was George Selwyn, later to be connected with the Walpoles through the Townshend family and destined for a life of idleness and wit; and among those not his relations two boys who shared his interest in history and antiquities, Charles Lyttelton who would one day be Bishop of Carlisle, and William Cole, never to be more than a country clergyman but to be Walpole's friend and correspondent until his death. Then there was George Montagu of whom very little can be said except that he was charming and indolent and was to receive from Walpole in the course of his life many fascinating letters to which he was usually too lazy even to reply. Already Walpole was beginning to form a circle of friendships many of which would be lasting. We shall meet most of them again.

His most intimate friends, however, were neither relations nor drawn from the exclusive world of aristocracy and privilege. They were bound together by a compatibility of tastes, a rather whimsical sense of humour, and a sentimental bond not unusual among sensitive, rather romantically inclined adolescents. They were all precocious, and perhaps a little precious, and called themselves the Quadruple Alliance. They wrote poetry, 'sighing some pastoral name to the echo of the cascade under the bridge', for to them the playing fields of Eton were food for all manner of flights of fancy far removed, as they liked to think, from the thoughts of those who usually disported themselves on those legendary acres.

Thomas Gray was the chief among the three who, with Walpole, formed this alliance. He was, like the others, a year older than his friend, already writing poetry, and already marked by the touch of melancholy that was to haunt him through life. His home was unhappy, his parents estranged, his mother having been forced to keep a shop with one of her sisters in order to maintain the boy at school. Richard West was also a budding poet, but showing signs of the ill health that cut short his existence while still in his twenties. He was the most scholarly of the group. The third friend was Thomas Ashton. He was later to develop into a self-seeking and ambitious clergyman, an unattractive figure who Walpole always believed to have lost interest in their friendship when his father was no longer in a position to dispense bishoprics. This later reputation makes it more difficult to envisage Ashton as a schoolboy, though at that time he must have had qualities to make him a welcome member of this exclusive little circle. Like Gray, he came from a very different and simpler background than Walpole's. His home was in Lancaster where his father was a schoolmaster. West's circumstances, in theory at least, were on a grander scale. He was a grandson of Bishop Burnet and his father had been Lord Chancellor of Ireland, but the father had died when he was only ten years old. His mother, to whom he was devoted, consoled herself in the arms of her late husband's secretary, and whether her son was at this period aware of it or not, the atmosphere at home must have been far from happy.

There was, then, this added bond between Gray, West and Walpole, that they were all three to some extent dominated by their mothers; in Walpole's case through the involvement of his father in affairs of state and that other less mentionable affair with Maria Skerrett; for Gray, through the persecutions of a cantankerous and half-crazy father who refused to have anything to do with his son's education and indeed who had virtually abandoned him altogether; and for West by reason of his mother's recent widowhood. This is not to suggest, however, that they were all the time lost in a mood of melancholy. They enjoyed many private jokes such as exist in all close relationships. Walpole had a mercurial temperament and knew how to dazzle his companions by his wit and by a show of learning lightly borne, for all that he was not over zealous in his application to school work and was reluctant to undertake any task that he considered as being more than he was absolutely forced to learn. Much better, he believed, to be reading a play, composing elegant occasional verses or following the story of some old French romance.

The happiness and sentimental nostalgia with which the members of the Quadruple Alliance could look back upon their schooldays in later years owed everything to the existence of their mutual friendship. Individually, without the embracing protection of the alliance, they would probably have been lonely and unhappy and almost certainly persecuted. As it was they lived in a sort of Arcadian dream, and even adopted secret names to distinguish each other: Orosmades for Gray, Amanzor for Ashton, Favonius for West, while Walpole was the pastoral shepherd Celadon. The Thames-side meadows became the happy hills and pleasing shades of Gray's *Ode on a Distant Prospect of Eton College*. For West, later a solitary figure at Oxford after his three friends had gone to the other university, even the walks of Magdalen could not compare with the scenes he had recently left and he recorded in a poem he sent to Walpole how

> The thought, which still my breast invades,
> Nigh yonder springs, nigh yonder shades,
> Still, as I pass, the memory brings
> Of sweeter shades and springs.

We get a glimpse of Walpole's feelings for Eton in a letter to West at Oxford shortly before the latter sent him this poem. Gray had been to visit an uncle at Burnham in Buckinghamshire, and Walpole wrote: 'Gray is at Burnham, and, what is surprising, has not been at Eton. Could you live so near without seeing it? That dear scene of our quadruple-alliance would furnish me with the most agreeable recollections.'

The Etonian idyll ended for Walpole in 1734 when his friends went up to the university. Being their junior by a year he had a brief period without their company until March 1735 when he joined Ashton at King's College, Cambridge. Gray was already an undergraduate at Peterhouse and West, as we have seen, was at Oxford, where he was entered at Christ Church. Cambridge did not weave the same spell for Walpole that Eton had done. Though he spent four years there as a fellow commoner before leaving without taking a degree, his residence was only intermittent and his attendance at lectures not over assiduous after the first year. He attempted to follow a course in mathematics but was dissuaded by the dim-eyed Professor Saunderson whose lack of sight did not blind him to the total incapacity of his would-be pupil to master the subject. After some tears of mortification and a year with a private tutor Walpole was forced to accept the professor's verdict. More profitable time was spent learning Italian and in attending lectures in anatomy and civil law, but at no time did he over-exert himself at his studies. He wrote to West from King's in August 1736: 'I have been so used to the delicate food of Parnassus that I never condescend to apply to the grosser studies of Alma Mater. Sober cloth, of syllogism colour, suits me ill; or what's worse, I hate clothes that one must prove to be of no colour at all.' He was unfortunate in going to Cambridge at a period when the English seats of learning were not noted for much intellectual activity. There were certain individual scholars of great merit, but the general tone of the place was summed up in William Cole's description of Walpole's tutor, of whom he wrote: 'Excessive Drinking, high and luxurious Eating, and other riotous Behaviour was the daily and Common Way of life with Mr. Whaley.'

Such lasting impressions as Cambridge made upon Walpole's intellectual development came not from his official tutors but from a different and more distinguished member of the university, the somewhat sceptical divine Dr Conyers Middleton, a former Fellow of Trinity who was at this time University Librarian, a post that had been created specially for him. It is very probable that Middleton first sought out Walpole, for though he held scant regard for many of the theological mysteries of the religion of which he was an ordained priest, he was by no means averse from the thought of preferment and was known to cultivate the friendship of those who could help him climb to some perch of comfortable ecclesiastical eminence. He was a difficult and disputatious character who had spent many years in an absurd quarrel with Dr Bentley, the formidable but no less eccentric Master of Trinity, over a fee of four guineas which the latter had extracted from him in dues when he received his degree of Doctor of Divinity. Middleton considered the charge unlawful, threatened litigation, and carried on the controversy for years with little profit to himself and much loss of dignity to both parties. This, however, was a side of his life that did not concern his young friend, who was probably first attracted to Middleton by his interest in classical antiquities. Some ten years previously he had spent a time in Rome whence he had returned with a collection of antiques as well as material for a pamphlet attacking as pagan the ceremonies of the Roman Church. Middleton's antiquarian interests were at once an attraction to Walpole, and indeed he was later (in 1744) to buy the former's collection and install it at Strawberry Hill.

Middleton, however, had another and more profound influence upon the younger man. When Walpole first went up to Cambridge he shared with his friend Ashton an evangelical faith and they would go together to pray with the prisoners in Cambridge gaol. These pious practices did not long survive his encounter with the Doctor of Divinity. Middleton was an eloquent expositor of the principles of deism, that rather cold and passionless religion which appealed so strongly to certain eighteenth-century minds and which went little beyond a belief in a benevolent First Cause and an attitude of moral rectitude in the conduct of public affairs. Conyers Middleton himself questioned the verbal inspiration of the Scriptures and turned a sceptical eye upon the evidence of miracles in the Early Church. His *Free Inquiry into Miraculous Powers*, written some years after Walpole's time at Cambridge, and considered by many people to lead to total unbelief, summed up the ideas that Walpole now found so congenial, though curiously enough it was this same book that was later to drive the young Edward Gibbon, if only temporarily, into the arms of the Roman Catholic Church. Middleton's views were reinforced for Walpole by his reading of Fontenelle's *Entretiens sur la pluralité des Mondes*, which he later told Pinkerton had first rendered him an infidel with regard to orthodox Christianity. Atheism, on the other hand, he deplored. 'It is gloomy,' he declared, 'uncomfortable, and, in my eye, unnatural and irrational. It certainly requires more credulity to believe that there is no God, than to believe that there is. This fair creation, those magnificent heavens, the fruit of matter and chance? O impossible!'

This rather arid deism sufficed him for the rest of his life. If any creed were required of him he provided it many years later in a letter to Madame du Deffand:

> I believe in a future life. God has created so much that is good and beautiful that we can trust him for the rest. We should not deliberately offend him. Virtue must please him, therefore be virtuous. But nature does not permit perfection. Therefore God will not condemn what is not according to nature. This is my profession of faith. It is very brief and very simple.

It was also, he might have added, the creed of many of his

contemporaries not a few of whom, like Dr Conyers Middleton, were beneficed clergymen of the Church of England. It seems almost unjust that the latter did not, in the end, derive any promotion in the Church from his friendly association with this apt and influential pupil.

Walpole's deistic beliefs were no doubt suitable for one who remained a detached observer of the human scene. He showed little interest in the religious controversies of his time, though he confessed to Pinkerton a 'real affection' for Bishop Hoadley whose view of the Church reduced it to little more than a department of state. 'My faith in him and his doctrines', he declared, 'has long been settled.' His curiosity was aroused by ecclesiastical gossip rather than by doctrinal problems. Episcopal appointments concerned him only from their political aspect: a Whig bishop was a good bishop. As to the Methodist revivalists, the effusion and unction of their utterances seemed to him no more than histrionics; he likened them to actors ranting on the stage. Neither Whitefield nor John Wesley much impressed him. The former he considered vain and not over scrupulous in money matters; the latter, though 'wondrous clean' in appearance was none the less 'as evidently an actor as Garrick'. When Dr Johnson's prayers were published Walpole (who never liked or appreciated their author) confessed himself bewildered and shocked: 'One laughs at every page, and then the tears come into one's eyes when one learns what the poor being suffered . . . Johnson had all the bigotry of a monk, and all the folly and ignorance too.' If Walpole's unemotional faith excluded any mystic flights, it also protected him from anything resembling the dark night of the soul.

It can be questioned, however, whether so intellectual a system of belief can be of much help at a moment of great emotional crisis, and it is no wonder that Gray doubted whether his friend's religious faith would be strong enough to support him through the ordeal of his mother's death. She died on 20 August 1737 and the blow was so prostrating to Walpole that for a time his closest friends trembled for his sanity. To others Lady Walpole had not seemed a very impressive character. Lady Mary Wortley Montagu found her 'an empty, coquettish, affected woman', and certainly one of the reasons for the breakdown of her marriage was that Sir Robert found more intellectual companionship in the society of his mistress; but to Horace Walpole she could do no wrong, she had been the centre of his existence. The love she gave him was the yardstick by which all other offers of affection must be measured and few would be counted worthy to come near it. It was the only comparison he could think of when he was later tormented by the thought that he might not see again that other mother-figure in his life, Madame du Deffand. The embarrassments which her endearments had so often caused him were forgotten in a moment of unconscious insight when he spoke of her as 'this best and sincerest of friends, who loves me as much as my mother did'.

The death of his mother just over a month before his twentieth birthday was the first and almost certainly the greatest loss he would ever suffer. It left a scar that never entirely healed. Never again would he risk so close an emotional relationship; indeed, from now on his deeper emotions would be kept under strict control. His life would continue to be full of friendships with both women and men, but all his personal relationships would fall short of any commitment of a more passionate nature. He found the friendship of women a stimulation. As Pinkerton remarked in the biographical sketch he prefaced to his volumes of *Walpoliana*, 'he was an elegant and devout admirer of the fair sex, in whose presence he would exceed his usual powers of conversation; his spirits were animated as if by a cordial, and he would scatter his wit and *petits mots* with dazzling profusion.' But the fact that his most favoured female companions for the greater part of his life were women older than himself suggests that his search was always for some replacement to fill the gap in his emotional life that his mother's death had caused.

His friendships with men, a significant number of whom, in particular Mann, Chute, Gray, Selwyn, Montagu and Cole were, like himself, all bachelors, were amicable, intimate, and usually long-lasting, and this coupled with his rather effeminate mannerisms and somewhat epicene wit has encouraged some observers to suggest that Walpole was homosexual. There is no doubt that the feminine side of his character was strong, but this is not in itself evidence of homosexuality. His friendships with men, like those with women, are characterized by a similar detachment. He does not seem, in short, to have had a passionate nature, and his distaste for any too intimate involvement with others increased with age. Love, even in the eighteenth-century sense of meaning no more than a close and warm affection, must be kept at arm's length. 'Consider how little

you have known me,' he wrote in March 1766 to John Craufurd, a
younger man who had hoped to form a closer friendship with him,

> consider my heart is not like yours—young, good, warm, sincere
> and impatient to bestow itself. Mine is worn with the baseness,
> treachery and mercenariness I have met with. It is suspicious,
> doubtful and cooled. I consider everything around me but in the
> light of amusement, because if I looked at it seriously I should
> detest it. I laugh that I may not weep. But don't love me, pray don't
> love! Old folks are but old women who love their last love as they
> did their first. I should still be liable to believe you and I am not at
> all of Madame du Deffand's opinion that one might as well be dead
> as not love somebody. I think one had better be dead than love
> anybody. I can go no further. I have taken the veil and would not
> break my vow for the world.

It is impossible now to penetrate behind that veil, drawn, as it was,
with such finality and such determination over the face behind the
urbane public mask. It might be said that for someone who
suppressed his sexuality as rigidly as Walpole that it is immaterial
whether the hetero- or the homosexual element predominated; the
question becomes almost irrelevant. 'Pray mind,' he told Sir Horace
Mann when describing how he was roused from sleep by an
earthquake tremor in 1750, 'Pray mind, I lie alone . . .' There was a
virginal quality about him which set him apart in a robust age when
even (according to Walpole's own testimony) an archbishop of York
could keep a mistress and appoint his illegitimate son as chaplain.
The true character of Walpole's emotional nature continues to elude
us as, during his lifetime, it appears to have eluded his contemporaries.

❖❯❯❯ 3 ❮❮❮❖

If Walpole fought shy of emotional attachments, it did not have the
effect of withering his feelings or of making him appear frustrated or
withdrawn. He had a light-hearted streak in his personality which
made him respond quickly and happily to the enjoyment of
others—sometimes in ways that startled his more staid contemporaries. One of his friends was Lady Mary Coke, who never forgot the
respect owed to her position as a duke's daughter and who professed

an almost religious admiration for members of the royal family. In June 1770 she was staying with Walpole's relatives, the Conways, at Park Place near Henley, where the company included the king's aunt Princess Amelia as well as Walpole himself. One evening, just as the party were getting ready for cards a group of morris dancers appeared on the lawn and displayed their skill with such abandon that Walpole, to show his delight, began to pirouette about the room in time to their music. Lady Mary was rather shocked, but the princess thoroughly enjoyed the spectacle of the gyrating fifty-three-year-old, and perhaps to administer a mild rebuke to the other for being so disapproving, asked her to dance as well. 'Not being able to obey her commands,' Lady Mary recorded rather smugly in her diary, 'she pulled me into the middle of the room, and would have danced with me, if I had not begged H.R.H. to honour me with any other commands.' There was an exuberance in Walpole's character that could even overcome his fear of ridicule, as when he astounded Lord Blandford's guests one spring evening by appearing among them with his head garlanded in sweetpeas, or when he welcomed some visitors at Strawberry Hill wearing a lace cravat carved in wood by Grinling Gibbons and an immense pair of gloves embroidered up to the elbows that had once belonged to James I. On the latter occasion, which occurred when he was entertaining some distinguished guests from France, Walpole was enchanted by the sensation his odd appearance caused, especially its effect upon the French servants who, he declared, 'firmly believed this was the dress of English country gentlemen'.

This was all a part of Walpole's way of presenting his life to others as though it were a light-hearted frolic, an endless masquerade in which nothing very serious was ever attempted or achieved, a view of his activities which he promoted with such success that many people took it for the truth. Thus in a letter to Lady Hervey, the former Molly Lepell whose charms had been praised by both Voltaire and Alexander Pope, he gives a sketch of a week in his life in June 1765 which those who knew him only superficially (and his nineteenth-century detractors after his death) would eagerly take as a picture of the whole.

I am almost as much ashamed, Madam [he tells her], to plead the true cause of my faults towards your ladyship, as to have been guilty of neglect. It is scandalous, at my age, to have been carried backwards and forwards to balls and suppers and parties by very young people, as I was all last week. My resolutions of growing old and staid are admirable: I wake with a sober plan, and intend to pass the day with my friends—then comes the Duke of Richmond, and hurries me down to Whitehall to dinner—then the Duchess of Grafton sends for me to loo in Upper Grosvenor-Street—before I can get thither, I am begged to step to Kensington, to give Mrs. Anne Pitt my opinion about a bow window—after the loo, I am to march back to Whitehall to supper—and after that, am to walk with Miss Pelham on the terrace till two in the morning, because it is moonlight and her chair is not come . . .

People reading such an account of how his time was spent, and unaware of his other more serious activities, might well come to Macaulay's wholly false opinion that Walpole was a man to whom 'whatever was little seemed to him great, and whatever was great seemed to him little. Serious business was a trifle to him, and trifles were his serious business.' In fact, well aware that one person's serious business is a great bore to someone else, he contrived to keep his more important concerns out of his correspondence except when it was addressed to those to whom he knew it would be of interest. His manners were just as good when he put pen to paper as when he was in the drawing-room and he would no more be tedious in correspondence than he would be in conversation. Furthermore, as we have already noted, he always played down his abilities and accomplishments, wondering indeed how a real genius could support the compliments he must meet with, knowing, as he told Lady Ossory, 'that when they tumble down to my sphere they make me sweat'.

In fact, whatever faults Walpole may have had, idleness was not one of them. He was always busy from the moment he got up until he finally retired to bed, often in the small hours of the morning. With his books and memoirs, his correspondence, his antiquarian research, his collections, his building and architectural plans, his gardening, his parliamentary attendance and political intrigues on behalf of his friends his days and hours were always full. Laziness in others he rather despised. Müntz, alas, was ultimately to fall from grace with his employer for this fault among others. Thus to Richard

Bentley, another culprit in this respect, Walpole wrote in a cautionary spirit in 1756:

> I have been here [at Strawberry Hill] this week with only Mr. Müntz; from whence you may conclude I have been employed— Memoirs thrive apace. He seems to wonder (for he has not a little of your indolence, I am not surprised you took to him) that I am continually occupied every minute of the day, reading, writing, forming plans: in short, you know me. He is an inoffensive, good creature, but had rather ponder over a foreign gazette than a pallet.

To the fashionable world, however, the fiction of a tranquil and retired existence must be maintained. In 1774, the year in which he first compiled the catalogue of his collection at Strawberry Hill, in itself evidence of his continuous activity as a tireless if somewhat eccentric connoisseur as well as an arbiter of taste, we find him writing to Lady Ossory with gentle irony:

> You yourself owned, Madam, that I am grown quite lifeless, and it is very true. I am none of your Glastonbury thorns that blow at Christmas. I am a remnant of the last age, and have nothing to do with the present. I am an exile from the sunbeams of drawing-rooms; I have quitted the gay scenes of Parliament and the Antiquarian Society; I am not of Almack's; I don't understand horse-races; I never go to reviews; what can I have to talk of? I go to no *fêtes champêtres*, what can I have to think of? I know nothing but about myself, and about myself I know nothing.

And yet, for all his real industry as a writer and chronicler of his times, there is more than a hint of *fêtes champêtres* in Walpole's life which now, in an uglier and more violent age, gives it a compelling and poignant charm. The echoes that come to us from the fretted and gilded traceries of the long gallery at Strawberry Hill, so gay and elegant in its interpretation of gothic gloom, the plaintive sound of french horns from the cloister below, the complimentary verses struck off the printing press to surprise a visiting Marquise du Châtelet or soften the heart of a formidable bluestocking, or that salute of fifty nightingales 'who, as tenants of the manor, came to do honour to their Lord' and speed with their song the departing guests, all combine to speak of a leisurely, cosmopolitan and cultivated civilization that has now vanished for ever.

How pleasant to inhabit such a world, to pass one's time in agreeable occupations, to acquire a reputation as a man of letters by the occasional writing of useful, sometimes original, and never wholly trivial publications, to be an acknowledged authority in all matters of taste and *virtù*. 'I can figure no being happier than Horry,' wrote his friend Gilly Williams, '*Monstrari digito praetereuntium* has been his whole aim. For this he has wrote, printed, and built.' 'To be pointed out by the finger of passers-by' (as Williams's tag translates) perhaps exaggerates Walpole's attitude to fame though, as we have seen, he never denied the pleasure his celebrity sometimes brought him. His real hope, however, was in the verdict of a larger audience, and it was a disinterested hope, for he could never know what the verdict might be. For while his novel, his play, his periodical ventures into historical controversy, his parables and poems were praised or condemned by contemporary critics, he knew that posterity alone would be able to judge his most important work when his letters and memoirs would be published after his death. It was to this unseen audience only that he addressed his major work, and it was their approbation alone that he really desired, and time has justified his aspiration.

From where, then, did the money come to sustain him in these occupations? As a younger son Walpole had no landed estate to inherit and he did not follow any of those professions then considered suitable for cadets of noble houses: the Church, the Army or the Law. His fortune, which by the end of his life was considerable, was derived from various patent places he held under the Crown to which he had been nominated during his father's years of power. The sinecures he held included the offices of Controller of the Pipe, Clerk of the Estreats, and Usher of the Exchequer. Where duties were to be performed these were undertaken by a deputy who was paid a salary from the funds of the office, but the bulk of the revenue went into the pocket of the patent holder who was neither expected nor required to do anything in return for his profit. Trying to secure such a place under government, like hoping to marry an heiress, was considered a perfectly legitimate activity for a young man of family at the period of Walpole's youth, but as the century wore on the custom came in for growing criticism.

Walpole answered his critics boldly. He held his places as much by law, he declared, as any gentleman held his estate, and more by ancient tenure than many of them. Nor, he added, with an eye to those families enriched at the time of the Reformation, was his source of wealth wrung from the Church in violation of the intention of the original donors. He had as much right to his income as deans and prebendaries had to theirs. It remained, however, a sensitive point with him, and when the whole system came under attack when Edmund Burke was paymaster during the Rockingham administration of 1782 he felt obliged to make some justification of his position.

It is very difficult to state my case, [he wrote in the course of a long memorandum] and not seem to defend it. But I am telling the truth, and not pleading for favour—at least, my object is to obtain a favourable opinion of my character. I am far more indifferent about my fortune. But surely any impartial man will reflect how grievous it must be to a disinterested mind to be held up to the public as a blood-sucker, under the invidious name of a placeman—to be one of those pointed at by country associations, as grievances that call for speedy correction and removal; in short, to be confounded with contractors and other leeches that have grown out of the profusions and abuses of the time, though my office has existed from the oldest times, and has existed under the best government. Public distress demands economy and correction. Be they exercised, I desire no exception. But being guilty of no servile, of no direct means in obtaining, augmenting, or retaining my office, I am ready to resign that office; but I will prove (and defy all mankind to detect me in a single falsehood) that I have held my place with honour, and have nothing to palliate or conceal in my execution of it.

To the nineteenth century, which never really warmed to Walpole, there was something additionally shocking in his being a placeman; and it remains an embarrassment to his present-day apologists.

Walpole at least could claim that in comparison with the literary legacy he left to posterity, which is now regarded, in addition to its intrinsic artistic merit, as an indispensable source for our knowledge of the period, his country had not done badly out of the bargain. In his own day he was always generous in the financial help he gave, or tried to give, to others. He twice offered to share his income with his cousin Henry Seymour Conway, once when the latter was hoping to get married, and later when he had been dismissed, unjustly as

Walpole thought, from his government appointments; and in later life he tried, with equal sincerity but equal failure, to make up the pension of his friend Madame du Deffand when he learnt that the French authorities were about to stop it. He also offered shelter in his house to a natural daughter of his father when he discovered that she was living in neglected and much reduced circumstances. She was not a very prepossessing individual, having been jilted in early life by a young man who later rose to become a bishop and was now, in her later years at Strawberry Hill, according to William Cole's description, of a 'squat, short, gummy appearance', so that she could hardly have added much to the charms of the place, but her half-brother made her welcome in his home for six months in every year for the remainder of her life.

He was, in fact, a humane and kind-hearted man who reacted with horror at many of the inhumanities of his age. He did not harbour resentment. When he heard that a highwayman who had nearly killed him in a hold-up and robbery had been caught and was standing trial for his life, he refused to give evidence against him. When the unfortunate Admiral Byng was under sentence of death, Walpole, though he did not know Byng personally and was not actually in Parliament at the time, made strenuous efforts to have the sentence reversed. Long before the anti-slavery movement had got under way he was already a vigorous opponent of the whole degrading institution. 'We have been sitting this fortnight on the Africa Company,' he wrote to Sir Horace Mann in February 1750, '*we*, the British Senate, that temple of liberty, that bulwark of Protestant Christianity, have this fortnight been pondering methods to make more effectual that horrid traffic of selling negroes. It has appeared to us that six-and-forty thousand of these wretches are sold every year to our plantations alone!—it chills one's blood. I would not have to say that I voted for it for the continent of America!' So, too, when he heard that Colonel Christopher Codrington had left estates in Barbados to the Society for the Propagation of the Gospel but had also stipulated that three hundred slaves should continue to work on them, his reaction was one of disgust. In a letter to Richard Bentley, he asked ironically:

Did one ever hear a more truly Christian charity than keeping up a perpetuity of three hundred slaves to look after the Gospel's estate? How could one intend a religious legacy, and miss the disposition of that estate for delivering three hundred Negroes from the most shocking slavery imaginable? Must devotion be twisted into the unfeeling interests of trade?

His horror would have been complete had he known that the pious beneficiaries of this bequest had branded their newly acquired slaves with the word 'Society' on their chests.

Walpole was unjustly accused of having been indirectly responsible for the suicide of Thomas Chatterton which, if indeed true, would have been a serious countercharge against his reputation for kindness of heart. The real reason for this whole unhappy episode lay, however, not in any act of Walpole's but in Chatterton's own devious personality, and in the deceptive approach he made to Walpole when sending his ingenious forgeries for the latter's critical opinion. If Chatterton had been able for an instant to throw aside his morbid fantasies and present himself to Walpole as he really was, a sick, indigent but immensely talented boy in desperate need of help, there can be little doubt that the help he needed would have been forthcoming. As it was, his dishonesty and intention to mislead involved Walpole in a situation where his own particular morbid fear, that of ridicule, added further confusion to the situation. To be the dupe of a confidence trick, be the trickster ever so much a genius, is not an enviable situation to be in. Walpole, who suffered deeply from the insinuations made against him, at least had the magnanimity to remain silent in the face of the slanders that assailed him, and left his justification to be published only after his death.

If Walpole showed any intolerance, it was towards the Roman Catholic Church, though not towards individual members of it, for he professed an admiration for Pope Benedict XIV whom he hailed as 'beloved by Papists, esteemed by Protestants . . . a Prince without favourites, a Pope without nepotism, an author without vanity . . .' and he showed a lively and sympathetic interest in the activities of the Cardinal of York, grandson of James II, as these were related to him by Sir Horace Mann. But he had a typical Whig prejudice against the Roman Church as an institution, considering its influence inimical to liberty. 'Papists and Liberty', he roundly declared, 'are contradictions.' For this reason he was opposed to any measure for Catholic emancipation. This attitude sprang largely from his strong political loyalties which made him less dispassionate than he might care to have admitted. If he could dismiss Catholics in a sweeping judgement he could do the same for the Tories. 'Whig principles', he maintained, 'are founded on sense: a Whig may be a fool, a Tory must be so.'

✦≫ 4 ≪✦

Walpole never seriously considered marriage, nor did he ever keep a mistress, though he may fleetingly have cast himself in the role of lover in Florence in 1740. He was a natural celibate. Marriage, or rather the thought of himself getting married, was a subject upon which he would occasionally jest. Thus a quip of Gilly Williams when the public inquiries of a certain Mr Gilbert had revealed the value of Walpole's Ushership of the Exchequer prompted him to write jokingly to Lady Ossory:

> Apropos to matrimony, I want to consult your Ladyship very seriously: I am so tormented by droves of people coming to see my house, and Margaret [his housekeeper] gets such sums of money by showing it, that I have a mind to marry her, and so repay myself that way for what I have flung away to make my house quite uncomfortable to me ... Mr. Williams said this morning that Margaret's is the best place in England, and wondered Mr. Gilbert did not insist on knowing what it is worth. Thank my stars, he did not!

But bachelors are solitary people, and Walpole was essentially gregarious; it was for this reason that friendship was so necessary to him. As the youngest son of his family by so many years, he was cut off from his elder brothers and sister, nor were his relations with his brothers always harmonious, though he remained on good terms with his younger illegitimate sister who became Lady Mary Churchill after her marriage. He disliked his namesake and uncle 'old' Horace Walpole upon whose rustic ways his nephew as a young man expended a good deal of ridicule. 'I really was charmed with Wolterton,' he wrote after visiting his uncle's Norfolk estate in September 1742, 'it is all wood and water! My uncle and aunt may, without any expense, do what they have all their lives avoided, wash themselves and make fires.' Not a remark, it will be agreed, to endear one to the older generation of the family, but the idea so amused

Walpole that he could not resist recasting it in verse, revealing, at the same time, the very unflattering nickname he had devised for his aunt:

> What woods, what streams around the seat!
> Was ever mansion so complete?
> Here happy Pug and Horace may,
> (And yet not have a groat to pay,)
> Two things they most have shunned, perform—
> I mean, they may be clean and warm.

But if he failed (in his more youthful days at any rate) to strike up a cordial relationship with the elder members of his family, he would in due course become a favourite uncle to a growing tribe of nieces, nephews, and ultimately great-nieces and great-nephews, so that at the end of his long life he could tell Lady Ossory in the last letter he wrote to her of the 'about fourscore of nephews and nieces of various ages, who are each brought to me about once a year, to stare at me as the Methusalem of the family'.

Family piety, too, inspired much of his antiquarian and genea-logical research. 'I am the antiquarian of my race—people don't know how entertaining it is,' he wrote to Cole in June 1775. 'Who begot whom is a most amusing kind of hunting; one recovers a grandfather instead of breaking one's neck—and then one grows so pious to the memory of a thousand persons one never heard of before.' Thus it was an agreeable discovery to find the ancient families of FitzOsbert and Robsart among one's ancestors and to have their escutcheons blazoned on the library ceiling. This in its turn gave way to pleasant fantasies, so that the old coats of mail, broadswords, quivers, longbows, arrows and spears that adorned the armoury were soon, as Walpole told Mann in the description of his house sent out to Florence in the summer of 1753, 'all *supposed* to be taken by Sir Terry Robsart in the holy wars'.

So we return to the library where we first surprised Walpole as he sat to Müntz's pencil in the summer of the year 1755. As a man whose whole life was spent in copious if rather disorganized study and in communicating his discoveries, spiced with contemporary gossip and anecdote, to his friends scattered over England, France and Italy, this room provided him with those sources upon which he relied for information and verification. It was essentially a working library; he was not interested in fine editions in themselves, and like any such collection it reflected his character and tastes. The Latin classics were well represented as in any eighteenth-century library, but Greek authors less so. History, antiquity and topography filled many shelves, as did titles connected with his special studies, royal and noble authors and the history of British art. There was a good collection of sermons; erotica hardly featured at all except for Payne Knight's *Worship of Priapus* which had caused such consternation among the prudish when it was published in 1786, and a book illustrating the Spintrian medals. Large folios of prints from various countries, views of palaces and gardens, descriptions of processions and fêtes filled the shelves on each side of the window that forms the background to Müntz's sketch.

Perhaps the largest section in the library consisted of French books: romances, poets (Boileau was his favourite French poet) and of course the letters of Madame de Sévigné, whom he revered as the greatest exponent of the art in which he himself excelled as brilliantly. She was his 'adored Madame de Sévigné' as he told one correspondent, while to another he praised her as one who 'spread her leaf-gold over all her acquaintance, and made them shine'. He never lost an opportunity to extol her gifts. When Cole met him in Paris in 1765, Walpole took him on a special pilgrimage to see the house where she had lived: 'a Corner House', Cole noted in his diary, 'which he carried me on Purpose to see, not far from the Port St. Antoine, at the entrance upon the Boulevarts, as well as I remember.' The gifts Walpole most prized in her are those which we now enjoy so much in his own correspondence: 'her allusions, her applications are the happiest possible. She had the art of making you acquainted with all her acquaintance, and attaches you even to the spots she inhabited.'

Here in his library Walpole spent his industrious mornings while in the evening he sat writing at his books, notes and letters, sometimes until two in the morning, refreshing himself with occasional cups of coffee. 'I pass all my mornings in the thirteenth century,' he once wrote to his friend John Chute, 'and my evenings with the century that is coming.' Though his eye was ever focused on posterity he was a person who felt a special affinity with past ages, with the gothic gloom and the 'true rust of the barons' wars' that he tried to recreate at Strawberry Hill. The future was so fascinating and

vague; the past now so safe and complete. In January 1766 he wrote
to George Montagu:

> Visions, you know, have always been my pasture, and so far from
> growing old enough to quarrel with their emptiness, I almost think
> there is no wisdom comparable to that of exchanging what is called
> the realities of life for dreams. Old castles, old pictures, old
> histories, and the babble of old people, make one live back into
> centuries, that cannot disappoint one. One holds fast and surely
> what is past. The dead have exhausted their power of deceiving—
> one can trust Catherine of Médicis now.

This nostalgia for the past sprang, of course, at least in part from a
distrust of, a certain shrinking from, the dangers of too committed an
involvement in the affairs of the present, especially in the business of
public life with all the disappointments of thwarted ambition and
frustrated hope. Better far, he believed, to stand aside and watch,
listen and record that some remote posterity might find the same
safety and escape in a past he was now rescuing for it from the
oblivion of time. So too with personal relationships. He must avoid
the wounds that love inflicts even if it meant denying himself the
fullest experience of love. Walpole was loyal and faithful to his
friends, but the relationship was always intellectual. He could end a
friendship abruptly if he feared deception, indifference or disappointment, and occasionally did so. He never again risked the
trauma he had suffered after his mother's death. The past no longer
has the power to hurt; no more have stones and mortar. If we are to
look for a real love in Walpole's life we shall find it, perhaps, not so
much in any special or particular friendship as in that strange and
unique manifestation of his dreams and fantasies, his 'castle' of
Strawberry Hill.

II
John Chute and the
Strawberry Committee

✦ 1 ✦

Strawberry Hill was anything but a castle when Walpole first lived there; indeed, it was little more than a cottage, a house of very modest proportions, low ceilings and small rooms. When Lady Townshend first saw it she must have wondered what on earth had possessed her cousin to purchase so cramped a place. 'Lord God! Jesus! what a house!' she cried out as she climbed up the stairs. 'It is just such a house as a parson's, where the children lie at the foot of the bed.' Its charm lay in its situation rather than in the house itself, near to Twickenham, not too far from London, and surrounded by pleasant meadows commanding an uninterrupted view of the Thames.

The neighbourhood, too, was one particularly suitable for a man of Walpole's sociable tastes. It is difficult today to imagine Twickenham as a small town surrounded by open fields, but its rural atmosphere combined with its close proximity to London made it at that period a favourite place for country retreats, and the presence there only recently of Alexander Pope and Sir Godfrey Kneller had attracted people of artistic or literary inclinations to settle there. Later on Walpole would celebrate his new home in a poem recording all the remarkable people who had lived there from Bacon to Pope and Fielding, beginning with lines identifying Twickenham as an abode of the arts,

> Where silver Thames round Twit'nam meads
> His winding current sweetly leads;
> Twit'nam, the Muse's fav'rite seat,
> Twit'nam, the Graces' lov'd retreat . . .

Across the river lay Richmond, and Petersham with its elegant villas; Syon with its ducal mansion; Marble Hill and Ham House introduced an aristocratic air while Hampton Court, Kew and Gunnersbury, where old Princess Amelia lived, proclaimed the nearby presence of royalty.

> The house is so small [Walpole wrote to Horace Mann] that I can send it you in a letter to look at: the prospect is as delightful as possible, commanding the river, the town, and Richmond park; and being situated on a hill descends to the Thames through two or three little meadows, where I have some Turkish sheep and two cows, all studied in their colours for becoming the view.

An altogether suitable place, it would seem, for 'Celadon' to make his country home.

Walpole had lived chiefly at his father's house in Downing Street following his return from the Grand Tour in September 1741. After Sir Robert's fall from office they moved to Arlington Street, a house that became Horace's property after his father's death in 1745, and was to remain his London home for many years. He was now a Member of Parliament and regularly attended the House of Commons during the acrimonious debates that raged around the old minister's head during his last year in office, speaking (for all his weak voice and poor delivery) in his father's defence and resolving never to forgive those former allies who had plotted and schemed to bring about the minister's fall. Like any young man of fashion he also threw himself into the pleasures of the town, though avoiding those tempting excesses that were to cause the ruin of both health and fortune in so many of his contemporaries. He enjoyed cards, and gambled mildly at the fashionable games of loo, cribbage and quadrille. He was a devotee of the theatre, visiting the playhouses as often as he could, collecting printed editions of plays and numbering one or two of the leading actresses of the day among his friends. But being neither a rake nor a libertine, he soon began to feel the need to escape occasionally from the allurements and time-consuming diversions of Mayfair and St James's and to look for some retreat where he could find solitude, which he valued increasingly with the passing of the years, and a quiet setting for his growing collection of books, prints, pictures and *virtù*. In 1746, he took a house in the precincts of Windsor Castle but it did not really answer his needs. The following year he discovered the little house at Twickenham and his problem was solved.

The house had been built by a coachman of Lord Bradford half a century or so before Walpole acquired the lease. The coachman was said to have paid for the building from the profits made by selling the hay from his employer's stables and feeding the horses on chopped straw, which gave the place the nickname of Chopped Straw Hall. The actor and dramatist Colley Cibber had been a previous tenant but Walpole's immediate predecessor was Mrs Chenevix, the proprietor of a famous toy shop, which enabled him to describe it to his cousin Conway as 'a little play-thing house' that he had purchased out of her shop, 'the prettiest bauble you ever saw'. It was just the place he had been looking for, only two hours by coach from London, yet completely rural in its aspect, giving him the calm and peace in which he could read and write in uninterrupted seclusion; for when all was said and done, a man who is to devote his life to a voluminous correspondence must of necessity be sometimes separated from his friends. Yet company was always near and fuel for a romantic imagination was at hand: 'Dowagers as plenty as flounders inhabit all around,' Conway was assured, 'and Pope's ghost is just now skimming under my window by a most poetical moonlight.' After little more than a year there as a tenant Walpole was able to buy the freehold together with the surrounding five acres, and having discovered from an old deed that the slight eminence upon which the place was built had been known as Strawberry Hill, gave the house the name that would eventually become so famous. 'I like to be here', he told his friend Horace Mann in Florence, 'better than I have liked being anywhere since I came to England.' He would not change this opinion.

Walpole almost at once set about getting the garden and surrounding acres into something like order. Gardening was a subject upon which he had pronounced ideas that he later set down in his essay *On Modern Gardening*, written in 1770. He was, in the main, a follower of William Kent, the first man, in Walpole's phrase, who 'leaped the fence, and saw that all nature was a garden', thus striking a death-blow at the old formal layout of parterre, terraces, marble urns, statued fountains and 'canals measured by the line'. This Frenchified or Italianate taste was, in Walpole's opinion, alien to the English climate, resulting in 'symmetrical and unnatural gardens'. Equally to be avoided were some of the extravagances in an opposite direction, the romantic grotto and that favourite eighteenth-century conceit, the hermitage. This, he considered, was an ornament 'whose merit soonest fades', adding that 'it is almost comic to set aside a quarter of one's garden to be melancholy in'. False ruins he occasionally approved but only if they conjured up a genuine feeling for the gothic past, like the sham castle at Wimpole Hall near Cambridge. All the same when Horace Mann, writing from Florence, dared to suppose that his friend's garden, like his house, was a gothic one, he received a sharp rebuke. 'Gothic is merely architecture,' he was informed, 'and as one has a satisfaction in imprinting the gloomth of abbeys and cathedrals on one's house, so one's garden, on the contrary, is to be nothing but *riant*, and the gaiety of nature.'

Work on improving and developing his grounds began before any alterations were made to the house. In August 1748 he told Conway:

> My present and sole occupation is planting, in which I have made great progress, and talk very learnedly with the nurserymen, except that now and then a lettuce run to seed overturns all my botany, as I have more than once taken it for a curious West-Indian flowering shrub. Then the deliberation with which trees grow, is extremely inconvenient to my natural impatience. I lament living in so barbarous an age, when we are come to so little perfection in gardening. I am persuaded that a hundred and fifty years hence it will be as common to move oaks a hundred and fifty years old, as it is now to transplant tulip-roots.

The lawn was the chief feature of his garden, coming right up to the house and sweeping gently down to the river, its extremities planted with trees and shrubs in 'natural' groupings to avoid the sort of effect where 'the compass and square were of more use in plantation than the nurseryman'.

As time went on more land was bought, so that by the end of his life the original five acres had grown to forty-six, and while the garden still remained innocent of such follies as a ruin or a hermitage, it was to acquire a rustic thatched cottage, a chapel in the woods, and a garden-seat carved to represent a large sea shell. The nearest thing to a formal garden would be a walled enclosure close to the Round Tower, the last major addition Walpole made to his house, in the centre of which was a round pond given the Chinese name of Po-Yang. Another feature which came after the addition of further rooms, when the place began to take on a more baronial or monastic aspect, was the Prior's Garden between the house and the road with its high protecting wall, overlooked by the windows of the Great Bedchamber. This secluded spot was entered through a delicate gothic screen visible to the right as one entered the house and which created a charming cloister-like effect.

It is very difficult to form an impression of what Strawberry Hill looked like when Walpole first saw it, as all we have to go on is his rough sketch showing the house before and after the gothic battlements had been added. It would seem to have lacked any coherent architectural plan, a small gabled structure of three storeys in the highest part with a smaller two-storeyed wing containing the kitchen. To transform this rather nondescript place into an elegant villa he decided to adopt the gothic style which had been in fashion for some time, encouraged as it was, among other things, by the popular works of Batty Langley, appropriately a native of Twickenham, whose *Gothic Architecture Improved by Rules and Proportions* had appeared in 1742, and by the works of such accomplished amateurs as Sanderson Miller, an exact contemporary of Walpole. Miller in 1745 had added pointed arches and pinnacles to his family home, Radway Grange in Warwickshire, and was busily constructing some gothic ruins and a tower in his grounds just about the time that Walpole decided to start his improvements at Strawberry Hill. It was a style Walpole considered suitable for a house of modest size. 'The Grecian is only proper for magnificent and public buildings,' he assured Horace Mann in February 1750 when the latter had reacted in some alarm at his friend's announcement that he was about to build a little gothic estate at Strawberry Hill:

> Columns and all their beautiful ornaments look ridiculous when crowded into a closet or cheesecake-house. The variety is little, and admits no charming irregularities. I am almost as fond of *Sharawaggi*, or Chinese want of symmetry, in buildings, as in grounds or gardens. I am sure, whenever you come to England, you will be pleased with the liberty of taste into which we are struck, and of which you can have no idea.

❧ 2 ❧

When Walpole was describing the plans made for his house he used the plural; it was 'the taste into which *we* are struck', for he was referring not only to himself but to the two friends whom he had co-opted into a committee of taste to help and advise him in his work. This 'Strawberry Committee', as he called it, consisted as well as himself of Richard Bentley, son of the Master of Trinity already mentioned, a man with a brilliant flair for rococo design, and John Chute, one of a distinguished Hampshire family, whom Walpole had encountered on his Grand Tour. The latter was very well known to Horace Mann, and was to become one of Walpole's closest friends.

Chute was the youngest of the ten children of Edward Chute of the Vyne near Basingstoke, and was born on 30 December 1701. The family was descended from Chaloner Chute who had been Speaker of the House of Commons at the close of the Cromwellian era, and were staunch supporters of the Whig party. Edward Chute had served in his turn as High Sheriff of Hampshire and his two elder sons were both to sit in Parliament in the Whig interest. Young John had had the advantage of being brought up in one of the most beautiful country houses in England, but beyond this his advantages were few. His health was delicate, his eyesight was poor and even as a young man he suffered from severe attacks of gout and subsisted, in a brave attempt to combat the disease, on a disagreeable diet of milk and turnips. As a younger son his financial position was, to say the least, insecure. The estate would pass to his eldest brother, with whom he had little friendship. Another brother, Francis, pursued a legal career in London, but John, after leaving Eton, seems to have followed no profession. He was an aesthete, had the instincts and knowledge, though not the resources, of a collector, and had sufficient architectural skill to draw plans and elevations if not to solve the more intricate problems of strains and stresses. He was later on to design a house for Walpole's half-sister, Lady Mary Churchill, and was responsible for the gothic elevations at Donnington, near Newbury, built for his friend Mr Andrews. Though endowed with an acute intelligence and a pleasant wit, his physical appearance was not very appealing; he had a long pointed nose and a receding chin and an affected, rather mincing deportment. To the bucolic fox-hunting squires who were his neighbours, he must have seemed very decadent and effete. He was the sort of man who easily managed to shock his more conventional contemporaries by the affectation of his manner which effectively hid, except to the most discerning, the more sterling qualities beneath which included, in addition to a well stocked mind, a strong gift for disinterested friendship.

This quality was to show itself in the devotion which Chute was to lavish upon a cousin, Francis Whithed, almost eighteen years his junior, who was to become his travelling companion in Italy and was to remain his intimate friend until the younger man's premature death in 1751. Born Francis Thistlethwaite, he had adopted the surname of Whithed from an uncle whose estate he had inherited while still a minor. In consequence of this inheritance he was a man of considerable fortune; but like Chute he was handicapped by a delicate constitution which, with the added burden of deafness, gave him a slightly defenceless quality that appealed to some protective instinct in his elder relation. A portrait in pastel by Rosalba Carriera, made in Italy when he was about twenty-two, shows him to have been very good-looking. His pleasant appearance and gentle temperament made him an agreeable companion; women found him attractive (in Italy he was to become the father of an illegitimate daughter) but his deafness prevented him from developing the sort of verbal wit that characterized the rest of the circle of friends he was soon to join with Chute in Florence.

Whithed reached his majority in 1740 and decided, as was customary for someone of his age and fortune, to make the Grand Tour of France and Italy. It was usual for a young man to take an elder person, a tutor or 'bear-leader', on these extended expeditions, but in Whithed's case both his delicate health and deafness made it advisable for him to travel with someone with whom he was more intimately connected than one who would at that time have ranked as a mere retainer. It was therefore agreed that he and John Chute should travel together. There was much in this arrangement that suited Chute. His father had died in 1722 leaving him very little, and since then he had been more or less dependent upon his elder brother Anthony who was now master of the Vyne and the lion's share of the property. He had nothing in common with this brother; his only friends at the Vyne were his sister Ann and his cat Geoffrey and these he was quite ready to part from, if only temporarily, when the chance of freedom and foreign travel were offered him. What, indeed, could be more pleasant for a confirmed bachelor nearing forty, an acknowledged devotee of the arts with no very rosy prospects for the future, than to have the chance to see Italy, that Mecca of the eighteenth-century dilettante, in the company of a personable young relative whose wealth and warm regard were at his disposal? Such relationships can, and often do, end in disaster. It speaks well for Chute's adaptability and genuine care for his young friend, and the latter's affectionate and placid disposition, that the friendship thus started was to remain unbroken.

The two travellers must have left England with some relief, for Whithed's family circumstances were no happier than Chute's. His brothers, as Gray was later to declare, were 'nasty People, that don't deserve mentioning', while Walpole was even more explicit: 'Whithed's younger brother, the clergyman,' he told Horace Mann, 'is the greatest brute in the world, except the elder brother, the layman.' From such a background, it must have been almost a pleasure to face the hazards of seasickness, venal and corrupt customs officers, footpads, highwaymen, dishonest and extortionate land-lords, dirty inns, bedbugs, lice and all the other perils that were the commonplace of travel in that age of elegance. Of these they had their share including, for Chute, a dangerous bilious attack in a grimy lodging-house at Marseilles. But the excitement of new experiences and, after they reached Italy, the joy of seeing the great treasures of art and venerable monuments of the past more than compensated for these inconveniences. A Grand Tour usually lasted about two years; Chute and Whithed, the 'Chuteheds' as Walpole was inevitably to christen them, were to remain abroad for the best part of six.

It was in Florence that the meeting with Walpole took place. Together with Thomas Gray he had set out for Italy in March 1739. In the summer of 1740, having been driven by heat and fear of malaria from Rome where they had hoped to see the outcome of the election following the death of Clement XII, they had returned to Florence and to the house of the British Resident, Walpole's distant relative Horace Mann, and there, also staying as guests of the hospitable minister, they encountered Chute and Whithed. If Mann had engineered this meeting hoping that the four men would find each other's company sympathetic, he could not have been more successful, for an instant rapport seems to have been established. Mann himself had many characteristics in common with the guests who were staying under his roof. He was also a bachelor, a connoisseur of the arts, and inclined to fuss about his health. Many years later Dr Johnson's former friend Mrs Hester Thrale, in her role as Mrs Piozzi, was to make some revealing comments about certain proclivities of the British minister, though without offering an atom of evidence in support of her charge. 'I call these Fellows Finger-twirlers,' she wrote, 'meaning a decent word for Sodomites: old Sir Horace Mann and Mr. James the Painter had such an odd way of twirling their Fingers in Discourse—and I see Suetonius tells us the same thing of one of the Roman Emperors.'

Whether or not 'finger-twirling' in the sense in which Mrs Piozzi intended it was a feature in the lives of any or all of these five men can now only be a matter for speculation, but they must certainly have presented a rather odd picture to the inhabitants of Florence and even more so to the philistine youths from Britain who were passing through the Tuscan capital at the time. Whithed alone must have seemed more or less normal, and he was soon to embark on a liaison with a local girl, but even he was capable of appearing dressed 'all over spangles'. Walpole was also romantically engaged as *cicisbeo* to a Florentine beauty, but his effeminate look and manner were none the less marked. Gray, though lacking the gaiety and high spirits that Walpole displayed at this time, was accustomed to walk with short mincing steps, and unkind undergraduates at Cambridge had been known to call him 'Miss Gray'. Chute, perhaps, presented the most extraordinary picture, for as well as his quizzing-glass he adopted, while in Italy, the practice of carrying a fan, and the sight of him with his long-nosed but chinless face darting up to some masterpiece in the Uffizi, adjusting his eyeglasses while assiduously applying his fan, and exclaiming shrilly on the merits of the canvas, was calculated to startle even the most phlegmatic of observers. Certain mannerisms of speech, also, must have struck a singular note, like his habit of calling his host 'Mini' which was short for 'Minister'. What perhaps added to the oddity of the spectacle was the fact that Chute was by some years the eldest of the quintet. He was now forty years old; Mann was thirty-four, Gray ten years younger, and Walpole and Whithed twenty-three and twenty-four respectively.

But for all their unusual appearance and unconventional behaviour they formed a convivial group. They could laugh at the oddities they observed in others, and they laughed a good deal at themselves, refusing to take things too seriously. Walpole could now pose as a seasoned traveller: 'I have left off screaming, Lord! this! and Lord! that!' he had written home, rather complacently, to West. They found great amusement at the presence of some quaint English females, intrepid searchers after culture or romance, who frequented Florence at the time, chief among whom were Walpole's own sister-in-law, the estranged wife of his eldest brother, and the 'she-meteor', Lady Mary Wortley Montagu. These two formidable ladies, with the would-be bluestocking Countess of Pomfret, formed a trio that rivalled Walpole's own group for eccentricity. 'Only figure', the absent West was asked, 'the coalition of prudery, debauchery, sentiment, history, Greek, Latin, French, Italian, and metaphysics; all except the second, understood by halves, by quarters, or not at all.'

For Chute in particular this period in Florence came like a renewal of youth. The years that separated him from the others seemed to vanish, and in Walpole especially he found a mind that was in harmony with his own. For Walpole himself it was a no less fortunate encounter. For all his quick perception and brittle humour, his mind was still to some extent unformed, and needed the guiding hand of a more mature personality. It was John Chute, with the advantage of age and more settled opinions, who was able to give form to the younger man's so far rather disorganized notions and a firmer foundation to his aesthetic ideas. The seventeen or so years of seniority in Chute were a distinct benefit, for Walpole needed some person who could fill the void which the remoteness of his father and the lack of accord with his much older brother had made in his life. Chute was to become his firm friend, the one 'to whom one speaks as confidentially as to one's own soul'. Time was to strengthen this relationship and when Chute died thirty-six years later, Walpole would write to Mann of his grief for the friend who had been the chief counsel in his affairs, his oracle of taste, the man whose 'wit and quickness illuminated everything'.

Various shadows were to be cast over this bright and cheerful Italian scene before Walpole returned home. In April 1741 he left Florence, making his farewells to Mann whom he would never see again though they were to write to each other for the next forty years. He was soon to quarrel with Gray and to be struck down by a serious illness at Reggio when his friends had gone on before him to Venice and, but for the timely arrival of Lord Lincoln, might even have died.

Still greater clouds were gathering over Europe. In October 1740 the Habsburg Emperor Charles VI had died leaving a disputed succession; in December Frederick II of Prussia invaded Silesia and the prospect of a general European war threatened. Letters from Downing Street reached Walpole from his father urging his return, and in July he set out from Venice for Genoa and the long journey back to England, leaving Chute and Whithed behind him.

The 'Chuteheds' were soon back in Florence where they remained for the next few years living with Mann at the Casa Ambrogi between the Arno and the via de' Bardi, Whithed returning to the arms of his *innamorata*, Chute following his artistic and musical tastes undisturbed by the distant thunder of war and wondering, as he explored the treasures of Florence, whether or not to spend the rest of his life in this most enchanting exile. He now had a new and very agreeable occupation in hunting out works of art for Walpole which they both hoped the latter's father might be persuaded to purchase for his collection at Houghton. Less serious topics also adorned their correspondence: Chute complained of a singer at the opera 'whose voice is exactly like that of an old lady's old lap-dog, who has caught an asthma of his mistress', or sent messages from his cat Geoffrey to Walpole's dog Patapan, the cat (for all that it was in fact at this time still at the Vyne and not in Florence at all) even addressing its canine friend, through its master, in verse:

> Pata is frolicksome and smart,
> As Geoffrey once was—(Oh my heart!)
> He's purer than a turtle's kiss,
> And gentler than a little miss;
> A jewel for a lady's ear,
> And Mr. Walpole's pretty dear . . .

Twenty-four lines followed in much the same vein, and it is not to be wondered at that in the course of Patapan's reply he complained, also through his master, that

> This very thing of Mr. Chute's
> Scarce with my taste and fancy suits.
> Oh! had it but in French been writ,
> 'Twere the genteelest, sweetest bit!

Such exchanges were, no doubt, trivial enough, but they helped to keep Chute feeling young and provided Walpole with an amusing outlet for that whimsical side of his nature which never left him but was to strike such a jarring note on the rising tide of earnestness that was to make its first dreary appearance in his extreme old age, leaving him refreshingly unrepentant. 'I have a true regard for nonsense', he would tell Mary Berry when he was seventy-six years old, 'on which I have lived man and boy for longer than I will say.' It is no surprise, however, that the nineteenth century never really appreciated him.

A warm friendship had developed between Chute and Horace Mann. Shortly after Walpole left Italy, Mann had to undergo an operation for an anal fistula, a risky and painful ordeal at that time, but he made a good recovery and Chute was able to report to Walpole that he had found the minister 'as well as you yourself can wish him', adding that 'he is most undoubtedly in a state of much more strong and perfect health than ever he was since I had the happiness of loving, that is knowing him . . .' The mild and sunny climate of Italy had a beneficial effect upon Chute's own delicate constitution, though he was still racked by agonizing attacks of gout which he now sought to allay by varying his diet of milk and turnips by a slightly more interesting one of ravioli and spinach tarts. He might well have prolonged his stay in Italy indefinitely had not various circumstances coincided early in 1745 to make him think that the time had come to return home. Whithed's state of health, never robust, had been undermined by a venereal infection; Chute's own affairs were affected by the news from England of the death of his second brother Francis; and the war, which had seemed so remote only a short time ago, was now beginning to encroach upon Italy with Milan threatened by Franco-Spanish troops.

Before leaving Italy, however, the two friends were determined to pay a final visit to Rome. Mann was eager to help, though no doubt reluctant to see them go, and wrote on their behalf to Cardinal Alessandro Albani, the handsome, genial and cultivated nephew of Clement XI, who was not only one of the richest and most discerning collectors in Rome and a powerful figure in the Curia, but was also the representative there of the interests of Maria Theresa, and thus a friend to the subjects of her ally George II. This was an important fact, for Rome was the home of the Stuart Pretender whose elder son

Charles Edward was at that very moment embarked on his adventure in Scotland, while Rome itself swarmed with his adherents and supporters. To jump into this nest of Jacobites without powerful protection would, at that particular juncture, have been imprudent, to say the least.

The travellers set out in May, reaching Rome by way of Bologna and Loreto. They were received by the Cardinal with affability. He had also met their friend Horace Walpole in 1740, though due to the circumstances of the conclave their encounter had been of the very briefest nature. Chute was now to find himself, somewhat uncharacteristically, involved in a web of political intrigue, all the more fascinating for being so unfamiliar. For some months Mann and Albani had been exchanging valuable political information, both making use of spies and informers who were never in short supply in Rome. But these rather shady individuals, who were often also employed in the lucrative antique trade, could not always be relied upon either for the veracity of the material they produced or as a safe and dependable means by which it could be transferred from Rome to Florence. Chute, mixing freely in the best society and frequenting the places where connoisseurs and dealers—the latter very often Jacobite agents—were accustomed to meet, was able to repay Mann for his hospitality and also prove his loyalty to the Hanoverian dynasty by doing a little spying on his own account and passing on what he gleaned to the Cardinal, a service for which Mann was later to commend him in a dispatch to the Duke of Newcastle. Albani also made use of him as a means for conveying to the British minister at Florence any information he did not think it proper to send directly himself.

This rather picaresque activity had its disadvantages, however. Roman society for the most part was ranged on the side of France and the Stuarts, and as a result both Chute and Whithed felt themselves rather isolated even if this meant, as a consequence, that the Palazzo Albani with its famous treasures was more often available to them than might otherwise have been the case. When the Cardinal gave a splendid entertainment there early in 1746 to celebrate the election of Maria Theresa's husband as emperor, The 'Chuteheds' were the only Englishmen present as Albani did not consider any of their other compatriots then in Rome sufficiently loyal to the House of Hanover and the cause of the Empress-Queen. The Jacobites, meanwhile, tried to denigrate Chute, spreading a malicious rumour that his social origins, and those of his friend, were somewhat obscure and that he was travelling only as Whithed's tutor. This brought an angry outburst from Florence when news of it reached Horace Mann. Both his friends, he assured the Cardinal, were of superior birth to the majority of their calumniators; they were in any case related and Chute, far from being dependent upon Whithed, travelled at his own expense.

On the whole, the atmosphere in Rome was tense and uncomfortable for men of their convictions, especially when news of Prince Charles's early successes in Scotland began to reach the ears of the exultant Jacobites, and they decided to move on to Naples. But even this simple operation presented its problems, for the Neapolitan ambassador, Cardinal Acquaviva, to whom they had to apply for passports, was a supporter of the Stuarts and only welcomed applications that were recommended by the Pretender's secretary Lord Dunbar, and it needed all the tact and diplomacy of Albani to secure the necessary documents for them. He was also able to render them another service. Chute had purchased on Walpole's behalf an antique eagle which had been excavated four years earlier in the Boccapadugli Gardens near the Baths of Caracalla. Thanks to Cardinal Albani's influence (aided by a hint from Mann) this valuable and unique sculpture was allowed to leave the Papal dominions and was later to be one of the most prized pieces in the Strawberry Hill collection, adorning first the library and later on the gallery where it stood on a sepulchral altar also decorated with eagles.

Chute and Whithed were back in England by the end of September 1746, returning by way of Vienna and the German states. In the Austrian capital they had been received in audience by the empress and Chute took the opportunity to pay fulsome compliments to Cardinal Albani, explaining the kindness and protection he had extended to her Imperial Majesty's allies in Rome. In London, they were reunited with Walpole whom they had not seen for over five years. 'I strolled to town one day last week, and there I found them!' he wrote to Mann on 2 October. 'Poor creatures! there they were! wondering at everything they saw, but with the difference from Englishmen that go abroad, of keeping their amazement to themselves.' Much had happened to Walpole in the interval: his father had died, so too had Patapan; he was now a Member of

Parliament, and was just about to acquire Strawberry Hill. It was from there that he wrote to Mann exactly a year later:

> The Chuteheds have been extremely good, and visited and stayed with me at Twickenham—I am sorry I must at your expense be so happy. If I were to say all I think of Mr. Chute's immense honesty, his sense of wit, his knowledge, and his humanity, you would think I was writing a dedication. I am happy in him; I don't make up to him for you, for he loves nothing a quarter so well, but I try to make you regret him less—do you forgive me?

❖❯❯ 3 ❮❮❖

When Chute paid his first visit to Strawberry Hill, it is fair to suppose that he and Walpole discussed plans for its extension, for it was plain that the latter could not be expected to exist for long in the cramped space and small rooms of the villa as they were when he first occupied the house. One of his reasons for thinking in terms of Gothic was, as we have seen, that he believed the 'Grecian' orders unsuitable for a small house, and indeed, for someone familiar with the classical splendours of Houghton, it would have seemed very ludicrous to try to reproduce anything like it on a 'cheesecake' scale. William Beckford was later to refer contemptuously to Strawberry Hill as 'a species of gothic mousetrap' and to a man as sensitive to ridicule as Walpole, this would have been a wounding remark had he ever heard it, yet while a gothic mousetrap is almost conceivable, the thought of a baroque mousetrap would really have belonged to the realm of the absurd. Even so, many of his friends must have been surprised by his choice of style when the first crenellations began to appear, for such pie-crust embellishments were considered at the time a rather middle-class taste, and they must have shared the bewilderment of Horace Mann who wrote from Florence asking 'Why will you make it gothic?'

In the course of his Grand Tour Walpole had seen the cathedrals of Amiens and Rheims in France as well as Siena in Italy, but had nothing in particular to say about them beyond criticizing Addison's opinion that Siena was one of the masterpieces of gothic architecture, declaring on the contrary that though the materials were richer the workmanship and taste were not nearly so good as in several others he had seen. When he did display what would later be recognized as a gothic taste (though only after the popularization of the literary genre started by his own novel *The Castle of Otranto*, which would not be written until 1764) it was in his response to wild and mountainous landscapes, scenery which his contemporaries still more generally regarded as 'horrid' rather than romantic or picturesque. 'Precipices, mountains, torrents, wolves, rumblings, Salvator Rosa—the pomp of our park and the meekness of our palace!' he had written to Richard West from a hamlet in the mountains of Savoy. 'Here we are, the lonely lords of glorious desolate prospects.' So, too, the journey to the Grande Chartreuse brought an ecstatic reaction to a view from which many an eighteenth-century traveller would have averted his eyes with a shudder of disgust:

> But the road, West, the road! winding round a prodigious mountain, and surrounded with others, all shagged with hanging woods, obscured with pines or lost in clouds! Below, a torrent breaking through cliffs, and tumbling through fragments of rocks! Sheets of cascades forcing their silver speed down channelled precipices, and hasting into the roughened river at the bottom! Now and then an old foot-bridge, with a broken rail, a leaning cross, a cottage, or the ruin of an hermitage! This sounds too bombast and too romantic to one that has not seen it, too cold for one that has. If I could send you my letter post between two lovely tempests that echoed each other's wrath, you might have some idea of this noble roaring scene as you were reading it.

It was this feeling for atmosphere that turned his thoughts in a gothic direction when he returned from his travels and settled down in his new home. When he came to discuss gothic architecture in the first volume of his *Anecdotes of Painting in England* he again reverted to this subjective approach, not so much emphasizing the glories of gothic buildings as such, as dwelling upon the mental impressions they created or suggested. He wrote:

> It is difficult for the noblest Grecian temple to convey half so many impressions to the mind, as a cathedral does of the best Gothic taste, a proof of skill in the architects and of address in the priests

who erected them. The latter exhausted their knowledge of the passions in composing edifices whose pomp, mechanism, vaults, tombs, painted windows, gloom and perspectives infused such sensations of romantic devotion; and they were happy in finding artists capable of executing such machinery.

This was the argument he still had in mind when, in 1774, he came to defend the architecture of his own 'small capricious house'. It was built, he maintained, to please his own taste and in some degree to realize his own visions, and the justification of all this, if any justification were needed, was that his house had become 'the proper habitation of, as it was the scene that inspired, the author of the Castle of Otranto'.

Chute seems to have fallen in with his friend's gothic preferences without much opposition or complaint. He had, after all, been brought up himself in a house of medieval origins so that the style had a domestic familiarity to him, and he was possibly just then in some reaction against classicism after his years in Italy, ending, as they had, with a period in the circle of Cardinal Albani, a milieu in which Winckelmann would soon be producing works that were to be the inspiration of Neo-Classicism. In any case a commitment to gothic at Strawberry Hill did not in any way imply a lack of commitment to classical forms elsewhere, as the ingenious and elegant staircase that he was later to design for the Vyne is an indication. That he responded whole-heartedly to his friend's plan of 'implanting the gloomth of abbeys and cathedrals' on his house we may assume from Walpole's tribute at the time of Chute's death that he was 'the genius that presided over poor Strawberry'.

Richard Bentley first appeared on the scene at Strawberry Hill about 1750 (the earliest mention of him in one of Walpole's letters was on 23 June of that year) and his arrival as a third to what had previously been merely the deliberations of two friends was no doubt what gave Walpole the idea of forming his committee of taste, for one of Bentley's chief recommendations was his artistic skill as a draughtsman. This gift, together with a pleasant wit and something of his father's scholarship—though none of his forcefulness of character—combined to produce a personality that Walpole declared he 'adored' telling George Montagu, his old Eton friend who probably introduced Bentley to him, how the latter had 'more sense, judgment, and wit, more taste, and more misfortunes, than ever met in any man'.

Among the misfortunes could be included a chronic impecuniousness, a lazy and disorganized disposition and, perhaps the worst of all from Walpole's point of view, a disagreeable and extravagant wife whose uneven temper and tiresome ways earned her the unflattering nicknames of 'Tisiphone', 'Mrs Hecate' and 'Hannah Cleopatra' from her husband's new patron. It was a mistake on Bentley's part to bring her a little too often to Strawberry Hill where her abrasive presence struck a discordant note. Her ever-increasing family was another problem. Some years later, when Bentley's fecklessness and domestic problems were beginning to cast a shadow over their relationship, Walpole would write to Montagu: 'You will ask where Mr. Bentley is; confined with five sick infants, who live in spite of the epidemic distemper, and as if they were infantas.' Financial calamity would ultimately force Bentley to seek refuge in Jersey, taking his wife and family with him, but for some years he remained in favour at Strawberry Hill, and probably would have continued to do so had it not been for his accumulating misfortunes and the doleful influence of 'Mrs Hecate' upon the lively spirits of his two friends.

After Bentley's departure his place on the Strawberry Committee was taken by Thomas Pitt, later Lord Camelford, a nephew of the Earl of Chatham, described by Mrs Thrale as 'a finical ladylike man' and by Walpole as 'very amiable and very sensible, and one of the very few that I reckon quite worthy of being at home at Strawberry'. He was twenty years Walpole's junior and had settled in the neighbourhood of Twickenham in 1761 after some time spent in foreign travel, visiting Portugal, Spain and Italy. In Florence he had met Sir Horace Mann, and had another link with Walpole through his relationship to Bishop Lyttelton of Carlisle, an Eton contemporary of the 'Quadruple Alliance'. He was to become an amateur architect of some talent, a member of the Society of Dilettanti, and was later to be an early patron of the young John Soane. Though he was to design some houses as well as a Palladian bridge at Hagley, a rustic bridge and gothic cottage at Park Place, Henley (for Walpole's cousin Conway) and a Corinthian arch at Stowe, his work at Strawberry Hill was to be mainly concerned, as was Bentley's, with interior features. Like Bentley, he was a married man, but there the resemblance stopped. Announcing the marriage (which did not take place until 1771) to his friend Lady Ossory, Walpole wrote: 'Tom Pitt is going to marry a Miss Wilkinson, a great fortune, sister of Jack Smith's wife. I don't believe your ladyship cares much about these Jacks and Toms.' There was obviously nothing of the Hannah Cleopatra about Miss Wilkinson. The only child of this union was the 'mad' Lord Camelford, a notorious profligate who was to be killed in a duel in 1804.

Thomas Pitt's work at Strawberry Hill was in fact not very extensive. He collaborated with Chute on the design of the chimney-piece in the Gallery and was responsible for the latticed door to the Tribune, but by the time he appeared on the scene, the greater part of the house was either built or (in the case of the Long Gallery and Great Cloister) already in process of construction, so that his help and advice were only needed in respect to certain decorative features. It was the trio of Walpole, Chute and Bentley who were the real creators of Strawberry Hill. Their talents were evenly divided and nicely complemented each other. Walpole provided the initial inspiration and was responsible for the archaeological research that provided the medieval originals upon which the various internal details were based; Chute drew up the plans and elevations so that the external appearance of the house may be said to be his work; Bentley's lively imagination produced the note of fantasy, adopting gothic forms, often with great freedom and a lack of authenticity that was later to be frowned upon by the other two, that created the atmosphere, the 'gloomth' so essentially associated in Walpole's mind with his idea of true gothic taste. This was particularly noticeable in the hall and staircase, Bentley's principal contribution, and in some early chimney-pieces where the mingling of gothic with rococo produced a style that was neither the one nor the other but was a characteristic ingredient of the style that was afterwards to be recognized as 'Strawberry Hill gothic'. It was, even when following ancient sources with some accuracy, a purely surface approach to gothic ornament that took no account of the constructional problems of medieval building or of the original materials used. There was no solidity in the designs that employed wood, stucco and papier mâché in place of masonry, but while this might horrify or amuse the purists of a later generation, it did give a delicate fairy-like quality to the whole, more suitable to the 'cloud-capp'd towers' and 'gorgeous palaces' of Prospero's insub-

stantial pageant than any Gothic cathedral or baron's keep. Walpole
was not building for posterity; his pinnacles were only constructed
of wood. No one would have been more surprised than he had he
known that his gothic folly would still be standing two hundred
years after the last stones were laid.

The first main additions to the original villa were started in 1752
with the construction of the hall and armoury, connected by
Bentley's staircase with its gothic balustrade and wallpaper with
traceries copied from the screen of Prince Arthur's tomb in
Worcester Cathedral. The box-like exterior created by this enlargement was at the same time clothed in gothic dress by Chute much in
the manner of Batty Langley, 'gothicizing' the windows and adding
crenellations and pinnacles to the roof. This earliest work established
some features of design that were to remain a characteristic of the
house as it grew from villa to castle; the application of gothic
architectural decoration to the exterior unrelated to any structural
requirements, and the use of archaeological sources, in this case
Prince Arthur's tomb, to totally unrelated objects, so that choir
doors could be adapted for bookcases or medieval tombs for
chimney-pieces. In the following year work began on two much
needed larger rooms, the Refectory or Great Parlour and the library
above it, entered by way of the armoury at the head of the staircase.
The familiar pattern of the later Strawberry Hill was beginning to
take shape, and Horace Mann, kept informed by letter of these
exciting developments, was urged to hunt for suitable remnants of
antiquity from Italy to embellish the new quarters, though without
much hope of success on the part of his friend in England. 'I thank
you a thousand times', Walpole wrote, 'for thinking of procuring me
some Gothic remains from Rome; but I believe there is no such thing.
I scarce remember any morsel in the true taste of it in Italy.'

In August 1752, while the workmen were still busy on this labour
of transformation, Walpole and Chute made a tour of Kent and
Sussex. It was to be a pilgrimage to 'this holy land of abbeys and
Gothic castles' while the two pilgrims were still inspired by the
enthusiasm of their first attempt to interpret and recreate gothic
'gloomth' in a contemporary idiom. Long and detailed accounts of
their progress were sent by Walpole to Bentley.

They visited Knole, admiring the 'ancient magnificence' of the
furniture and noticing the fact that 'there is never a good staircase',

and then went on to Bayham Abbey, to Battle Abbey where 'the situation is noble, above the level of abbeys', and to Herstmonceux where Chute, an amateur of heraldry, was delighted to find the coat of arms of Lord Dacre with all his alliances displayed over the drawing-room chimney-piece. 'Mr. Chute was transported,' declared Walpole, 'and called cousin with ten thousand quarterings.' Sissinghurst was a disappointment for all that most of the great Elizabethan quadrangle was still standing. It struck them as 'a park in ruins, and a house in ten times greater ruins', though Walpole admitted that the sight of the courtyard was 'perfect and very beautiful'. Leeds Castle also failed to satisfy their exacting taste. This was before the restoration of the main castle, and such modern additions as they did see were quickly condemned. 'Never was such a disappointment . . .' Walpole pronounced, 'the moat is the only handsome object, and is quite a lake, supplied by a cascade which tumbles through a bit of a romantic grove.' But the newly fitted-up apartments were dismissed as 'pert' and bad: 'They had a gleam of Gothic in their eyes; but it soon passed off into some modern windows, and some that never were ancient.' Penshurst they found in a rather fallen state, though the apartments, albeit furnished in 'a tawdry modern taste' were the finest Walpole had seen in an ancient palace. As a break from gothic, they paid a visit to Mereworth where Colen Campbell's masterpiece in the manner of Palladio almost made them unfaithful to their original quest. It was, wrote Walpole, 'so perfect in a Palladian taste, that I must own it has recovered me a little from Gothic.' Such rebellious ideas were soon quelled, however, and the general impression made by their tour was summed up in Chute's remark after their visit to Battle: 'What charming things we should have done if Battle Abbey had been to be sold at Mrs. Chenevix's, as Strawberry was!'

On tours such as this the travellers' eyes would be quick to notice anything that could be adopted for use at Strawberry Hill, though for the most part they used ecclesiastical models, so that hardly a chimney-piece did not claim descent from some bishop's tomb or chancel screen. In one room, the Holbein Chamber, added in 1758, and in Gray's estimation in the best taste of anything Walpole had done, the chimney-piece was based on Archbishop Warham's tomb in Canterbury Cathedral, the ceiling was taken from the queen's dressing-room at Windsor and the screen that divided the room in

two from the gates to the choir at Rouen. The effect produced by this
eclectic selection of domestic and ecclesiastical odds and ends was in
fact highly successful. Gray's opinion would be shared by many
today, and the Holbein Chamber is certainly one of the most
charming rooms in the house. Though it now seems strange to adopt
the sacred to the secular and turn tombs into familiar domestic
objects, it was this practice on Walpole's part of providing reliable
gothic ancestors for his architectural whimsicalities that made the
gothic revival not only fashionable but also respectable, so that his
house became itself a place of pilgrimage, some visitors, indeed, being
quite overcome by what they saw. When George Montagu inspected
the earlier improvements in 1754, he 'was in raptures, and screamed,
and hooped, and hollaed, and danced, and crossed himself a thousand
times over'. Eighteen years later, visiting the virtually completed
house, Lady Mary Coke reacted more soberly. It was, she
considered, the most amusing house she ever was in, 'so many
pictures and things to help one to ideas when one wants a fresh
collection; entertainment without company'.

From the time of the first extensions in 1752 additions and
improvements were carried out in one form or another for the next
twenty-four years, though Bentley's contribution ceased after 1759
when he left England for Jersey. As no member of the committee of
taste was a qualified architect, technical building problems were
managed for them by William Robinson, clerk of the works at
Greenwich Hospital and later on, after 1754, at Westminster and St
James's, whose job was to interpret the committee's plans in practical
terms. Following the completion of the Holbein Chamber, whose
main features reflect Bentley's work as adaptor or designer, the Long
Gallery was the next addition, built to Chute's design during the
years 1761–2. It was the most spectacular room in the house, and also
the largest, being 56 feet long, 15 high and 13 feet wide. Once again
various different sources were utilized to create a general effect. The
ceiling, in fan vaulting, was copied from one of the side aisles of the
Henry VII Chapel at Westminster Abbey, the canopied recesses
along the north wall, the most striking feature of the room, were
derived from Archbishop Bourchier's tomb at Canterbury, and the
doors were copied from the north door of St Alban's Abbey. In
treatment, however, an impression of surprising lightness was
achieved by the lavish use of looking-glass covered in gold net-work

to line the walls of the recesses and by the contrast between the white and gold modelling of the gothic traceries and the brilliance of the intervening wall spaces which were hung with crimson damask. There was no 'gloomth' in this room despite its gothic embellishments. It was bright and cheerful, having five south-facing windows whose upper panes were filled with heraldic glass displaying all the quarterings of the Walpole family. This painted glass, however, did not obscure the greater part of the windows whose light was reflected back from the mirror-glass walls of the recesses opposite.

It was while building the Gallery and the cabinet, or Tribune, that led out of it that Walpole had his first experience of industrial trouble, and though irritated by the delays that resulted from it, showed a characteristic sympathy with the grievances of the workmen. On 1 July 1762 he wrote to Mann:

> I am in distress about my Gallery and Cabinet. The latter was on the point of being completed, and is really striking beyond description. Last Saturday night my workmen took their leave, made their bow, and left me up to the knees in shavings. In short, the journeymen carpenters, like the cabinet-makers, have entered into an association not to work unless their wages are raised; and how can one complain? The poor fellows, whose all the labour is, see their masters advance their prices every day, and think it reasonable to touch their share.

Perhaps his sympathy with the workmen sprang from his own financial worries. 'You would be frightened at the dearness of everything,' his letter continued. 'I build out of economy, for unless I do now, in two years I shall not be able to afford it.'

A letter to Mann of 9 July 1761 suggests that Walpole intended to build the Round Tower, which terminated his extension to the west, at the same time as the Gallery and Tribune, but in fact the tower was not built until the years 1768-9. The delay was probably due more to the need to recoup financially himself than from any more problems with his workmen, for the job, he assures Mann, will 'cost immensely'. Here for the first time Walpole brought in a professional designer from outside his Strawberry Committee, employing Robert Adam to design the frieze and fireplace for the round drawing-room on the principal floor of the tower, which was approached from the end of the Gallery. Even so, he still remained faithful to his idea of

1   Horace Walpole in the Library at Strawberry Hill,
by J. H. Müntz. (Private Collection)

2   John Chute, by Gabriel Mathias. (National Trust, The Vyne, Hampshire)

3   George Selwyn, Gilly Williams and Lord Edgcumbe, by
Sir Joshua Reynolds. (City of Bristol Museum and Art Gallery)

4 Henrietta, Countess of Suffolk, by Charles Jervas.
(National Portrait Gallery)

5   Thomas Gray, by J. G. Ecchardt. (National Portrait Gallery)

6 General Conway, Lady Ailesbury and their daughter Anne,
by J. G. Ecchardt. (Private Collection)

7 Horace Walpole, Earl of Orford, by Sir Thomas Lawrence. (National Portrait Gallery)

8   Strawberry Hill from the south-east, by Paul Sandby.
(Castle Museum, Nottingham)

copying from ecclesiastical sources, and the chimney-piece was based very freely on the tomb of Edward the Confessor at Westminster and executed in white marble inlaid with scagliola, while the ceiling was copied from a rose-window in old St Paul's. In the Great North Bedchamber, built 1771–3, the last major addition except for the Beauclerk Tower of 1776, the former team was back again, Walpole himself designing the chimney-piece—this time from Bishop Dudley's tomb at Westminster—and Chute providing the design for the doors. Chute's choice was probably also responsible for the ceiling, for it was based on one dating from 1520 at his old home, the Vyne. The transformation that Walpole had planned so many years ago was now virtually complete. 'The Round Tower is finished, and magnificent,' Mann was told in June 1771, 'and the State Bedchamber proceeds fast; for you must know the little villa is grown into a superb castle.'

Even before it was finished, Walpole's 'superb castle' attracted the curiosity of connoisseurs as well as more simple sightseers, and he was constantly bothered with visitors wishing to admire or criticize his new creation.

I have but a minute's time for answering your letter, [he complained to Mann in September 1763] my house is full of people, and has been so from the instant I breakfasted, and more are coming; in short, I keep an inn; the sign, 'The Gothic Castle'. Since my Gallery was finished I have not been in it a quarter of an hour together; my whole time is passed in giving tickets for seeing it, and hiding myself while it is seen. Take my advice, never build a charming house for yourself between London and Hampton-court: everybody will live in it but you.

In applying the adjective 'charming' to his house, Walpole was using the most suitable word to describe a place that has both fascinated and irritated architectural historians ever since; too fragile and fanciful, in a way, to justify stern condemnation, yet too important in its influence upon the development of taste to be ignored. It has, indeed, something of that quality of 'Herculean weakness' that Walpole once claimed for himself in the way that it has survived while more massive structures like Fonthill Abbey have crumbled into dust. It established Walpole's reputation as an arbiter upon all questions concerning the use of gothic in his day, as when, in

1769, the Bishop of Ely asked for his advice on the design of an east window for his cathedral; and though almost wholly the work of amateurs, it was soon influencing the work of professional architects. When James Wyatt rebuilt Lee Priory near Canterbury in the gothic style for a friend of Walpole's, the latter acknowledged the house as being 'a child of Strawberry prettier than the parent'. More children were to spring into being on both sides of the Atlantic during the next hundred years. For a 'small capricious house', it was not a bad record.

❖❖ 4 ❖❖

Chute was suddenly overtaken by tragedy in the spring of 1751 by the death of Francis Whithed. Whithed's health had never been good; he had a weak chest and possibly suffered from tuberculosis. Despite a bad cough he had been out riding with his two brothers with little regard to his state of health or the very cold weather, and had then almost at once started on the long ride to Hampshire to visit his friend. He collapsed upon arrival and all Chute's care and nursing were of no avail. He died shortly afterwards at the Vyne at the age of thirty-three. For John Chute the loss was overwhelming. Whithed had been like a son and a brother to him; he had also provided a refuge for Chute, still living in straitened circumstances, where he could escape from too much dependence upon his elder brother. When Walpole heard the sad news late in March, he wrote at once to Chute offering what comfort he could in the circumstances, at the same time assuring him of his own continuing friendship:

> I can't expect to replace him, [he wrote] but at least you will in me see one who loves you as sincerely as he did and who will omit nothing that is possible to alleviate your grief . . . I shall never have a home that will not be yours—we have both seen enough of the world, to care little about it, or how soon we have done with it—but among the very few satisfactions that remain for either of us, I am persuaded we have mutually that of knowing each other's friendship—You have lost what you loved best, what have I to lose?

Whithed left Chute a legacy of £1,000 in his will, but there were those who thought that this showed a lack of proper gratitude for all the older man had done for him. Chute himself does not seem to have shown any concern on this score for all that he now had to find rooms of his own, being no longer able to avail himself of Whithed's country or town houses as had previously been his custom. In a letter to Walpole that April, Gray in particular expressed himself as being 'ashamed, but not astonish'd' at what he described as Whithed's insensibility, declaring that he thought Chute should have received five hundred a year, though even that sum he considered 'at least by half too little'. £1,000, however, was a much greater sum in 1751 than it would be today, and it should be pointed out that when Whithed made his will he probably never for a moment thought that he would predecease a man so many years his senior in age.

At the time of Whithed's death, Chute had been hoping to arrange a marriage between his friend and a certain Miss Margaret Nicoll, described in the frank manner of the eighteenth century in such matters as being worth 'above £150,000'. With the sudden removal of the prospective bridegroom, Chute, whose better judgement seems to have been undermined by his grief, decided that so handsome a fortune should not go begging, and entered into a wild scheme to transfer the young lady's hand and wealth to Walpole's impecunious nephew who had recently succeeded to the earldom of Orford and the mountain of debt that went with it. Walpole rather foolishly joined in the scheme, which soon took on the character of a comic opera with all those opportunities for public ridicule which should have warned him against it from the start. Miss Nicoll was no more than sixteen and lived with guardians who, according to Chute, gave her more blows than money. He tried to abduct her from these bawdy guardians (as he later described them) and place her in the care of his sister-in-law, the widow of Francis Chute. When the girl refused to leave he first fell down on his knees in an effort to make her change her mind and then, having no success, flew round the room in a frenzy denouncing her as a base and ungrateful creature. When this, too, failed to move her he announced that she had broken his heart, adding ominously and a shade hysterically: 'I will go where you shall never see me more. I'll hang myself. I only wish to live to serve you.'

Walpole, meanwhile, had made the mistake of involving his uncle 'old' Horace Walpole in the scheme, but the uncle, seeing that a great fortune was the stake, thought it much more sensible that Miss Nicoll should marry one of his sons, and so embarked on a sub-plot of his own devising that succeeded in frustrating Chute without securing the heiress, and added a further cause of enmity between himself and his nephew Horace whom he had never liked in any case. Finally, Lord Orford managed to sabotage the entire scheme by declaring that he had no intention of marrying Miss Nicoll under any circumstances as he had heard that she was both bad-tempered and plain. He preferred the company of his mistress Patty Turk. So it was that poor Chute's plan to help his friend Walpole and his family came to grief in a tableau of ridiculous situations. As for Margaret Nicoll, she later married the Earl of Caernarvon and, it must be hoped, lived happily ever after.

Chute's extraordinary and rather unbalanced behaviour in this burlesque business can only be explained as a reaction from his grief over Whithed's death, which represented the lowest ebb in his affairs. He was fifty, and must have thought that he had very little to look forward to in the years that lay ahead. His financial resources were now more severely limited than ever; his recurring attacks of gout were so sharp as to make him sometimes cry aloud in agony and have recourse to opiates; he had no home of his own and was compelled, when not accepting such hospitality as Walpole and other friends generously offered, to take modest rooms in London. With all the flair and taste of a connoisseur, he must for ever reconcile himself to the fact that the enjoyment he derived from the study and contemplation of works of art—one of the few consolations of his life—must always be derived from the possessions of others more fortunate than himself. It is greatly to his credit, and a mark of his courage, that with so dismal a prospect before him he still managed to maintain his reputation for wit and that he continued to be such good company to his friends, never allowing his problems to depress anyone except himself.

The shadows were gathering round him and must only, it would seem, grow denser. That they should suddenly be dispersed was hardly to be credited, yet so it was to happen. On 20 May 1754, his brother Anthony died intestate and Chute found himself master of the Vyne. Three days later, Walpole wrote in jubilation to Mann:

That tartar his brother is dead, and having made no will, the whole, and a very considerable whole, falls to our friend . . . As the whole was in the tyrant's power, and as every art had been used to turn the vinegar of his temper against his brother, I had for some time lived persuaded that he would execute the worst purposes—but let us forgive him!

Chute had sent his Italian servant Francesco to Strawberry Hill with the happy and unexpected news and Walpole, sure as he was that his friend had been disinherited, was so taken by surprise that, as he informed the new owner of the Vyne, 'I started up and embraced him and put myself in such an agitation that I believe I shall not get over it without being blooded.'

Walpole first visited the Vyne as Chute's guest in the August of that year, finding the old house very damp, so much so, indeed, that he hinted to George Montagu that if he went again in the autumn he would need some persuading to go there on stilts. However, late October found him there again with Montagu and the latter's brother the Colonel—a rather unmilitary colonel it would appear, for the two of them 'screamed with approbation through the whole *Cu*-gamut'. One can imagine Chute's pride and pleasure as he showed his friends the beauties of his new inheritance, at last able to entertain them under his own roof and feel the glory of being a man of property. Bentley, still an active member of the Strawberry Committee, was unable to be present, and it was to him that Walpole sent his description of the visit upon his return to Strawberry Hill in the first days of November:

> Do you think we wished for you? I carried down incense and mass-books, and we had most Catholic enjoyment of the chapel. In the evenings, indeed, we did *touch a card* a little to please George—so much, that truly I have scarce an idea left that is not spotted with clubs, hearts, spades, and diamonds. There is a vote of the Strawberry Committee for great embellishments to the chapel, of which it will not be long before you hear something.

Walpole was full of ideas for 'improvements' to the Vyne which he hoped his friend would put quickly into operation, but Chute was in no hurry, content, for the present at any rate, to enjoy his new possessions in peace. He was also rather lazy over his correspondence and did not always answer his letters as promptly as was expected. As Walpole complained to Montagu some weeks after their visit: 'Mr. Chute, I believe, was so pleased witht the *tenebrae* in his own Chapel, that he has fairly buried himself in it. I have not even had so much as a burial-card from him since.' It was in this chapel, as Walpole had told Bentley, that the deliberations of the Strawberry Committee were to be realized, for in the following July we find him writing to tell Mann of 'the most heavenly chapel' which only needed a few pictures to give it a true Catholic air. 'We are so conscious of the goodness of our Protestantism', he adds, 'that we do not care how things look.' Could Mann find 'a tolerable Last Supper' for them, or failing that have one copied? If he could, Walpole assured him, 'we will say many a mass for the repose of your head-aches.' Mann obligingly sent a work by Giovanni Domenico Feretti, which it may be hoped also fulfilled the stipulation that it must be very cheap. It can still be seen today in the Ante-Chapel where it now hangs.

It is in this latter room, leading from the wainscoted Chapel Parlour into the chapel itself, that the spirit of Strawberry Hill most prevails. The 'gothic' effect is achieved by a fretwork pattern superimposed on the walls, painted dark brown but with some details picked out in gold and blue. The result has a certain fragile charm, but manages to look rather flimsy in comparison with the solid oak panelling of the first room and the genuine late gothic of the chapel itself with its Renaissance choir-stalls and the fine medieval glass of the three windows in the apse. The chapel and its furniture were left untouched by the committee except for the wall space above the stalls where an Italian of the name of Roma was employed to paint a fresco in *trompe-l'oeil* to represent a vista of fan vaulting reminiscent of the roof of King's College Chapel at Cambridge.

Beyond the chapel, Chute designed a Tomb Chamber in honour of his ancestor Speaker Chaloner. It was an unusual thing to do in that Age of Reason; it is difficult to say what prompted him to build it, unless the motive was family piety and a sense of gratitude to the great-grandfather who had brought into their family this house to which John Chute, the last of his line in direct male descent, had so unexpectedly succeeded. Here again the influence of the Strawberry Committee was seen in the attempt to create a sense of the Perpendicular style in the carving of the wainscot and in the cusped lozenges of the ceiling where plaster masquerades as stone. But it is the actual monument to the Speaker that is the most striking feature of the room: a recumbent figure carved in marble reclines on the altar-like sarcophagus, clad in a legal gown with a book and hat lying by its side, the face young and handsome as though the Speaker had been depicted in his earlier years when as a courageous barrister he had defended Archbishop Laud at his trial for treason. In contrast to its surroundings the monument is strictly classical, having four fluted Ionic columns on each side grouped in pairs with elaborate escutcheons between them, and inscribed tablets in the centre, one on each side, with swags in high relief carved below. The tomb shows Chute's interest in heraldry and also indicates that his taste was beginning to move away from gothic towards the classical influences of his earlier years in Italy.

Chute contemplated various other plans for the Vyne, some gothic, some Palladian, and he seems to have hesitated between the two, for the latter was still the accepted style for large country houses, especially with the Whig aristocracy. One plan for a gothic facing to the south front he must surely have intended to carry out, for in Gabriel Mathias's portrait of him painted in 1758 he is shown holding the design in his right hand as though he intended to record his authorship of it for posterity, but fortunately nothing was done to alter the mellow early Tudor appearance of the external elevations. This dilatoriness exasperated Walpole who was to write with some irritation that he had done advising his friend as he would never execute anything. It was not until 1770 that Chute finally decided to remove the old staircase and replace it with what was described as a 'Grecian theatric staircase', a beautiful and subtly designed classical construction using the Corinthian order, more Roman in fact than Greek. It was his masterpiece, a brilliant exploitation of the available space, and correct in style for the site, for it is approached from the outside by the only post-Tudor feature of the north front, the portico said to have been designed by a pupil of Inigo Jones, the earliest example of a classical portico in English domestic architecture. Even Walpole had to praise this departure from the 'true Gothic taste'.

Chute's inheritance of the Vyne and his emergence in middle age as a rich country squire made no difference to his relationship with Walpole, though the latter had written jokingly:

if I should grow to love you less, you will not be surprised—you know the partiality I have to the afflicted, the disgraced, and the oppressed, and must recollect how many titles to my esteem you will lose, when you are rich Chute of The Vyne, when you are courted by chancellors of the exchequer for your interest in Hampshire; by a thousand nephews for your estate, and by my Lady Brown for her daughter.

They still saw each other constantly and it was to Chute that Walpole still turned for help and advice. Müntz was commissioned to paint Chute's portrait for Strawberry Hill where 'Mr. Chute's room' was always available for his use. At the Vyne, a small panelled sitting-room next to the Print Room was named the Strawberry Parlour and was Walpole's special retreat when he visited. So for the next twenty-two years their friendship continued interrupted by nothing more serious than the attacks of gout from which by this time they both suffered. Advancing years no doubt toned down the more eccentric affectations of Chute's Italian days; he became a sober country gentleman, High Sheriff of Hampshire as his father had been before him. But like Walpole he retained his love for art, his sense of humour and his zest for life, and despite the bandages and the gout-stools the Strawberry Parlour must often have echoed to their laughter.

When John Chute died on 26 May 1776, in his seventy-fifth year, Walpole realized that he had lost his greatest friend. That this was so is made quite plain from the words he wrote in the course of a long letter to that other old friend in Florence who had first brought them together:

> I saw him oftener than any man; to him in every difficulty I had recourse, and him I loved to have here, as our friendship was so entire, and we knew one another so entirely, that he alone never was the least constraint to me. We passed many hours together without saying a syllable to each other; for we were both above ceremony. I left him without excusing myself, read or wrote before him, as if he were not present. Alas! alas! and how *self* presides even in our grief! I am lamenting myself, not him!—no, I am lamenting my other self. Half is gone; the other remains solitary. Age and sense will make me bear my affliction with submission and composure—but for ever— that little *for ever* that remains, I shall miss him. My first thought will always be, *I will go talk to Mr. Chute on this*; the second, *alas! I cannot*: and therefore

judge how my life is poisoned! I shall only seem to be staying behind one who is set out a little before me.

Walpole would not write like this for anyone else. It was a tribute to the depth of his friendship and an answer to those who would say that he had no heart.

III

George Selwyn and the
Out of Town Party

On Christmas Eve in 1754, Horace Walpole wrote from
Strawberry Hill to Richard Bentley: 'I am here quite alone; Mr.
Chute is setting out for his Vine; but in a day or two I expect Mr.
Williams, George Selwyn, and Dick Edgcumbe. You will allow that
when I do admit anybody within my cloister, I choose them well.'
The group of friends to whom he referred had been meeting at
Strawberry Hill for some years past at Christmas and Easter. Though
they were essentially what would be described as 'men of the world',
and were more usually to be seen in the card-room at White's in
St James's Street, they had formed the habit of escaping at least
twice a year to stay with their friend in rural Twickenham and
these little gatherings came to be described by Walpole as 'my out-
of-town'.

Like the Quadruple Alliance, the Out of Town party had its
origins in friendship made at Eton, but there the resemblance ended.
Unlike Gray and Ashton, both Edgcumbe and Selwyn came from
aristocratic backgrounds with strong connections with Parliament
and the Court. Williams, like West, was the son of a successful
lawyer, but was a man of independent financial means with no need
to follow a profession. Though all three were interested in literature
and the other arts (they would hardly have belonged to Walpole's
intimate circle otherwise), they were strictly amateurs. Edgcumbe
and Selwyn were both members of the Society of Dilettanti, which
had originally been founded to encourage a taste in England for those
arts which flourished in Italy and were so much the inspiration of the
more intelligent travellers to that country in the early years of the
century; but though they were connoisseurs, they were not
collectors, and Selwyn, if not the others, was later to be mildly
satirical at the expense of Walpole's ever-growing accumulation of

objects of art and curiosity. He declared to Lord Holland that Strawberry Hill had become a catacomb or museum rather than a habitation, while its master was 'one of the most carefully finished miniatures and best-preserved mummies in the whole collection'. Such criticism was, however, only of the sort that is permissible among old friends and was in character with Selwyn's reputation for mordant and somewhat sepulchral humour. Alone among Walpole's circle the members of the Out of Town party made use of Christian names in addressing each other; for the rest, even for so intimate a friend as John Chute, the customary formalities of the eighteenth century were observed. Selwyn and Edgcumbe were thus always George and Dick while Williams, who had been named George James at the font, was invariably known as 'Gilly', and none but these three would ever (except perhaps behind his back) have ventured to address the master of Strawberry Hill as 'Horry'.

We see the three members of the Out of Town group in a conversation piece painted by Sir Joshua Reynolds in 1759. The scene is set in Walpole's library. To the right of the picture Edgcumbe and Williams are seated at a table; the former, who had some skill with his pencil, is looking directly out from the canvas and would appear to be drawing a sketch or caricature of the artist, while Williams, seated beside him, looks on admiringly at his work. To the left stands Selwyn, leaning rather languidly for support on the back of a chair in an attitude which admirably suggests the drowsiness and indolence for which he was famous. He has an open book in one hand which he has just been reading, but his attention has wandered to his two friends whom he regards with sleepy interest. Walpole, who commissioned the work, was highly delighted with the result; he wrote to Montagu after Edgcumbe's untimely death in 1761: 'Did you see the charming picture Reynolds painted for me of him, Selwyn, and Gilly Williams? It is by far one of the best things he has executed.' In fact the work is unique in being the only picture of its kind that Reynolds painted except for the two large groups of the Dilettanti Society executed some years later. Though uncharacteristic of the artist's usual style, it is full of perception, cleverly conveying the differing spirits of the sitters, all of whom were well known to him. Selwyn's easy, lounging expression of lassitude and world-weariness; Edgcumbe absorbed in his drawing but so much the well dressed man of the world; Williams, lively, bright, and boyish as he looks over his friend's shoulder; it is a masterly representation of three highly original personalities.

Edgcumbe was the eldest of the three, being a year older than Walpole. He was born in 1716, the son of the first Lord Edgcumbe of Mount Edgcumbe in Cornwall. As a youth he had made the acquaintance of a boy seven years his junior, the son of a local clergyman and schoolmaster who lived not too far from Plymouth. The lad showed a remarkable talent for art and under Dick Edgcumbe's encouragement painted a portrait of the latter's tutor, the Revd Thomas Smart, making his first rough sketch in church without the sitter's knowledge and finishing the picture on a canvas cut from an old sail. The youthful artist was then about twelve years old and as far as is known this was the first portrait from the brush that about a quarter of a century later was to paint the conversation-piece set in Horace Walpole's library and which was to hang above the spiky pinnacles of the gothic chimney-piece in the Great Parlour.

This boyhood friendship with Edgcumbe was to have fortunate consequences in Reynolds's life, for it was through this connection that he was able to make his first trip to Italy and study art in Rome. This happy chance came his way in 1749, by which time he had made some local reputation as an artist, and was firmly established as a friend of the family at Mount Edgcumbe. It was to the house of these friends and early patrons, in this year, that capricious winds brought Commodore Keppel, the future admiral. His ship, the *Centurion*, was bound for the Mediterranean, but some storm damage to both topmasts had caused him to put in to Plymouth and to pay an unexpected call upon his friend Lord Edgcumbe. Here artist and seaman met and the two young men, both about the same age, became such fast friends that by the time the *Centurion*'s topmasts had been repaired, Reynolds had been offered a passage to Italy as the commodore's guest. It has generally been assumed from the early friendship with Joshua Reynolds that it was Edgcumbe who first introduced him to Walpole, and it would seem likely that this was so. The artist was to paint a striking portrait of Walpole in 1757, and in the course of his life he painted Selwyn no less than five times. The most beautiful work he was to do for Walpole was the charming group of the latter's three great-nieces, the Ladies Waldegrave, painted in 1781 and exhibited at the Royal Academy. It was later to hang in the Great Parlour at Strawberry Hill near the earlier picture of the three men.

Dick Edgcumbe was a small man, so small that he stood shorter than his strutting little sovereign George II, who was so often obliged to look up at his subjects that he was quite delighted to discover at least one that he could look down upon. Edgcumbe's natural talents and wit, together with the privileged circumstances of his birth and position in society, should have destined him for a useful and distinguished career. He had great charm. In addition to his abilities as an amateur artist, he was skilled in throwing off slight but amusing sets of verse, and had all the social graces upon which the polite world of the eighteenth century set such store, but unfortunately all these virtues were vitiated by his passion for the gambling tables. He was, in Walpole's phrase, a man 'who thinks nothing important that is not decided by dice'. As a young man, so Gilly Williams was later to tell the diarist Lord Glenbervie, Edgcumbe had been so ruined by play that his father had smuggled him on board a ship bound for Constantinople where he remained for some years in the care of the British Ambassador, Sir Everard Fawkener. But even this expedient had hardly served its purpose, for during the voyage the young scapegrace had engaged the captain at cards to such an extent that £22,000 was lost and won between them. This eastern interlude was referred to many years after Edgcumbe's death in a letter from Selwyn to the Earl of Carlisle. In 1781 the Emperor Joseph II had just been visiting Flanders where he had received Lord Malden with whom Selwyn dined on his return to England. Selwyn wrote:

> He [the emperor] reads all our papers in English, so I asked Lord Malden if he said anything of my jokes, and was mortified to find that they had escaped his Imperial Majesty's observations. But he has read some of them, *sans doute*, so I may have the same vanity as poor Dick Edgcumbe had, of thinking that the Emperor of Constantinople had from the windows of his seraglio heard him play upon the kettle drums.

What else Edgcumbe did at Constantinople beyond playing at cards and on the drums has not transpired.

It was at play that the greater part of his life was frittered away, though in an age when so many hours were spent at cards or other games of chance, and when vast sums of money were regularly wagered and lost, this was not held against him, and he even managed to hold a succession of government posts. He was in the House of Commons from 1742 until 1758, when he succeeded his father in the House of Lords; he was a Lord of the Admiralty in 1755-6 and Comptroller of the Household and Privy Councillor from 1756 until his death five years later. But his interest in politics came a poor second to his interest in gambling. 'Is Mr. Pitt out?' Walpole once asked him, eager to know the fate of the ministry. 'Yes,' answered Edgcumbe, totally absorbed in his game, 'I called at his door just now and his porter told me so.'

Edgcumbe, like so many of Walpole's friends, was unmarried, but very far from being a celibate. Highly susceptible to the charms of the opposite sex, he probably never married because he was usually involved in some affair of a less regular nature. In the problems that arose from these amorous adventures he found in Walpole a sympathetic ear into which he could pour his troubles, someone who, he maintained, had 'more feeling and had given better advice about his mistresses than the rest of his acquaintance'. In 1744 when both men were still in their twenties, he wrote to Walpole: 'I do not choose you before the rest of my acquaintance only because I had rather talk with you than any body else, and upon a subject I love most, but because I think you have more feeling, and will be more sensible of my present uneasiness.'

The cause of his uneasiness on this occasion was a young woman to whom he had lost his heart and who has survived only as 'the Kitten', the nickname by which she was known to her friends and admirers. The affair did not last long as infidelity and death seem to have intervened almost simultaneously. The 'feeling' that Walpole could express as the understanding confidant of his lovesick friend shows him in an interesting and sympathetic light. He did not, however, display very much of it when he passed on the news of the Kitten's sad plight to his friend Sir Charles Hanbury Williams. 'Oh!' he wrote on 25 June 1745, 'I forgot to tell you, that Dick says he has just quarrelled with the Kitten: you will stare and cry, why she has been dead these two months! That is nothing: he has just discovered a deathbed infidelity with my Lord Belfield.' Later on, Edgcumbe settled down to a more steady relationship with a certain Anne Franks by whom he had four children. His faith in Walpole's genuine concern and disinterest is demonstrated by the fact that he made him a trustee for the children under his will.

Edgcumbe's reputation as an amateur artist was sufficiently well established among his own circle for Reynolds, as we have seen, to show him at work on a sketch in the conversation piece he painted for Walpole. None of his sketches has survived, however, so his artistic abilities cannot be judged. A facetious coat of arms devised by the Out of Town party for White's Club and painted by Edgcumbe, is all that has come down to us. It once hung at Strawberry Hill and earned for its artist the mock title of first heraldic painter or 'Strawberry Herald'. His poetry has suffered the same fate. Most of it was passed round in manuscript and has perished with the passage of time; such fragments as have survived suggest no more than a minor 'drawing-room' talent. This did not prevent Walpole from including him in his *Catalogue of Royal and Noble Authors*, though admitting that he had 'a slenderer portion of fame than his genius deserved and promised', and that this poetry suffered from being 'the production of his most careless hours'. He was, Walpole wrote,

a poet from fancy, not from meditation; yet he possessed those graces which study cannot give, ease and harmony, the fruits of taste and a good ear. What elegance might he not have attained, had application been added to strong parts, to humour that was the result of truth, and to wit that never was the offspring of ill-nature!

It is difficult to believe that Richard Edgcumbe had a true place in any pantheon of the arts. It was, of course, Walpole's generous loyalty to the memory of a friend that made him include his name in the *Catalogue*. It was judgements such as this, dictated more by generosity than taste, that earned for Walpole the reputation for tempering his criticisms by merely snobbish considerations. 'It seems as if he had no real sympathy for genius,' Eliot Warburton was to write, 'and could scarcely be brought to recognise it, unless the possessor had certain pretensions to the character of a fine gentleman.' Walpole certainly allowed some licence to his critical faculties where his close personal friends were concerned, but this did not obscure (despite some idiosyncratic opinions) his appreciation of true genius when he saw it. Edgcumbe himself does not seem to have shared the same perception. Williams in old age described to Lord Glenbervie (who was married to his great-niece) how Dick

Edgcumbe had been present at Strawberry Hill when Gray had read from the manuscript of his *Progress of Poesy* to Walpole and a group of his friends. 'When Gray got to the second stanza,' Glenbervie recorded in his diary, 'Mr. Edgcumbe leant towards Mr. Williams who sat near him and said "What is this? It seems to be English, but by G-d I don't understand a single word of it." '

Walpole's inclusion of Dick Edgcumbe's name in the *Catalogue of Royal and Noble Authors* was his public tribute to the memory of a friend who died tragically, if failure to fulfil the promise of youth is a tragedy, at the early age of forty-five. His private feelings were expressed in a letter to Horace Mann on 14 May 1761:

> I have lost one of the oldest friends I had in the world, Lord Edgcumbe; a martyr to gaming. With every quality to make himself agreeable, he did nothing but make himself miserable. I feel that loss much, though long expected; and it is the more sensible here where I saw most of him. My towers rise, my galleries and cloisters extend—for what? For me to leave, or to inhabit by myself, when I have survived my friends! Yet, with all these ungrateful reflections, how I wish once to see you here! And of what should we most talk?—of a dear friend we have both, alas! survived.

Gilly Williams was to recall his friend more tersely but no less vividly, and without the note of self-pity that Walpole so often struck and as quickly repented, on similar sad occasions. Edgcumbe was, according to Williams, 'a most extraordinary mixture of art and absurdity, parts, folly, business, idleness and dissipation of every sort'. In this curious mixture of worthiness and folly he had much in common with the generation that was to follow immediately after him, as typified in the career of Charles James Fox, whose course in life was to cause so much fascination and astonishment to older men such as Walpole and George Selwyn.

Gilly Williams was the only member of the Out of Town party who had not been to Eton. He was born at Denton in Lincolnshire in 1719 and had been sent to Westminster for his schooling. From there he had won a studentship to Cambridge, but for some reason or other, perhaps because of his Tory leanings, his father had preferred that he should go to Oxford, and so he was entered at Christ Church, where he would have been a younger contemporary of Richard West.

His father, William Peere Williams, was an eminent lawyer and a prominent member of a class which in this period had many opportunities for social advancement, as was demonstrated by the fact that Williams himself was able to lead a life of patrician idleness, marry the daughter of an earl, and that his niece, granddaughter of the old lawyer, could marry Lord North, son and heir of the Earl of Guildford and later to be George III's chief minister. These useful connections enabled Gilly Williams to enrol himself in the privileged circle of patent place-holders, being appointed Receiver-General of Excise in 1774 through the influence of his noble nephew-in-law.

Williams was an easygoing sort of fellow who took as his motto a saying of the seventeenth-century diplomatist Sir William Temple: 'Old wood to burn, old friends to converse with, and old books to read'. He was observant and witty, an amusing letter-writer capable of shrewd comments on persons and events, all recorded without malice in the most entertaining way. He was received everywhere for his good humour, his anecdotes, and his almost boyish lack of solemnity. He did not take himself at all seriously. Speaking of Madame du Deffand's circle in Paris, he once wrote to Selwyn: 'I always found myself treated in that set as a *jeune garçon, qui n'avait point encore l'habitude du monde*. Faith! there may have been some ground for it.'

He had so much the character of a gay bachelor that his marriage has passed almost without notice, and indeed in some books he has been described as a single man. Yet he was very definitely married on 30 July 1752 at the age of thirty-three. His wife was Diana, daughter of William, fifth Earl of Coventry—or so she has been described. But something of a mystery hangs over her birth and this, and the fact that the marriage was childless, is perhaps why so little is heard of her. Was she in fact Lord Coventry's daughter? In one opinion at least, that of Williams's own niece Lady Guildford, she was not. At Lord Glenbervie's, whose wife was Lady Guildford's daughter, they were once discussing cases of natural children who had been accepted and brought up in their father's family among his legitimate offspring. Lady Guildford advanced the view that this could also happen where the wife's illegitimate children were concerned, declaring that 'her own uncle, the present Mr. George Williams, married a Miss Dye or Diana Bertie, a natural daughter of Lord Coventry's wife'. This conversation took place in the mid–1790s when Williams was an elderly man and his wife, presumably, already dead. It is about the only scrap of information we have about her.

It was primarily as George Selwyn's great friend that Williams was welcomed at Strawberry Hill, a category in which he came second only to the Earl of March, of whom we shall soon hear more. Indeed it was only with some reluctance that Williams conceded first place, writing to Selwyn with a hint of touchiness: 'Thank you, my dear George, for including me in your pacquet of friends. Not even March himself is worthier of that appellation, for no one can esteem and love you better.' His London house was in Cleveland Court, almost next door to Selwyn's, and they were much in each other's company, especially in their younger days. When Selwyn first took his seat in the House of Commons, his friend wrote an amusing letter imagining the budding orator rehearsing before a glass: 'I must intimate to you not to forget closing your periods with a magnificent stroke of the breast; and recommend Mr. Barry [a well-known actor] as a pattern, who I think pathetically excels in that beauty.' The advice was the more absurd in that Williams knew well enough that Selwyn was unlikely to raise his voice in Parliament to any effect at all, nor indeed is it recorded that he ever did so. The letter is a good example of Williams's method of combining gentle mockery with light-hearted wit and the merest whisper of flattery, a gift that won him a ready acceptance among the young bloods who frequented White's as well as in the more rarefied atmosphere of Strawberry Hill. With these gifts so effortlessly employed, helped by the modest affluence provided by his inheritance and government place, Williams was able to drift through life in comfort, becoming in his genial old age something of a legend for his stories of the great and famous people he had once known so well. He was to outlive all his companions of the Out of Town party, dying in November 1805 at the age of eighty-six.

❖ 2 ❖

George Augustus Selwyn, like his friend Gilly Williams, was born in 1719. He came of an old Gloucestershire family which had gained wealth through the law in the reign of Elizabeth I, when one Jasper Selwyn was a Bencher and later Treasurer of Lincoln's Inn. The next two generations of the family continued to practise at the Bar or, in the case of younger sons, hoped for preferment in the Church, without losing contact with their county background, keeping up the family home at Matson just outside Gloucester, which Jasper Selwyn had purchased in 1597. It was not until the time of William Selwyn, George's grandfather, that the legal tradition was broken. He entered the army, and after a distinguished career reached the rank of brigadier-general. He died in 1702 as Governor of Jamaica. His son John followed him into the army, consolidating his military position by marrying his cousin Mary Farrington, the daughter of a general. He was to fight at Malplaquet where he was aide-de-camp to the Duke of Marlborough, and by the end of the war was able to purchase a colonelcy, a promotion that cost him £7,000. With the coming of peace, the Colonel abandoned the army for various Court appointments, becoming Groom of the Bedchamber to George II and later Treasurer to Queen Caroline. He also entered Parliament, sitting as Member for Gloucester from 1734 until his death in 1751. His wife also held a position at Court as a Woman of the Bedchamber to the Queen. Lord Hervey in his *Memoirs* describes Mrs Selwyn as 'a simple cunning woman about the Court who loved Sir Robert Walpole, as he himself knew and often would say.' According to Horace Walpole she was 'of much vivacity and pretty' and could at times display 'all the wit of her son George'.

George Selwyn was the younger son of this marriage of first cousins. His parents' friendship with Sir Robert Walpole would naturally recommend him to Horace when he came to Eton as a schoolboy, and their lifelong friendship indeed began at this early period in their lives, though Walpole was probably closer to the elder brother John during his school-days. John Selwyn seems always to have been delicate, and his precarious health, for which Walpole showed considerable concern, was one of the topics in the latter's correspondence with Henry Conway while he was away on his Grand Tour. A closer family link was forged when Selwyn's only sister Albinia (the eldest of the family) married a cousin of Horace Walpole, Thomas Townshend, a younger son of the second Viscount Townshend, himself married to Sir Robert Walpole's sister Dorothy. This marriage not only gave Walpole and Selwyn a degree of kinship but secured for the Selwyn family a place in that complicated but influential cousinage of great Whig families who exercised so much political power at that time. Virtually nothing is known about

Selwyn during his time at Eton. The only anecdote that has survived from his boyhood has nothing to do with his school. In 1733 on a visit to Goodwood, he saw an old lady who struck even so unsophisticated an observer as a fourteen-year-old boy as being remarkably well preserved. She was Charles II's mistress Louise de Kéroualle, Duchess of Portsmouth, then aged eighty-five. She died the next year. How Horace Walpole, with his fascination for dowagers, must have envied his young friend this experience!

Someone with Selwyn's Whig background one would have expected, in the reign of George II, to go to Cambridge, but in 1739 we find him an Oxford undergraduate at Hart Hall, which changed its name to Hertford College the year after he went up. His university career was not a distinguished one. He seems to have been one of those young men, more numerous in those days than they are now, who look upon a university as a place of amusement rather than scholarship; one of the few letters that survives from his father, written in 1740, begins: 'I am disposed once more to pay your debts, which is what you have no pretensions to ask,' and gives some impression of the sort of life he was living. George replied with due filial submission, but added a note to the copy of the letter which he preserved that it had in fact been composed not by himself but by Dr Newton, who was none other than the Principal of his college. It is not surprising that he imagined that he could do what he liked at Oxford.

In 1741, halfway through his university career, he left Oxford for a period of over three years, much of which was spent in France. Whether he was temporarily rusticated for some unspecified offence, or whether he went of his own free will, has never been made clear. The letters he wrote home from Paris, like those from Oxford, were almost constantly upon the theme of his need for more money, though his father made him an allowance, generous enough for that period, of £220 a year. One phrase which he used in mitigation of his importunity does not present a very reassuring picture of what his life had been like at Hertford College. 'In respect to my circumstances,' he wrote to his father's agent in London, 'when I consider how much all kind of economy was a stranger to me, and that carelessness and dissipation were by long use become almost natural, it is surprising to me that I have been able to keep within bounds as much as I have.' Selwyn was a lifelong gambler, though to a lesser degree than his friend Edgcumbe, and this no doubt was one cause for his financial distress, but at least he made use of his opportunities to perfect his knowledge of French, which became his second language. Paris made a cosmopolitan of him. During the rest of his life he paid many visits there, his wit giving him the entrée to the exclusive society of the salons. It was he who would later introduce Walpole to Madame du Deffand.

The exact date of Selwyn's return to England is not clear. In March 1744 France had declared war on England, and though in that civilized age this would not have required his leaving the country, it may well have been one of the contributory causes. Certainly by 1745, the year of the death of Sir Robert Walpole and the invasion of England by Prince Charles Edward Stuart, Selwyn was back at Oxford and up to his neck in trouble. On 21 May he had met various young friends including Lord Harley and two other peers' sons who had formed themselves into a convivial drinking club. The meeting took place in the house of a wine-seller called Charles Deverelle who lived near St Martin's Church. According to the depositions made later by the various witnesses, at the height of their revels George Selwyn—who some, but not all, present considered to be 'very much disordered by Liquour'—sent out to a neighbouring goldsmith for a cup which much resembled a chalice. He then took a bottle of wine and pretending to cut his arm poured the wine down his arm and into the chalice, declaring at the same time: 'Here's my body, Hoc est corpus meum.' He then passed the cup to the somewhat astonished Deverelle with the words: 'Take or Do this in Remembrance of Us.' He was also said to have remarked as the wine flowed into the cup, 'It bloods freely', and to have crossed himself on the forehead, saying that it was what Roman Catholics did when they went to church. He also announced for the benefit of those present who were unaware of the fact that 'Hocus Pocus' came from 'Hoc est corpus' intending— according to the testimony of Richard Leveson Gower, one of his companions—to ridicule the Roman Catholic Mass.

When Selwyn, whether drunk or sober, performed his tasteless ritual, he could hardly any longer lay claim to the thoughtlessness and recklessness of extreme youth. After three years or so away from the university he was considerably older and more experienced than the average undergraduate. He was in fact just three months short of his twenty-sixth birthday, a circumstance that makes his conduct all the more inexplicable. As an act it was also entirely out of character with anything else in his life, for he was a mild, peaceable, unaggressive and good-natured man. Though a certain mockery of Catholic ceremonies was not uncommon at the time, there is nothing to indicate that Selwyn himself held particularly strong anti-Catholic views; he was, if anything, irreligious and equally indifferent to the various sects and divisions of Christendom as they then existed. The most charitable explanation is that he was indeed very drunk at the time, that he was recently back from Paris where he must often have seen the Roman Catholic ceremonies performed, and that some unfortunate impulse made him indulge in this crude parody.

The university authorities, however, were not disposed to take a charitable view of the situation when news of this deplorable frolic reached them. It was all very well to claim that the episode had been some sort of anti-Catholic demonstration; the whole thing came too near to a general travesty of official religion for them to be able to countenance it. After an examination of all those present by the Vice-Chancellor, the heads of colleges and proctors, it was announced that George Augustus Selwyn, Gentleman Commoner of Hertford College, was to be 'utterly expelled and banished from our said University and the precincts thereof' and that he be deprived of 'all and singular the Rights and Privileges of our said University, both now and hereafter'. Considering the nature of the offence, and the fact that the university at that time was a wholly clerical corporation, the verdict was not surprising. Selwyn protested violently, none the less, at the severity of his punishment and tried to have the edict annulled. If academic opinion generally supported the Vice-Chancellor, some merely fashionable opinion in London gave support to the culprit, one friend expressing a hope that the university might burst into flames so that 'one could hear the proctors cry like roasted lobsters', while another registered mild surprise that the authorities at Oxford were capable of showing any principles at all 'for you must know that they never had any, human or divine—party only governs', which was meant, of course, to refer to the Tory party.

In effect there was nothing Selwyn could do but accept the situation with as good a grace as he could muster. He could afford to dismiss Oxford with a shrug. Had not his cousin Sir Charles Hanbury Williams, a man of the world if ever there was one, written to him before it had all happened: 'I hope you divert yourself well at the expense of the whole university, though the object is not worthy of you. The dullest fellow in it has parts enough to ridicule it, and you have parts to fly at nobler game'? He would follow his cousin's advice. He retired to London where letters were to be addressed to him at White's Chocolate House. By the beginning of December, the Pretender's army was approaching Derby and George II was wondering whether or not to pack his bags; so small an event as the expulsion of an idle young man from Oxford could hardly survive as a topic of interest against such competition, and the whole episode was quickly forgotten.

Selwyn's expulsion from Oxford must have come as a severe blow to his father, who was already exasperated by his younger son's extravagances. His hopes were centred in his elder son John, that delicate young man, who now sat as Member of Parliament for Whitchurch and showed promise of carrying on the family tradition of public service. We know very little about him, but he seems to have been an amiable person. 'He deserves so much love from all who know him,' Walpole had written during one of his serious illnesses. In June 1751, however, his father's hopes were shattered when John Selwyn died of a heart ailment. Colonel Selwyn, who had already lost his only daughter some years previously, did not recover from the shock of this bereavement and followed his favourite son to the grave five months later, but not before he had made a new will in which the direct entail to his estate was broken. Matson and the property that went with it were re-entailed on the descendants of his daughter. George Selwyn was not disinherited, but he was only given a life interest in the estate.

✦✦✦ 3 ✦✦✦

There is something rather strange about Colonel Selwyn's action in breaking the entail when he made his will in August 1751. At that time, his only surviving son was in robust health, only thirty-two years old, and in the normal course of events more than likely to marry and produce a family. He had already started to show some signs of settling down when in 1747 he had been returned to Parliament for his father's pocket borough of Ludgershall, and had secured his first 'place' as early as 1740 when he had been appointed

Clerk of the Irons and Surveyor of the Meltings at the Mint. It was, admittedly, only a modest post which brought in barely £100 a year, but he would in due time add to it the registrarship of the Court of Chancery of Barbados and the office of Paymaster of the Works. When this last post, which was worth £400 a year, was abolished by Edmund Burke late in Selwyn's life, so accomplished a place-seeker had he become that he was able to compensate himself after a brief interval with the Surveyorship-General of Crown Lands, which brought in exactly twice as much. Indeed almost his entire time in Parliament, where he rarely spoke but often slept, was spent in supporting the administration of the day for the sole purpose of protecting the various sinecures he held under government patronage.

Selwyn's predilection for the gaming table, what he himself described as his 'ungovernable passion for play', may have been one of the causes for his father's action, but this is unlikely. Gambling in all its forms was the vice of the day. It was so common and so widespread in Selwyn's class that if all fathers had disinherited their sons for that reason there would have been few people left to inherit. Selwyn, moreover, never gambled to excess; he always exercised control, and despite a lifetime spent in this particular foible—even playing at lotto with the Papal nuncio in Paris—he never came anywhere near to ruining himself as did so many of his contemporaries. It is more likely that the Colonel was guided by the knowledge that his son was unlikely ever to present him with grandchildren. Whether George Selwyn was impotent or not is something that can now never be discovered, but his total indifference to the charms of the female sex was widely known, often commented upon, and indeed something of a joke among his friends. It was not the sort of joke that might be made at the expense of a suspected homosexual; it was just that everyone knew that George Selwyn was about as complete a misogynist as could be met with. Thus, when he was in Paris in 1764 with his friend Lord March, Gilly Williams wrote to him:

How you fare upon the Continent, I know not, but with us it is one of the coldest Christmasses I ever passed. I hope the Earl of March takes care to keep himself warm with the largest — of the Most Christian King's subjects; but you, who lie whole nights alone, what you can do to amuse yourself is, and will be, a mystery to me.

Perhaps it was no less a mystery to his father, but one that he was aware of, and so he took care to secure the succession of his property to his grandchildren by his daughter's marriage.

Selwyn had the gift for attracting friends and for preserving their friendship. He was loved for his wit, his oddness, and a warm-heartedness which did not, possibly, go very deep. The more acute observers detected a certain coldness beneath the urbane and rather blasé exterior. This was more evident to women, if only because he made no effort to flatter or make love to them. 'Of all the English whom you see in Paris,' Horace Walpole wrote to Madame du Deffand, 'Mr. Selwyn has the most wit. But you must draw him out; you must make him speak bad French. He makes so many efforts to speak your tongue like a true academician that he totally forgets to throw in ideas.' To this, that very shrewd woman replied: 'What you tell me of Mr. Selwyn is perfect; I add to it that he has only intellectual brilliancy (*de l'esprit de tête*) and not a scrap of heart.'

With his lack of heart went an almost total lack of any kind of commitment. His political career (if one can call so negative an approach to his House of Commons duties by such a name) consisted in little more than maintaining the status quo. He was shocked by the exuberance of the younger generation of Whigs, especially Charles James Fox, whose father had been about the only politician he had admired. 'You will not believe it, perhaps,' he once wrote to Lady Carlisle, 'but a minister of any description, though served up in his great shell of power, and all his green fat about him, is to me a dish by no means relishing, and I never knew but one in my life I could pass an hour with pleasantly, which was Lord Holland.' Behind such a remark one hears a sigh of boredom, of ennui, that occupational hazard of the eighteenth-century upper classes which was the other side of the coin to their craze for gambling. In Selwyn's case this gave birth to physical and intellectual lassitude and a rather cynical gift for discovering in the example of others an excuse for his own lack of achievement. 'They were talking before George Selwyn of genius,' Lord Glenbervie noted once in his diary.

He said, 'Genius is an indefinite term. I never think a man really an able man, unless I see that he has attained the object of his pursuits, whatever they may be. I try Charles Fox by that test. He had had three favourite pursuits—gaming, politics, women. He addicted himself to play and thought himself a skilful player, but lost an immense fortune almost before he was of age. Power was his grand object, yet he has never been able to keep possession of it, scarcely for a twelvemonth. He was desirous of shining as a man of gallantry, and he married a whore.'

It was in remarks of this sort, so cynical and cruelly observed, yet uttered with a bored detachment that took the sting out of them, that Selwyn's reputation for wit was made. It was a reputation that all his friends acknowledged, yet hardly any example has come down to us in a way that we can appreciate or savour. So much of his wit depended upon the manner of its delivery which could be visualized at once by Horace Walpole's correspondents when he tells the latest good thing that had fallen from George's lips, yet falls so flatly on the ears of posterity. One example that has survived with a little more sparkle than most also concerned Charles James Fox. A namesake of his had been executed at Tyburn and Fox asked Selwyn whether he had attended the ceremony. 'No,' he answered, 'I make a point of never frequenting rehearsals.' When the chief minister Henry Pelham died and his effects were being sold, Selwyn observed, as a fine silver dinner service came under the hammer, 'Lord! How many toads have eaten off these plates.' Walpole gave another example in Selwyn's answer to Lord George Gordon when he had asked to be put up for Parliament at Selwyn's borough of Ludgershall; they would elect him with Selwyn's recommendation, declared Lord George, even if he came from the coast of Africa. 'That is according to what part of the coast you came from,' answered Selwyn. 'They would certainly, if you came from the Guinea Coast.'

None of these quips strikes us as an example of true wit for they contain no germ of comic inspiration or invention in themselves but depend upon some property to trigger off the response, such as the dinner service or some fortuitously offered remark like Fox's or Lord George's question. Selwyn had an impassive expression, was rarely known to laugh, and had a drawling way of speaking that made his remarks sound all the more amusing, a quality that could not be reproduced when they were written down; and the fact that these remarks, so often indicating a very sharp retort to some unfortunately expressed or ill-conceived observation, came from someone who had an extraordinary aptitude for drowsiness or even actually falling asleep in public, gave them an added element of surprise. He could be likened to a cat sleeping, or apparently sleeping, on the hearth that suddenly reaches out a deft blow with its sharp-clawed paw.

Selwyn's somnolence was liable to overcome him at any moment, in a crowded drawing-room, in the House of Commons, or when among his chosen friends. It was a curious characteristic that sometimes gave an impression of stupidity. In fact he was very far from stupid. In later life, his long correspondence with the Earl of Carlisle shows a man of many interests, well read in English and French, with a shrewd if rather disillusioned view of the contemporary political scene where he was on familiar terms with most of the principal actors. He was, however, a profoundly lazy man and one completely lacking in worldly ambition. In 1767, in an analysis of his character for their mutual friend James Craufurd, Madame du Deffand wrote of Selwyn:

I am far from thinking him stupid, but he is often in the clouds. Nothing strikes him or wakens him save ridicule; though he catches even that on the wing. His words are graceful and delicate, but he cannot carry on a conversation. He is *distrait*, indifferent. He would often be bored, but for an excellent recipe against boredom which he possesses: that of going to sleep whenever he wishes. It is a talent that I envy him: if I had it, I should make good use of it. He is sarcastic without being spiteful; formal, but polite; he loves nothing and nobody but his Lord March; one would never think of forming a close relationship with him, but one is very glad to meet him and be in the same room with him, although one has nothing to say to him.

The friendship between William Douglas, third Earl of March, and George Selwyn, to which Madame du Deffand here refers, was a curious example of the attraction of opposites. March, who succeeded as fourth Duke of Queensberry in 1778 and became notorious in his dotage as the libidinous 'old Q', who would sit on the balcony of his Piccadilly house ogling any pretty girl who passed, was the very paradigm of the eighteenth-century rake. He was five years younger than Selwyn, a small rather ugly man with a sharp tongue, capable of swearing 'like ten thousand troopers', but at the same time having unmistakably the air of a *grand seigneur*. He had an insatiable appetite for the pretty young dancers of the Italian opera, girls not yet out of their teens, who passed through his hands with a remarkable rapidity, the Zamperini, the Rena, the 'poor little Tondino', the very thought of whom filled his sentimental eyes with fresh tears, his heart so full he could 'neither think, speak, nor write' as he conducted her to Dover that her place might be taken in his fickle affections by someone else. His life was dominated by women, cards and horses, but in spite of his reputation in a permissive age as a notorious womanizer he was not merely a libertine. He was a man of shrewd judgement in the affairs of the world, something of a connoisseur, and an enthusiastic amateur of music. Lady Louisa Stuart, who remembered him in his debauched old age, was to write of him in the days of his prime that 'he was then the most brilliant, most fashionable, most dissipated young man in London, the leading character at Newmarket, the support of the gaming table, the supreme dictator of the Opera house, the pattern whose dress and equipage were to be copied by all who aimed at distinction, and (need we ask?) the person most universally admired by the ladies.' He was a Lord of the Bedchamber to George III from the king's accession in 1760 until 1789 when he lost his post after having supported the cause of the heir to the throne a little too warmly during the regency crisis following the king's symptoms of mental illness.

March was a man of boundless vitality, his sensual appetites lasting, it would seem, into his eighties, while he was capable of spending long hours at the gaming table or on the turf at Newmarket. It would be difficult to find a character more entirely different from the sleepy, lazy and apparently sexless Selwyn. Yet the strongest bond of friendship existed between them and lasted without a break until the elder man's death. March was the more dominant character, but Selwyn willingly submitted to his sometimes inconvenient whims. 'March promised that I should be in London again today,' Selwyn wrote to Lord Carlisle from Newmarket in February 1768, 'but you know his irresolution, and the little opposition which I can give to what he desires . . .' Yet March, for all that he liked to have his own way, was quite genuine in his devotion to the other. He once wrote:

How can you think, my dear George, and I hope you do not think,

that anybody or anything can made a *tracasserie* between you and
me? I take it ill that you even talk of it . . . I must be the poorest
creature upon earth—after having known you so long, and always
as the best and sincerest friend that anyone ever had—if anyone
alive can make any impression upon me where you are concerned.
I told you, in a letter I wrote some time ago, that I depended more
upon the continuance of our friendship than anything else in the
world, which I certainly do because I have so many reasons to
know you, and I am sure I know myself.

What was the secret of this strong but somewhat ill-assorted
friendship? Was it that Selwyn, so frigid himself, one who would so
notoriously 'lie whole nights alone', found in March's raffish
carnality some sort of proxy to compensate for his own emotional
sterility? Would this account for the anxiously protective feelings he
was later to show for March's natural daughter? He certainly had a
gift for finding surrogates for those family ties and responsibilities
that his temperament had denied him. This was especially marked in
his relations with a much younger man than either March or himself,
Frederick Howard, fifth Earl of Carlisle, born in 1748, and thus as
much as twenty-nine years his junior. Selwyn became his confidant
and mentor from about 1767 when the younger man was only
nineteen and just about to leave Cambridge for the Grand Tour.
When Carlisle later married, Selwyn without any difficulty extended
his affection to include his friend's wife and children. He had a way of
winning the confidence and affection of men of a younger
generation, but in Carlisle's case the relationship was of a much
closer and more intimate nature than any other, except perhaps for
that with March. They corresponded constantly, Selwyn advising his
young friend in his career with the sort of affection and concern that
might come from a devoted uncle or much older brother, if not
indeed from a father. Sir Joshua Reynolds recorded them together in
a charming picture in which the two men sit at a table, the young
nobleman in his star and ribbon holding an open book in his hand
and Selwyn seated at the side of the table with a paper in front of him,
in the act of caressing his dog who jumps at his knee. There is a
suggestion in the scene of tutor and pupil and it is only the
intervention of the dog, Selwyn's favourite Râton, that gives it a more
domestic and informal flavour.

Relationships such as those with March and Carlisle, as also his friendship with Walpole and Williams, were important to Selwyn. They filled the emotional void in his life and enabled him, if only at second-hand, to experience some of those aspects of ordinary existence which his peculiarly withdrawn nature prevented him from knowing more intimately and directly himself. They also helped him to dispel the spectre of loneliness that occasionally haunted his solitary bachelor state. He could joke about this, as he could about anything, but fear lurked behind the pleasantry. 'This is the second day I am come home to dine alone,' he once wrote to Carlisle, 'but so it is, and if it goes on so I am determined to keep a chaplain, for although I do not stand in need of much society, I do not much relish being quite alone at this time of day.'

Yet there was another even stranger side to his character that was again something both of a joke and a cause of perplexity to his friends. This was his fascination with death, crime, and executions. Public executions were popular spectacles at the time and people of all classes thronged to see them, but Selwyn's taste for witnessing the grim ritual of the scaffold and for gazing on the faces of the dead was sufficiently marked for it to be a matter of general comment and the origin of some of his more sombre strokes of wit. Walpole records an occasion when some women scolded Selwyn for going to watch an execution and asked him how he could be such a barbarian as to see a head cut off. Selwyn was quite unrepentant. 'If that was such a crime,' he answered, 'I am sure I have made amends, for I went to see it sewed on again.' His friends, no less than Selwyn himself, could make jokes about this unusual propensity. When Lord Holland lay fatally ill, he was told that George Selwyn had come to enquire after his health. 'The next time Mr. Selwyn calls,' he replied 'show him up: if I am alive I shall be delighted to see him, and if I am dead he will be glad to see me.'

Selwyn's morbid inclinations were no doubt exaggerated by gossip. It was difficult to resist the temptation to improvise upon so bizarre a theme. 'You know George Selwyn never thinks but *à la tête tranchée*,' Walpole wrote in October 1747 to Montagu. 'He came to town t'other day to have a tooth drawn, and told the man that he would drop his handkerchief for the signal.' If we are to believe all the reports that circulated about the necrophiliac leanings of this enigmatic character, then we must accept that there were indeed morbid depths to his imagination that 'afforded him a painful and unaccountable pleasure' (the phrase is that of his first biographer J. H. Jesse) in delving into all the gory particulars of suicide and murders, in looking upon disfigured corpses, or in observing the last agonies of the condemned criminals on the scaffold. Yet it is clear that in some of the stories told about Selwyn invention plays a more prominent part than truth. Can we really believe that he would sometimes disguise himself as a woman in order to avoid being recognized among the crowds at an execution, or that he made a special journey all the way to Paris just to see Damiens, the would-be assassin of Louis XV, broken on the wheel? It was on this occasion that someone observing the close attention he paid to the proceedings is supposed to have asked him whether he was a professional hangman himself, to which he answered modestly (so the story goes) that he did not have that honour but was merely an amateur. In fact there is no record of Selwyn having been in France at the time and the very same story is told of the French geographer and explorer La Condamine.

It is perhaps revealing that many of the stories supporting Selwyn's penchant for executions came from friends such as Gilly Williams, eagerly describing such scenes for his benefit when Selwyn himself was not there. Even Lord Carlisle was not above watching a hanging for this vicarious purpose. 'Hackman, Miss Ray's murderer, is hanged,' he wrote somewhat ingenuously to Selwyn on 19 April 1779. 'I attended his execution, and from no curiosity of my own. I am this moment returned from it: everybody enquired after you—you have friends everywhere.' Accounts such as this tell us more about the general popularity of such occasions than of Selwyn's special relish for them. He was, however, sufficiently celebrated for the morbid streak in his character for a great many anecdotes to be told at its expense. Even George III allowed himself to indulge in a mildly jocular reference to the subject when Selwyn was seen to leave the royal drawing-room just before the king dubbed a new knight. He was surprised, the king declared, that Mr Selwyn had not remained behind to watch the ceremony as it looked so like an execution. Selwyn was not greatly amused by the story when it reached him, but upon the whole he took such sallies in good part. In 1777 he had been satirized in a poem called *The Diaboliad*. The theme of the skit was that the Devil, having grown old, was searching for a suitable successor. Several candidates in London were considered, including George Selwyn:

> The murmurs hush'd—the Herald straight proclaimed
> S–l–n the witty next in order nam'd,
> But he was gone to hear the dismal yells
> Of tortur'd Ghosts and suffering Criminals,
> Tho' summoned thrice, he chose not to return,
> Charmed to behold the crackling Culprits burn.
> With George all known Ambition must give place
> When there's an Execution in the case.

Selwyn's reaction to these lines was resigned rather than angry. 'I forgive him his mention of me,' he told Carlisle, 'because I believe that he does it without malice, but, if I had leasure to think of such things, I must own the frequent repetition of the foolish stories would make me peevish.' Whether he liked it or not, the stories would persist, and Selwyn's memory has always been accompanied by this dark shadow. Would he have been equally peevish had it been revealed to him that he would be resurrected ninety years after his death in the character of 'Georges Selwyn', a morbidly sadistic Englishman, in Edmond de Goncourt's novel *La Faustin*?

❖ 4 ❖

It is a relief to turn from Selwyn's sepulchral pleasures to something more healthy and agreeable, for this man who hated to miss a public hanging was also noted for his love of children and animals. These were tastes he shared with Horace Walpole, some of whose most charming stories and poems were addressed to children, and who was never without a pet dog, from the plump little spaniel Tory who had the misfortune to be devoured by a hungry young wolf on his journey to Italy in 1739, to the spoilt, bad-tempered old Tonton he inherited from Madame du Deffand and who snapped at so many of his friends. Selwyn's favourite Râton had the distinction of being twice painted by Sir Joshua Reynolds, once, as we have seen, in the conversation piece with Lord Carlisle, and again when still little more than a puppy in a portrait of his master finished in 1764. He was a constant companion. 'I have no one with me but Râton,' Selwyn wrote to Lord Carlisle from Matson in 1764, 'but he is in great health and beauty.' Walpole's dog at this period was a black and tan spaniel bitch called Rosette. His amusement may well be imagined when he discovered on a visit to Paris in 1771 that a farce was playing at the Comédie Italienne called *Râton et Rosette.* He managed to procure a playbill and sent it to Selwyn when he got back to Strawberry Hill that September. He wrote:

> Would you ever have thought that Râton and Rosette would be talked of one for another? But neither innocence nor age are secure. People say that there never is a smoke without some fire: here is a striking proof to the contrary. Only think of the poor dear souls having a comic opera made upon their loves. Rosette is so shocked that she insists upon Râton's posting to Paris and breaking the poet's bones, *sauf à les ronger après.* If he is a *preux chevalier,* he will vindicate her character *d'une manière éclatante.*

Selwyn had always liked young people, and adopted the role of benevolent uncle to his friends' children. 'Heaven is remarkably indulgent to you to secure you a nursery *in perpetuo,*' Gilly Williams once wrote to him in a mocking vein. 'The moment the old one is fledged, and takes wing, you have another, with clouts, and pap-spoon, to which you are equally attentive.' There was something of the pedagogue in Selwyn, and he was no doubt pleased when a five-year-old girl, in thanking him for a present, wrote him a letter in very proper French. He took a great interest in the education of Lord and Lady Carlisle's children, hoping that Lady Carlisle would find suitable masters for her daughter, and commending their eight-year-old son George to his father for his intelligence and application to study. 'What I tell you of his reading is literally true,' Carlisle was told,

> but it is not reading that expresses it, for I could have said as much if he had read nothing but the History of Cinder Breech and that kind of biography. He read with me English History, and stopped for information, and showed an uncommon thirst for it. He asked me as many questions in the history of George I concerning the South Sea Scheme, the prosecution of Lord Macclesfield, and the Barrier Treaty, as another boy would have asked me about Robinson Crusoe. He likes other books too, and it is agreeable to hear him talk of them.

He suggested that the boy should have his own choice of books, 'a little library—as many as would fill a small bookcase.'

It was not until Selwyn was fifty-two that he found a true outlet for his pent-up paternal feelings; someone upon whom he could concentrate the affections that had previously been dispersed among his Townshend nephews and nieces and the children of his close friends. On 25 August 1771 the Marchesa Fagnani, an Italian lady of distinguished family but rather easy virtue, gave birth to a daughter in London. The father of this child was almost certainly the Earl of March, who from the first showed a concerned regard for its welfare, though the lady's husband appears to have acknowledged the infant as his daughter, presumably for the sake of his wife's reputation. Here, however, he might have saved himself some trouble for all fashionable London was aware that the child was not his. The only doubt, from their point of view, was whether the father was in fact March or Selwyn, for both took an immediate proprietary interest in the little girl who was to be baptized Maria but would always be known as 'Mie Mie'.

Everything we know about Selwyn's frigid nature and his general aversion from the society of women makes the possibility that he was himself Mie Mie's father wholly unlikely. He was never known to have had a love affair in his life even as a young man and not, as was now the case, a middle-aged misogynist. Such doubt as there might be, in view of his lifelong affection for the girl, he himself dispelled in a letter to his favourite niece Mary Townshend, written in June 1778. Referring to Mie Mie, he wrote,

> It is an insuperable difficulty to make people comprehend that one can love another person's child as much as one's own, although it is in common speech often allowed. If that was once admitted, I should expect that no one would think extraordinary what I have done and suffered and exposed myself to for her sake.

March's paternity is as certain as can be in such matters, and is now generally accepted without question. Why else should so selfish and hedonistic a man take so much notice of the birth of someone else's child or at the end of his life make her the heiress to a fortune? And if Selwyn were looking for someone to whom he could be proxy-father, who else but the daughter of the man who was his greatest friend? At the beginning of her life both March and Selwyn vied with each other in watching over Mie Mie's welfare, but March's interest soon gave way to Selwyn's. He was not the kind of man to waste any time on another person, even his own daughter, if someone else was prepared to do it for him; and there was nothing in the world that Selwyn wanted to do more.

The Marchesa Fagnani left England soon after her daughter's birth, leaving the child in the care of March and Selwyn. Relations between mother and daughter were always somewhat equivocal, but at this period the marchesa seems to have had no qualms about leaving the child in the charge of these two bachelors, one an infamous rake (for all that he was the girl's father), the other hardly versed in the mysteries of the nursery even if one were to overlook his widely known tendency to morbidity. There is a touch of complacency in one of her surviving letters to Selwyn which suggests that she did not take her maternal duties very seriously. As Mie Mie was approaching her first birthday, she wrote:

> I am enchanted to learn that my daughter is in good health, though I fear she will suffer much in cutting her teeth. I venture to beg of you to continue to give me tidings of her, as without your kindness in writing to me from time to time I should have been ignorant, for the last three months, of the fate of *ma petite*. My Lord [March], on his part, is a little indolent; but I forgive him this little fault on account of the many good qualities of his heart which he has to counter-balance it.

The marchesa perhaps knew Selwyn's character better than this superficial correspondence would suggest, for in fact Mie Mie had found in him a substitute father who would not only lavish affection upon her, but suffer all the agonies of uncertainty and insecurity that arose from the unofficial nature of his wardship over her. The ominous presence of the mother in the background, likely at any moment to snatch Mie Mie away from him, and having all the legal power and authority to do so, was a thought that often reduced him to a state of nervous despondency.

It is interesting to contrast the marchesa's rather formal inquiries about her daughter—let alone the apparent indifference with which she allowed three months to pass without news of her daughter and yet made no effort to initiate any inquiries herself—with the anguished notes that Selwyn sent to Mie Mie's schoolmistress when the little girl was first parted from him to attend at an establishment run by a Miss Terry on Campden Hill, Kensington. The long-suffering woman was submitted to a constant stream of querulous interrogations: yes, Mademoiselle Fragnani was quite well, and engaged in a game of romps; no, the child's spirits were not depressed, she was lively and had eaten a good dinner; yes, she had slept well, Mr Selwyn had no cause to feel uneasy. On days when visits were allowed, he was there to vouch for himself that all was well; when away, anxious notes and inquiries continued much, one must imagine, to the irritation of Miss Terry, in whose replies one detects a slight note of weariness as she assures the worried guardian that his young friend behaves exactly like other children. Selwyn had never been so happy. His devotion to Mie Mie was almost maternal in the way he fussed over her. She very soon became the centre of his existence. The idea that he might one day have to part from her permanently was almost more than he could bear to think of, yet he must have known, however much he managed to banish the notion from his mind, that sooner or later the blow must fall.

In August 1776, the marchesa and her husband returned to England on a visit and Selwyn was in a frenzy of suspense. An interview with the parents took place. Madame Fragnani herself was quite content with the way things were going; she was prepared for the break to be as gentle as possible—let Mie Mie remain for at least another year with Selwyn before she need think of returning to Italy—but the marchesa made it clear that the girl's grandparents in Milan were insistent that she should return before long, that they were worried lest she was perhaps not being educated in the Catholic religion, and were determined to have her back when the year was up. Selwyn had no alternative but to agree, though he began almost at once a desperate but forlorn rearguard action in a vain attempt to keep Mie Mie with him, even going to the extreme of writing to the Imperial ambassador and the governor of Milan hoping to enlist their support. It was all to no avail. In August 1777, when the year's grace had expired, Mie Mie left England for Italy, to parents who were almost strangers to her and to grandparents whom she had never met. From Paris he received a pathetic little note from his young friend who was just six years old: 'My dear Monsieur Selwyn, God bless you and preserve you, with all my heart, and let me see you as soon as I can. I am your Mie Mie.'

Selwyn was in despair, and began again to plot for Mie Mie's return. His friends were amazed at the effect the parting had upon him and were sincerely worried by the depth of his dejection.

> I never thought your attachment extraordinary [Carlisle wrote]. I might, for your sake, have wished it less in the degree; but what I did think extraordinary was that you would never permit what was most likely to happen ever to make its appearance in your perspective. March speaks with great tenderness and real compassion for your sufferings.

He advised a change of scene: 'Gratify every caprice of that sort, and write to me everything that comes into your head. You cannot unload your heart to anyone who will receive its weight more cheerfully than I shall do.' Madame du Deffand, who acknowledged her own dislike of children, was more frank in her reaction to what was, to her, a slightly grotesque situation, as she made quite clear when she wrote to Walpole from Paris about this latest escapade of 'Lindor', as she called Selwyn. 'I believe if they refuse Lindor his Mimie,' she declared, 'he will kill himself: it is a folly without precedent.'

Fortunately Selwyn did not have to take so fatal a step and Mie Mie was eventually returned to him, but only after many tortuous negotiations including a visit to Milan and his promise, at first rebuffed by the supposedly indignant parents and then accepted, that he should make a financial settlement in Mie Mie's favour—something he had in any case planned to do before she first left England. One cannot avoid forming the impression that the marchesa was playing fast and loose with him in the hope of striking the best bargain possible. Her reputation, which was somewhat tarnished already, was not improved by these mercenary schemes, and in the long run they worked against her, as we can gather from a letter Selwyn wrote to Lord Carlisle in January 1781, a couple of years after Mie Mie's return to England. 'From Milan things are well: at least, no menaces from thence of any sort, and I am assured, by one who is the most intimate friend of the Emperor's minister there, that he was much more likely to approve than disapprove of Mie Mie's being with me, knowing as he does the turn and character of the mother.' Mie Mie in fact remained in his care until his death, when she inherited £33,000 from him. Not only did 'Lindor' not kill himself but he lived very happily with his adopted daughter, suffering nothing more alarming than a 'bastard hooping cough' which he caught from a too assiduous attendance in her sickroom in 1780. To Madame du Deffand, the whole thing was all very strange and she thought Selwyn a great fool, but as she wrote to Walpole, at least 'Lindor' had someone to love, even if it was only a doll and, as no doubt she enjoyed pointing out to the friend who always shied so at the very mention of love, that was better than having an empty soul.

Selwyn's remaining years were certainly brightened by the presence of Mie Mie who provided him with a *raison d'être* that he had not noticeably possessed before, and over whom he watched with tender care. He always preferred living in London, only going to the country when business connected with his constituency at Gloucester (which he represented for some years while other nominees sat for his borough of Ludgershall) necessitated a visit there. To represent Gloucester actually involved an election, so that there were occasions when he was called upon to placate the city fathers, a duty which he found exceptionally tedious. It was his hope at such times that some congenial friend might come to visit him and distract his mind from the boredom of having to dine with the mayor and corporation and deliver an address which, as he confessed to Carlisle, he was glad nobody heard but themselves. What a relief, then, when Horace Walpole turned up at Matson in August 1774. He wrote to Carlisle: 'At night I heard that Mr. Walpole is here. I was then at Gloucester; so I hurried home, and have now some person to converse with who speaks my own language.' Fortunately a neighbour owned 'some charming ruins of an abbey' within a mile of Matson which was just the thing to interest his visitor, and if that was not enough he would 'throw in' what he described as the *masure* or ruin of his own old house which, he believed, would not hold out the century.

Walpole, of course, was enchanted with Selwyn's 'ruin' which he had already visited some twenty years before when he described it as 'small but neat'. Now, in a letter to the antiquary clergyman William Cole, one of his few friends who was a staunch Tory, he began:

You will not dislike my date. I am in the very mansion where King Charles the First and his two eldest sons lay during the siege; and there are marks of the last's hacking with his hanger on a window, as he told Mr. Selwyn's grandfather afterwards. The present master has done due honour to the royal residence, and erected a good marble bust of the Martyr, in a little gallery. In a window is a shield in painted glass, with the King's and his Queen's arms, which I gave him. So you see I am not a rebel, when *alma mater* antiquity stands godmother.

Walpole also visited Gloucester cathedral and the old manor house at Prinknash, once the country retreat of the abbots of Gloucester. 'I wished you there with their mitre on,' he assured Cole, who had decidedly High Church leanings.

Walpole was always happy if there was some ancient site to visit or if he could puzzle over the problem of why the effigy of Edward II in Gloucester cathedral depicted him with a beard when he could recall a story of the king being shaved in cold water from a ditch when he was carried off to Berkeley Castle. Here was exciting material for some more historic doubts. Selwyn could discover no such diverting pursuits to enliven his existence when in the country, which bored him so much that he found it difficult to prolong his stay even for the purpose of encouraging the electors of Gloucester. 'I can hardly save appearances,' he confessed to Carlisle, 'either by staying, or by forbearing while I do stay to show them what a pain it is to me.' The only justification he could find for his visits to Matson was that the country air was good for his beloved Mie Mie. Even so he fretted for London, for his club, for the latest political gossip, and for the society of friends whose presence would banish the spectre of solitude.

The only place he could tolerate that had some air of the country about it was Kingston-upon-Thames where in 1780 his friend March, now Duke of Queensberry and a millionaire, had bought a villa. Here was the guarantee of constant company, for the gregarious duke was lavish in his entertainment, dining peers and bishops and members of Parliament and later on some of the more distinguished refugees from the French Revolution, though the public preferred to imagine his villa as the scene of unspeakable orgies. No doubt there were still occasions in the duke's life that he would not choose to share with bishops, but the general impression we get of life at his Richmond house from the letters of Walpole and Selwyn, depicting, as they do, pleasures that are entirely aesthetic, is hardly one to shock or scandalize the reader. In a letter to Carlisle, Selwyn wrote:

> The Duke dines with me when he is here a little after four, and when we have drunk our wine, we resort to his Great Hall, *bien éclairée*, *bien échauffée* to drink our coffee and hear Quintettos. The hall is hung round with the Vandyke pictures (as they are called) and they have a good effect. But I wish that there had been another room or gallery for them, that the hall might have been without any other ornament but its own proportions.

Horace Walpole, dining with Queensberry in the year of Selwyn's death, presents an equally innocuous picture in a letter to Mary Berry:

> The next evening I was again at Queensberry-house, where the Comtesse Emilie de Boufflers played on her harp, and the Princesse di Castelcigala, the Neapolitan minister's wife, danced one of her country dances, with castanets, very prettily, with her husband. Madame du Barry was there too, and I had a good deal of frank conversation with her about Monsieur de Choiseul; having been at Paris at the end of his reign and the beginning of hers, and of which I knew so much by my intimacy with the Duchesse du Choiseul.

This was the atmosphere that Selwyn liked to breathe, worldly, sophisticated and cosmopolitan, and he continued to inhale it as long as there was any breath in him, until at the close of his life he gave the impression to young William Wilberforce of the waxwork figure of a corpse as he made his appearance in some fashionable drawing-room more dead than alive. But he was not quite the skeleton at the feast for his wit did not desert him and his friends continued to repeat the cynical, slightly cruel, and always ironical comments that fell from his lips. It was this wit, so much of which is now lost, that made Selwyn memorable to those who outlived him and established the legend that still survives. When Walpole heard that his old friend was on the point of death late in January 1791 he wrote to Mary Berry, 'these misfortunes, though they can be so but for a short time, are very sensible to the old; but him I really loved, not only for his infinite wit, but for a thousand good qualities.' When the sad news was confirmed he told Lady Ossory: 'I have had another and grievous momento, the death of poor Selwyn! His end was lovely, most composed and rational. From eight years old I had known him so well, and consequently few knew so well the goodness of his heart and nature.'

In many ways George Selwyn was the least typical of Walpole's circle, for no one who formed a part of that élite group was quite so completely idle or left so little behind in terms of positive achievement. He was, however, a curiously complex and fascinating character, a real psychological enigma, with his morbid necrophilist tastes that contrasted so curiously with his innocent but compulsive love for little girls; with the emotional frigidity which he himself acknowledged when he once admitted that he had had sexual relations with women only seven times in his life and none since the age of twenty-nine; and with the strong, possessive attachment he felt for men like March and Carlisle that even to his contemporaries appeared like 'a sort of sentimental sodomy'. If the wit that his friends recalled with such delight has now for the most part evaporated, the strange riddle of his personality remains for us to puzzle over. Rarely have so many incompatibles been united in one personality.

IV
Dowagers: The Countess,
the Actress and the Marquise

It was, as we have already noted, Gilly Williams who once recorded in a letter to George Selwyn what he considered to be the ridicule of Horace Walpole's moving from the society of 'old Suffolk on the Thames to another old goody on the Tyne'. For Walpole himself, sensitive as he was to the sneers of derision, there was nothing at all absurd in his enjoyment of the company of these old ladies whose memories, when stimulated by his eager questions, could enlighten him so entertainingly upon the customs, the scandals, and the gossip of an earlier age. Indeed, he often found their conversation a good deal more interesting and amusing than the vapid topics of the young. He was already forty-six and, as was his custom, behaving as though he were a good deal older, at the time when Williams's letter was written. Two years earlier he had given his opinion upon the relative conversational merits of the old and the young in a letter to his cousin Henry Seymour Conway that left little doubt as to which he preferred. He wrote from Strawberry Hill:

My nieces, Lady Waldegrave and Mrs. Keppel, were here five days, and discussed the claim or disappointment of every miss in the kingdom for Maid of Honour. Unfortunately this new generation is not at all my affair. I cannot attend to what concerns them—not that their trifles are less important than those of one's own time, but my mould has taken all its impressions, and can receive no more. I must grow old upon the stock I have. I, that was so impatient to all their chat, the moment they were gone, flew to my Lady Suffolk, and heard her talk with great satisfaction of the late Queen's coronation-petticoat. The preceding age always appears respectable to us (I mean as one advances in years), one's own age interesting, the coming age neither one nor t'other.

When Walpole came to Strawberry Hill in 1747 the Countess of Suffolk had been living in retirement at her neighbouring villa of Marble Hill for many years. She was then sixty-six years old, twice widowed, and had about her that peculiar glamour that must always belong to anyone who has once been the mistress of a king. It was the memory of this all too intimate connection with the Court of George II that had inspired the reference to her in the poem called *The Parish Register of Twickenham* that Walpole had written in about 1758 when he referred to the spot

> Where Suffolk sought the peaceful scene,
> Resigning Richmond to the queen,
> And all the glory, all the teasing,
> Of pleasing one not worth the pleasing . . .

Certainly her arduous term as *maîtresse en titre* to the irascible little monarch had brought her few of the spoils and none of the power usually associated with the difficult and, in her case, always rather precarious place she occupied in his life, where habit rather than affection gave her such security as she had. It is interesting in the context to compare her lot with that of her much younger contemporary Madame de Pompadour, whom she was to survive by some three years. While the French marquise in her time governed the king, dismissed and appointed ministers and was courted by the Empress of Austria, the English countess suffered the angry abuse of her lover, the jealousy of the queen and the contempt of ministers, including Horace Walpole's father, who knew that she had neither influence nor power. As Lord Hervey was to express it in his *Memoirs*, Lady Suffolk had to reconcile herself to the unflattering truth that 'a mistress who could not get power was not a much more agreeable or respectable character than a minister who could not keep it'.

Lady Suffolk was born Henrietta Hobart in 1688, one of the seven daughters of a Norfolk baronet, Sir Henry Hobart, and spent her childhood at Blickling Hall, the beautiful old Jacobean manor house near Aylsham, some fifteen miles north of Norwich. Misfortune came early in life, for her father was killed in a duel when she was only ten years old and her mother died three years later. While still in her teens, she was married to Charles Howard, youngest son of the fifth Earl of Suffolk, a captain of dragoons with few prospects and no money beyond his army pay. According to the cynical testimony of Lord Chesterfield, they had married for love but afterwards hated each other for the rest of their lives. Their characters would certainly seem to have had little in common; they were, as Lord Hervey observed, an 'ill-matched, unfortunate couple', for this pretty, good-natured and intelligent girl found herself tied to a husband who the same witness summed up as being wrong headed, ill-tempered, obstinate, drunken, extravagant and brutal, and in this sorry catalogue of vices Lord Hervey does not seem to have exaggerated.

From the start, their marriage was haunted by the spectre of poverty. Henrietta's marriage portion was not large and was well tied up in trusts; her husband's entire capital would appear to have been the £700 he obtained from the sale of his commission in the dragoons which he effected only three months after their marriage. As this left him with no employment as well as no regular income, he occupied his new-found leisure by bringing a suit at law in the Court of Chancery against his wife's family in an attempt to gain control of her modest fortune. As a result of the procrastination peculiar to that court, the case was not settled for nearly seven years, by which time most of the money had vanished into the pockets of the lawyers. Meanwhile the couple, to whom a son had been born in 1707, passed a dreary existence in cheap lodgings, at times using an assumed name in order to evade their creditors. Such a life is only bearable if the burdens are shared, but Charles Howard would leave his wife in wretched and squalid surroundings while he squandered such money as they possessed or had been able to wheedle from relatives in what Henrietta later described as 'drinking or other pleasures which a wife is entitled to call crimes', and he would often stagger home 'in surfeits' when she had spent the day without proper food.

There seemed no solution to the predicament in which the Howards found themselves except flight abroad. Henrietta was the driving force in this enterprise, but the first time she contrived to raise the money for their passage her husband managed to spend it all on himself before the scheme could be put into effect. Eventually, however, enough money was saved and some time towards the end of 1713 they left England for Hanover. It was an obvious choice. Queen Anne was a sick woman and not likely to live much longer, and in Hanover the Electress Sophia, though so much older, did not conceal the eagerness with which she looked forward to succeeding to her ailing cousin's throne. The Howards were not the only English subjects who took the opportunity to ingratiate themselves with their future ruling family. Lack of money continued to be a serious embarrassment all the same, and loyalty to the Hanoverian succession was no substitute for hard cash. 'Still so narrow was their fortune,' Walpole wrote in his *Reminiscences*, 'that Mr. Howard finding it expedient to give a dinner to the Hanoverian ministers, Mrs. Howard is said to have sacrificed her beautiful head of hair to pay the expenses,' adding for the benefit of the Miss Berrys, for whose amusement the *Reminiscences* were written, that 'it must be recollected, that at that period were in fashion those enormous full-bottomed wigs, which often cost twenty and thirty guineas.' The main purpose of the visit to Hanover was successful despite these unfortunate humiliations for Henrietta. 'Mrs. Howard,' Walpole continues, 'was extremely acceptable to the intelligent Princess Sophia; but did not at that time make further impression on the Electoral Prince, than, on his father's succession to the crown, to be appointed one of the bedchamber women to the new Princess of Wales.' Her husband at the same time became groom of the bedchamber to the king.

Henrietta Howard's career at the Court of George II, both as Prince of Wales and as king, can be followed in the respective memoirs of Lord Hervey and Horace Walpole, the latter's account being based almost entirely upon the long, 'extremely agreeable' conversations he had with her many years later when, elderly and deaf, she would spend the autumn evenings with him exchanging anecdotes and recalling earlier days. 'Each of us knew different parts of many Court stories,' he wrote, 'and each was eager to learn what either could relate more; and thus, by comparing notes, we sometimes could make out discoveries of a third circumstance, before unknown to both.' Apart from the degree of financial security which her post at last brought her, Henrietta's troubles were by no means over when she became a Woman of the Bedchamber to the shrewd, intelligent but formidable Caroline of Ansbach; they merely took on a new dimension in which Court intrigues assumed the place of previous matrimonial harassments. Her position was not especially enviable even before the prince's amorous advances added further complications. She had that elusive quality of charm in a Court that conspicuously lacked it, and was cultivated and witty in an environment that was essentially philistine and shallow. The only place in the drab Court where some gaiety prevailed was in the room reserved for her colleagues in waiting on the princess, where her companions in those early days when George I still lived were the beautiful Molly Lepel, who would later marry Lord Hervey, the vivacious Mrs Selwyn, mother of George Selwyn, the very pretty Mary Bellenden who was Henrietta's particular friend, and Horace Walpole's own mother, Lady Walpole. Their apartment, the latter's son was to record, 'became the fashionable evening rendez-vous of the most distinguished wits and beauties'. Away from this charmed circle, however, all was tedium and drudgery. The princess (who later as queen would boast of how she could assume '*mon grand ton de Reine*') treated all her maids of honour and women of the bedchamber, however well-born, as one might some upper servant scolding them peevishly when annoyed and referring to them always as 'my good Howard' or 'my good Bellenden'. It was not a very agreeable existence at the best of times, and when the princess was displeased her sharp tongue made life decidedly unpleasant. Nor were their living conditions, for all that they were housed in a palace, exactly ideal. 'My Lady Yarmouth has an ague,' Walpole wrote in 1749 of Henrietta's successor in the royal bed, 'and is forced to keep a constant fire in her room [in Kensington Palace] against the damps. When my Lady Suffolk lived in that apartment, the floors produced a constant crop of mushrooms.'

Mrs Howard (she did not become Countess of Suffolk until 1731, when her husband succeeded his elder brother in the family honours) became the Prince of Wales's mistress about the time that the prince and his family were banished from St James's Palace in 1717 and set up a rival court at Leicester House. George had at first cast some languishing glances at Mary Bellenden, one of the maids of honour, but that vivacious beauty had avoided the royal embrace because, in her opinion, 'the Prince's gallantry was by no means delicate, and his averice disgusted her'. She escaped into matrimony, marrying Colonel Campbell, a kinsman of the Duke of Argyll, and retired from the Court leaving the field open to her friend Mrs Howard who, in Walpole's unromantic phrase, 'on Mrs. Campbell's eclipse succeeded to her friend's post of favourite—but not to her resistance.'

There was certainly little, if indeed any, romance in the situation.

'From the steady decorum of Mrs. Howard,' Walpole later noted, 'I should conclude that she would have preferred the advantages of her situation to the ostentatious éclat of it . . . nor do I suppose that love had any share in the sacrifice she made of her virtue. She had felt poverty, and was far from disliking power.' Of the prince (or king as he became in 1727) he wrote:

> The King, though very amorous, was certainly more attracted by a silly idea he had entertained of gallantry being becoming than by a love of variety; and he added the more egregious folly of fancying that inconstancy proved that he was not governed; but so awkwardly did he manage that artifice, that it but demonstrated more clearly the influence of the Queen.

Caroline herself, though she resented what had happened and persecuted the new mistress with jealous jibes and cutting innuendoes, was prepared to accept the liaison as she knew that her 'good Howard' was no real rival when it came to influencing the king in any political decision, and that her own ascendancy over him was unchallenged. Few royal mistresses can have gained less from their position than Lady Suffolk did, or have had such a grim time of it while her period as favourite lasted. As Lord Hervey neatly summed it up:

> she was forced to live in the constant subjection of a wife with all the reproach of a mistress and to flatter and manage a man whom she must see and feel had as little inclination to her person as regard to her advice; and added to this she had the mortification of knowing the Queen's influence so much superior to hers, that the little show of interest she maintained was only a permitted tenure dependent on a rival who could have overturned it any hour she pleased. But the Queen, knowing the vanity of her husband's temper, and that he must have some woman for the world to believe he lay with, wisely suffered one to remain in that situation whom she despised and had got the better of, for fear of making room for a successor whom he might really love, and that might get the better of her.

And so, while submitting to the graceless gallantries of the king, who visited her apartment promptly at nine o'clock every evening, Henrietta remained at the beck and call of the queen, who saw no reason to conceal the dislike and slight contempt she felt for this harmless rival. The king was so ruled by the nicely timed schedule of his activities, which he followed with military precision, that if he arrived at his mistress's door a few minutes early, he would pace up and down, watch in hand, until the exact moment of nine, when he would enter her room and harangue her for hours in his thick Westphalian accent with a recital of his political grievances, a tirade from which her growing deafness was her only protection. If he bored her in private, he could be downright rude to her in public. It was one of her duties as woman of the bedchamber to assist at the queen's toilet. On one occasion the king happened to be present as Mrs Howard was arranging a scarf or handkerchief round the queen's neck. To everyone's astonishment, the king suddenly snatched it away, telling his mistress that because she had an ugly neck herself was no reason for her to hide the queen's.

Henrietta's only security lay in the queen's dread, to which Lord Hervey had referred, that her husband might find some new mistress whom she could not herself trust and who might really undermine her powerful influence over the king. Knowing her husband's slavery to habit and routine, she realized that she was fairly safe so long as her 'good Howard' was always available, and for this reason she resisted vigorously any attempts that Henrietta made to retire from the Court. The king was well aware of this manoeuvre on his wife's part and probably only accepted things the way they were because, as Walpole put it, 'it is certain that the King always preferred the Queen's person to that of any other woman; nor ever described his idea of beauty but he drew the picture of his wife.' Even so, his response to the queen's efforts to keep his mistress at Court was characteristically brusque and unflattering to the supposed object of his affections. 'I don't know', he declared, 'why you will not let me part with an old deaf woman, of whom I am weary.'

Henrietta's own weariness must often have exceeded that of the king's. She certainly achieved very little in material terms from her intimacy with her august lover beyond a gift of money to help pay for her villa at Twickenham and the award of a barony and the Order of the Bath for her brother. Lord Bolingbroke and Dean Swift both made much of her, hoping to rehabilitate themselves in the royal favour, the one eager to return to active political life, the other hoping to exchange an Irish deanery for an English bishopric, but better informed courtiers knew that the mistress was the last person one should apply to in matters of political or ecclesiastical patronage. Her influence in such matters was virtually nil and it was a sign of political *naïveté* to suppose that she had any. 'Her credit', as Walpole was to explain to Miss Berry, 'had always been extremely limited by the Queen's superior influence, and by the devotion of the minister [his father, Sir Robert] to her Majesty.'

A further embarrassment came Henrietta's way when her husband, who had ignored or ill-treated her before she became the king's favourite, started to make a nuisance of himself and publicly demanded that his wife be restored to him in an ugly and clamorous scene in the courtyard of St James's Palace. Later on, when the Court was moving from London to Richmond, he threatened to pull his wife out of her coach, and Henrietta had to leave surreptitiously in the early hours of the morning under the protection of the Duke of Argyll and his brother Lord Islay. It was not, of course, that Charles Howard really wanted to have his wife back; he hoped, and eventually succeeded in achieving, a useful financial settlement, or, as Horace Walpole more plainly expressed it, 'he sold his own noisy honour and the possession of his wife for a pension of twelve hundred a year.' He was, however, still able to render one involuntary and unexpected service to his wife. When his brother died without an heir and he succeeded to the earldom of Suffolk his wife's new rank of countess delivered her from the menial duties of a woman of the bedchamber and she was promoted Mistress of the Robes to the queen. After that her life became a bit more peaceful, though rows and scenes, often over the merest trifles, continued to plague her.

Her liaison with the king lasted until 1734, by which time they were both thoroughly tired of each other and only the queen, for her own peace of mind, tried to keep the relationship going. When Lady Suffolk finally asked permission to retire from the Court her request was only granted after a plea from the queen for her to remain at her post had been turned down. Lady Suffolk had been for a short visit to Bath where Lord Bolingbroke had also been taking the cure, and George II's daughter Princess Amelia had mischievously suggested that they were intriguing together against her father. When Lady Suffolk returned, the king ostentatiously refused to visit her room. Henrietta protested to the queen and offered to go rather than be accused of disloyalty. Caroline tried to brush her fears aside, telling her that she had got the idea 'out of *Celia* or some other romance' and begged her to stay at least one more week. Lady Suffolk stayed her week while Caroline hoped that habit and familiarity would soon restore her husband to his familiar routine. The king, however, still refused to visit his mistress and when the queen attempted to intercede on her behalf she was soundly snubbed for her pains. At the end of the week Henrietta left the Court for ever, and within a year the king had fallen in love with one of his Hanoverian subjects, Amelia von Walmoden (later created Countess of Yarmouth), inanely informing his wife, 'I know you will love Madame Walmoden because she loves me.' Perhaps what best illustrates the lax atmosphere at this bickering and discordant Court from which Lady Suffolk, surely to her great relief, had at last escaped, was the remark of the king's eldest daughter Princess Anne during the brief interval between mistresses. 'I wish with all my heart that he would take someone else,' she said of her father to Lord Hervey, 'then Mama might be a little relieved of the ennui of seeing him in her room.' It did not occur to her that Lady Suffolk might have felt some ennui too.

⟫ 2 ⟪

To see Lady Suffolk as she appeared at Court, where she was both exploited and ill-used by the king and queen, was to see but one side of her personality, and that the most negative. A whole aspect of her character had to be kept repressed, and only blossomed when she could escape into her own private world and chosen circle of friends. Lord Hervey was probably the only person in the royal entourage who was able to appreciate her true worth, for the portrait he draws of her in his *Memoirs* helps us to understand how this woman who pleased an absurd little king (silly and immature at least in his personal relationships) could also appeal to such people as Alexander Pope, Jonathan Swift and John Gay; and how the more serious and cultivated members of the aristocracy, men like Lord Islay, Lord Pembroke, the 'architect earl', and later on Horace Walpole himself, were immediately attracted by her sympathetic nature.

Good sense, good breeding, and good nature [Lord Hervey

wrote], were qualities which even her enemies could not deny her;
nor do I know any one good or agreeable quality which those who
knew her more intimately would not as readily allow her. She was
civil to everybody, friendly to many, and unjust to none: in short,
she had a good head and a good heart, but had to do with a man
who was incapable of tasting the one or valuing the other, one who
seemed to look upon a mistress rather as a necessary appurtenance
to his grandeur as a prince than an addition to his pleasures as a
man, and thus only pretended to distinguish what it was evident he
overlooked and affected to caress what it was manifest he did not
love.

Away from the Court, in the retirement and tranquillity of
Twickenham, whether walking in the gardens of her beautiful little
villa by the Thames or reclining by the fire in the elegant
white-and-gold Great Room, exchanging gossip and reminscences
with the young Horace Walpole on those autumn evenings, we
recognize at once the 'certain Lady at Court' to whom Pope
addressed the lines

> I know a thing that's most uncommon;
> (Envy be silent and attend!)
> I know a Reasonable Woman,
> Handsome, witty, yet a Friend . . .

and can understand how that eccentric old warrior Lord Peter-
borough when well over sixty, and already secretly married to a
singer from the opera, fell under the spell of this 'wonderful creature,
a woman of reason', and in lines more suitable to some feverish
adolescent Cherubino than a veteran of many amorous and military
campaigns declared his passion for her in turbulent verse:

> I said to my heart, between sleeping and waking,
> 'Thou wild thing, that always art leaping and aching,
> What black, brown or fair, in what clime, in what nation,
> By turns has not taught thee a pit-a-patation . . .?'

At Marble Hill she could be herself, enjoy the company of her
literary friends, and forget the endless intrigues, the vicious quarrels,
the royal spite and anger that seemed an inescapable element of the
Court of King George and Queen Caroline. Here she could escape

from the restrictions and tedium of that life, and when she retired from St James's it became her permanent home. It was her refuge in every sense of the word, and after the death of her long estranged husband was to be the setting of her brief but happy second marriage to George Berkeley, a gouty old bachelor who was devoted to her and with whom she spent ten happy years.

Marble Hill had one thing, and one thing only, in common with its neighbour Strawberry Hill, and that was that it had been built by a 'committee of taste', though one much stricter in its application of architectural rules than the trio of Walpole, Chute and Bentley was to be; for while Strawberry was the eclectic creation of intentional gothic muddle, Marble Hill was an essay in strict classical terms, aiming at a perfect harmony of proportion in the manner of the rural villas of Andrea Palladio, a style that Inigo Jones had introduced into England a century before and which Lord Burlington was now making fashionable. It had been started in about 1723 when Lord Islay, a distinguished patron of art and architecture, had purchased some plots of land near the Thames at Twickenham on Henrietta's behalf. The design of the house was in the hands of her friend and fellow courtier Henry, Lord Herbert, whose plans were interpreted by the builder Roger Morris. Herbert, who later succeeded as ninth Earl of Pembroke, was an acknowledged arbiter of taste, and about the same time was also concerned with the plans of the White Lodge in Richmond Park for George II. According to Walpole's fanciful opinion, the soul of Inigo Jones had assisted the muses in Herbert's education. 'No man', he claimed, 'had a purer taste in building than Earl Henry.' When the house was finished, Alexander Pope gave his expert attention to the planning of the garden (which, like his own, included a grotto), assisted by the professional gardener Charles Bridgeman, while Lord Bathurst sent a gift of lime trees from his park at Cirencester.

Horace Walpole came to know Lady Suffolk in the year she lost her second husband, and his visits must have helped her through that period of sadness. He would sit near her chair and shout his questions into her long tortoiseshell ear trumpet and listen eagerly to her replies in the quiet, almost whispering voice of the very deaf. He would appeal to her in matters of etiquette; upon such questions she was his 'oracle'. Never was her advice more urgently needed than in the embarrassing business of the queen's kinsman, the Prince of

Mecklenburg, in August 1764. Walpole, who had overslept, was wakened by the sound of the doorbell. Who could it be? His Swiss servant told him that two men had called and asked if they could see the house, but as the master was still in bed they had been told to come back in an hour's time. Who were they? The Prince of Mecklenburg, and Dr Witz! But this was not all; the queen herself was there with them, waiting in her coach which stood in the road outside. 'I am shocked to death, and know not what to do,' Walpole lamented in a letter to his cousin Lord Hertford. 'It is ten times worse just now than ever at any other time: it will certainly be said that I refused to let the Queen see my house. See what it is to have republican servants!' What was he to do to put things right? 'I shall go this evening and consult my oracle, Lady Suffolk. If she approves it, I will write to Dr Witz, and pretend I know nothing of anybody but the Prince, and beg a thousand pardons, and assure him how proud I should be to have his master visit my castle at Thundertentronk.'

There could be no greater contrast in architectural styles than that between the 'gloomth' of Strawberry and the chaste classical perfection of Marble Hill. Walpole, with his keen artistic sensibility, must often have pondered on this as he made his way from one to the other, for Lady Suffolk's house with its almost academically correct proportions yet modest domestic scale was a direct contradiction of his pronouncement that classical or 'Grecian' styles were only suitable for 'magnificent and public buildings'. Perhaps this was why, as a tactful concession to his gothic susceptibilities, Lady Suffolk agreed in 1758 at least to having a Gothic 'prospect' and allowed the Strawberry Committee to convert one of her barns into a 'priory of St Hubert'. There was the hint of a cloister, a nave and chancel with triple lancet window, and rising above the roof an octagon lantern in two pinnacled tiers topped by a short spire. The 'priory' was designed by Bentley, but John Chute was kept in touch with the details of its progress. 'My Lady Suffolk', Walpole wrote to him on 29 June, 'has at last entirely submitted her barn to our *ordination*. As yet it is only in *Deacon's orders*, but will very soon have our last imposition of hands.' The octagon and spire has a strong resemblance to the one which James Wyatt was to build forty years later on his first version of Fonthill Abbey, which is chiefly famous for its fall. The fate of St Hubert's priory was hardly happier. As a note in Walpole's hand on one of Bentley's surviving drawings sadly informs us, the priory was indeed built but pulled down after Lady Suffolk's death.

Comparisons of another sort, that had nothing whatsoever to do with architecture, took place later on between Walpole and Chute when they were attempting to guess the age of the Princess Craon whom they had known in their younger days on the Grand Tour when her husband had been Regent of Tuscany. The princess, whose supper parties they had attended in Florence, had, like Lady Suffolk, once been a royal mistress, having in her day been the lover of Duke Leopold of Lorraine. 'Mr. Chute and I have been computing her age,' Walpole wrote to Mann in August 1765, 'and find her completely ninety, for Prince Craon, in the year 1746, owned that she was seventy-one.' He then went on to compare her with his neighbour:

> 'Tis very wholesome to be a sovereign's mistress! My neighbour and friend Lady Suffolk is little short of fourscore, and except her hearing, which she lost early in her reign, has all her senses as perfect as ever; is clean, genteel, upright; and has her eyes, teeth, and memory in wonderful conservation, especially the last, which, unlike the aged, is as minutely retentive of what happened two years ago as of the events of her youth.

It was that marvellously retentive memory, of course, that most fascinated Walpole, with his passionate interest in the past; and it is pleasant to picture these two firm friends, a generation apart in age, absorbed in their discussion of the days when the elder, using such power as she then possessed, had sought with determination though without any notable success to frustrate the political schemes of that great minister, her young friend's father, for such indeed had been her intention when she was the king's mistress. Walpole usually pursued his father's former enemies with venomous scorn, but Lady Suffolk he not only forgave (perhaps because her efforts had been so very fruitless) but also came to bless her for the way she could illuminate a vanished world for him and thereby help him in his ambition to be the chronicler of the age. The talks he had with her were carefully noted down afterwards in his Commonplace Books and were of value to him in writing his memoirs of the reign of George II as well as the *Reminiscences* written in 1788 for Mary and Agnes Berry in which he paid special tribute to the accuracy of his friend's memory as well as to her strict love of the truth.

The visits to Marble Hill were not, of course, solely devoted to Court and political reminiscences. There were many lighter moments. In September 1761 we find Walpole writing to tell his friend George Montagu how he helped to arrange Lady Suffolk's hair for the coronation of George III and gave a helping hand in making Lady Hertford's dress, 'for you know,' he adds, 'no profession comes amiss to me, from a tribune of the people to a habit-maker'. Earlier that year, in April, there had been a scare when a fire broke out near Lady Suffolk's London house in Saville Row. Walpole, who declared himself to be as constant at a fire as George Selwyn was at an execution, walked from his house in Arlington Street to see the fire-fighters at work. When a change in the wind seemed to put Lady Suffolk's house in some peril from the flames, he struggled to her door, though up to his ankles in water from the fire engines and pumps, and remained with her until about three in the morning by which time the danger was passed. He had meanwhile persuaded her to be ready to transport her most valuable effects to safety should the need arise, but fortunately the fire was brought under control and this was not necessary. His old friend, who was then over seventy, behaved with great composure while the danger lasted, but complained to him how much worse her deafness grew with the alarm.

When Lady Suffolk had a serious attack of gout (or whatever passed under the name of gout at that period) at the beginning of 1764 and very nearly succumbed, it brought home to Walpole how much he valued her friendship. He confessed to Montagu, 'Her loss will be irreparable to me at Twickenham, where she is by far the most rational and agreeable company I have.' Only a short while before they had both been conspiring together in a New Year's surprise for her young great-niece Henrietta Hotham, hiding a diamond ring in a small round box and placing it on a table where the little girl would see and open it 'with all the eagerness and curiosity of eleven years'. Inside she found a short poem written in a tiny elf-like hand announcing that the ring was

> Sent by a sylph, unheard, unseen,
> A new-year's gift from Mab our queen . . .

The lines had been written by another of Walpole's dowagers, Lady Temple. That evening, at Lady Suffolk's request, he dashed off some verses appointing Lady Temple poet laureate to the fairies, though by then he was himself feeling so unwell with a stomach ache that (as he told Montagu) he felt 'fitter to write verses like a Poet Laureate than for making one'. Next day, the poem was solemnly presented to Lady Temple by the excited Henrietta Hotham who acted out an appropriate little scene for the occasion. The whole charade, which delighted Walpole as much as the child, had been devised by Lady Suffolk though she too had been ill for the past three weeks with eye trouble that had caused her much discomfort and prevented her from sleeping. 'What spirits, and cleverness, and imagination at that age, and under those afflictions . . .' Walpole wrote in admiration. 'Do you wonder I pass so many hours and evenings with her?'

On the evening of 23 July 1767, some three years after these happy events, Walpole made his habitual journey from Strawberry Hill through the village of Twickenham to Lady Suffolk's. It was a cold night for the time of year and he found her complaining of gout and rheumatism, but sitting downstairs when he thought she should really have been in bed. They spent a couple of hours together before he returned home, feeling sufficiently concerned about her to send next day to inquire after her health. She had passed a bad night, his messenger was told, but otherwise was much better. Later that evening, after a visit from their mutual friend Lady Dalkeith, she decided to have supper in her bedroom, but as Walpole wrote a few days later to Lady Dalkeith's brother-in-law Lord Strafford, 'she had scarce sat down in her chair before she pressed her hand to her side, and died in half an hour'. Walpole sadly missed this kind friend and neighbour who was seventy-nine years old when she died, and was horrified to learn after her death that she had been living for some time in very straitened circumstances, deeply anxious that she would be able to make proper provision for her niece Henrietta after she was gone. When her will was opened, he declared, it would surprise those who thought her rich.

It was Walpole's custom to hang portraits of his close friends in the various rooms of Strawberry Hill, some of which he had himself commissioned from the artists, others he had received as gifts from the sitters. Lady Suffolk's portrait by Charles Jervas was placed in the Round Bedchamber in the tower. Beside it hung a picture of Marble Hill, once the property of Alexander Pope, that Lady Suffolk had given to him herself. 'She had seen, known, and remembered so much, that I was seldom not eager to hear,' he told Horace Mann. 'She was a sincere and unalterable friend, very calm, judicious, and zealous.' Four years later, visiting her nephew at the house by the river that still spoke to him of his old friend, he felt the loss as acutely as ever. 'I have been dining at Lord Buckingham's at Marble Hill,' Mann was informed in June 1771. 'He has three fine children by his first wife; and has got a pretty, agreeable young wife; but it was all a melancholy day to me, who have passed so many agreeable hours in that house and garden with poor Lady Suffolk.'

❧ 3 ❧

In July 1761 when Walpole was busily engaged upon the third volume of his *Anecdotes of Painting* and, as usual, had men at work upon some improvement to his house (the interiors of the Gallery and Tribune were in process of construction at this period) he sent a brief account of his activities to his cousin Henry Conway: 'All the morning I play with my workmen or animals, go regularly every evening to the meadows with Mrs. Clive, or sit with my Lady Suffolk, and at night scribble my Painters—what a journal to send you!' Catherine Clive, more usually known as Kitty, would hardly qualify as a dowager though she formed, with Lady Suffolk and others, part of his intimate circle of women friends at Twickenham and for that reason may perhaps be included under the heading in an honorary capacity. She was, and had been for many years, the leading comic actress of her day, a jolly red-faced, good-natured woman with a loud infectious laugh. When Walpole came to live in Twickenham she was already established there as an occasional resident when she could escape from her theatrical duties, and they soon became friends. Later on, when he bought a small property just to the south of Strawberry Hill in the direction of Teddington, which he called Little Strawberry Hill, Mrs Clive became his tenant and was to remain his neighbour until her death.

Kitty Clive was six years older than Walpole. She was born in 1711 in London, the daughter of William Raftor, a soldier of Irish extraction who had served under James II and then turned to the law, a profession he had practised with such little success that his family had known the meaning of poverty, and it was said that his daughter had been in service as a maid before she began her career on the stage.

As an actress she specialized as what was known as a 'romp', those rather bouncing characters, either skittish or hoydenish, and usually appearing as serving girls—'singing chambermaids' was the contemporary name for them, for the part usually included a song—who were so popular in eighteenth-century farce. Her skill, however, was not limited to those boisterous roles; Henry Fielding applauded her ability to heighten all 'characters of humour' she attempted, adding 'nor is she confined only to the hoyden Miss or pert chambermaid, but in spiritous gay characters of high life she always appears with such air, mien, and action as speaks the gay, lively and desirable.' It was probably in such a role that Walpole first saw her, for one of his earliest references to her, when he was twenty-five years old, was in a play called *Miss Lucy in Town*, acted at Drury Lane in 1742. Another of her performances was to provoke one of George Selwyn's dry witticisms. He was eager, he declared, to see *High Life below Stairs* as he was weary of low life above stairs.

There are many testimonies to Kitty Clive's talents as an actress. 'What Clive did best,' Dr Johnson pronounced, 'she did better than Garrick; but she could not do half so many things well; she was a better romp than any I ever saw in nature.' Oliver Goldsmith was another admirer. 'Without exaggeration,' he wrote, 'she has more true humour than any actor or actress, upon the English or any other stage, I have seen.' Behind the scenes, however, her reputation was slightly different. She was a great one for rows and squabbles; she had a long-standing dispute with Garrick, and was always up in arms if she thought her rights were being infringed. And woe betide any other actress whom she considered to be trespassing on her territory. She had a tremendous row with Mrs Cibber (daughter-in-law of Colley Cibber, the dramatist and poet) when she discovered that this rival was going to play Polly in *The Beggar's Opera*, a part which Mrs Clive considered her own. Her furious reaction to the news caused such a stir that a poem was written about it, ending with the lines:

> 'Who is it thus,' in rage she cries,
> 'Dares rob me of my claim?'
> With that she to the green room flew,
> Where Cibber meek she found;
> And sure if friends had not been by,
> She had fell'd her to the ground.

She was, in short, in the words of the contemporary stage historian Tate Wilkinson, 'a mixture of combustibles; she was passionate, cross, vulgar, yet sensible; a very generous woman, and, as a comic actress of genuine worth—indeed, *indeed, indeed*, she was a diamond of the first water!'

She had started her career as Miss Raftor but had adopted professionally the surname by which she is best known to history after her marriage in 1732 to George Clive, a barrister and second cousin of Lord Clive of Indian renown. The marriage did not last. Perhaps her husband, like the unfortunate Mrs Cibber, fell a victim to her impatience or one of her stormy tantrums. In any event, a separation followed soon after her marriage and when she settled in Twickenham she was to all intents and purposes a single woman. After 1770, the year following her retirement from the stage, she was joined at Little Strawberry Hill by her brother James Raftor. Raftor was described as a wretched actor, who no doubt owed such success as he enjoyed to his sister's fame, but was none the less (according to Walpole's friend Lord Nuneham) a man of 'some information, of much observation, and possessing an extraordinary fund of original humour'. Everybody seems to have liked him. Some of his amusing anecdotes found their way into Walpole's correspondence, and when the prevalence of highwaymen made the neighbourhood of Strawberry Hill rather unsafe in the early 1780s so that it was 'as dangerous to go to Petersham as into Gibraltar', Walpole, who said that he comforted himself with the 'gothicity' of it all and found it 'delightful not to dare stir out of own's castle but armed for battle', jokingly announced that he would become a knight and appoint Raftor his esquire as he was 'as great a coward as Sancho Panza and has more humour'.

One of Kitty Clive's most noticeable features especially as she grew older, was her bright red face, a merry face that glowed all the redder when she laughed, which was often. It caused a good deal of waggish comment among Walpole's friends. Strawberry Hill, Lady Townshend observed, 'would be a very pleasant place if Mrs. Clive's face did not rise upon it and make it so hot.' Walpole himself could not resist a few sly comments at the expense of his friend's rubicund appearance. When she received a small bequest after the death of her friend Lord Radnor, another Twickenham neighbour, Walpole informed John Chute that 'you never saw anything so droll as Mrs.

Clive's countenance, between the heat of summer, the pride of legacy, and the efforts to appear concerned.' Writing to Montagu in the summer of 1766, he informed his correspondent: 'Strawberry is in perfection: the verdure has all the bloom of spring: orange-trees are loaded with blossoms, the Gallery all sun and gold, Mrs. Clive all sun and vermilion.' Her red face was an indication of her volatile temperament and no doubt was also a mark of those rages which she had sometimes visited on her professional rivals and colleagues when they had dared to cross her, but while her rages were like summer storms that passed as quickly as they rose, her laughter had an enduring quality, the sign of an essentially jovial nature. She was indeed a 'laughter loving dame', as Walpole later expressed it in some lines written in her memory, one whose home at once became 'mirth's consecrated ground'.

Walpole's uninhibited friendship with Mrs Clive belies the accusation sometimes brought against him that in relation to certain professional people he maintained an attitude of aristocratic aloofness, if not of actual disdain; that, as his biographer R. W. Ketton-Cremer expressed it, he 'could never quite forget, however familiarly he met them in social life, that Reynolds was a painter and Garrick a player'. It is true that he could mock at Garrick for being what he called '*sur un assez bon ton* for a player' when he dined at the ambitious actor's house in company with a duke, an earl, two countesses, a diplomatic envoy and the wife of a Secretary of State, but this was more because he felt out of sympathy with Garrick's *folie de grandeur* and his habit of flattering Walpole himself a little too obviously than because he earned his living on the stage. For that matter, James Raftor also flattered him quite unashamedly, so much so that Walpole said he would be 'a cormorant for praise' if he swallowed it, and could laugh at it instead; but in Garrick's case it was, he considered, just a shade calculated and it was this that he found distasteful. On the other hand, he never doubted Garrick's genius any more than he doubted that of Reynolds (though he could be sharp in his criticism of both) and for artistic genius in all its manifestations he always had a profound respect, acknowledging his sense of inferiority to those who possessed it. Had Walpole really been a snob he would never have dined with Garrick at all or lived on terms of the closest social intimacy with Kitty Clive and her brother.

In fact Walpole loved the theatre and was a frequent and

enthusiastic playgoer. He always relished a good performance and made a considerable collection of contemporary plays which he had bound up in stout volumes. He also wrote various prologues and epilogues including the lines Mrs Clive spoke upon her retirement from the stage. His five-act tragedy *The Mysterious Mother* was never performed, largely because the theme of incest, which would have suited the Jacobean palate, was rather too strong meat for the bland taste of eighteenth-century theatre audiences, but his one-act comedy or 'moral entertainment' as he described it, *Nature will Prevail*, was performed with success at the Little Theatre in the Haymarket in 1778. It was a charming, rather fragile little piece set on a desert island where two castaways, Current and Padlock, and a country girl Finette are involved in a serious of comic misunderstandings and confusions contrived by the fairy Almadine and an Echo, all to show that nature prevails in the same way everywhere and human beings are just as much subject to their own absurdities and follies on a desert island as they are back in their own homes. Walpole did not exploit his gift for comedy in writing for the theatre, perhaps because, as he explained to John Pinkerton, he considered the difficulty of writing a good comedy to be greater than that of composing a good tragedy. 'Not only is equal genius required,' he held, 'but a comedy demands a more uncommon assemblage of qualities—knowledge of the world, wit, good sense, etc., and these qualities superadded to those required for tragical composition.'

Walpole liked to read his works to certain of his friends. Lady Mary Coke was treated to a recitation from *The Mysterious Mother* as they both returned by coach from a breakfast party at Lady Cadogan's at Caversham Park near Reading. 'It pleased me very much,' she recorded in her diary, adding rather vaguely, 'you know how well he writes on all subjects.' Whether Kitty Clive was treated to a similar recitation we do not know, but he must surely have read *Nature will Prevail* to her. She was certainly given his *Letter from Xo Ho to his friend Lien Chi* to read, a political satire in which he was able to criticize some of the absurdities of government by pretending that his comments were those of a Chinese philosopher visiting England for the first time and sending his impressions back to a friend at Peking. 'Lord, you will be sent to the Tower!' was Mrs Clive's comment upon reading it, to which Walpole replied: 'Well, my father was there before me.'

Kitty Clive was a good neighbour for Walpole with her down-to-earth humour and cheerful laughter. She was also an intelligent woman who could enter into his more serious concerns. 'Clive, Sir, is a good woman to sit by,' Dr Johnson had maintained, 'she always understands what you say,' and though Walpole did not usually find himself in agreement with Johnson's opinions on any subject he would certainly have agreed in this. Kitty Clive took an interest in Strawberry Hill, embroidering chair covers and curtains for him and working a carpet with a design of blue tulips and yellow foliage for the Holbein Chamber. His friends found her quite as delightful as he did himself, and when Montagu visited Strawberry Hill she would sing Purcell's airs to him, something he would appreciate more than his host did, who was not endowed with an ear for music.

Mrs Clive and Walpole were constantly in and out of each other's houses. The two were so close and happy together that it was almost inevitable that malicious tongues would suggest that they were lovers. Chatterton, who hated Walpole, linked their names in some scurrilous lines, and the *Town and Country Magazine* lampooned them as Mrs Heidelburg and Baron Otranto, names derived from the part Mrs Clive played in George Colman's comedy *The Clandestine Marriage* and from Walpole's novel *The Castle of Otranto*. For once Walpole's fear of ridicule was not awakened by this obvious libel which was so plainly untrue; he could laugh at it, for were they not both, after all, between fifty and sixty years old at the time this attack on the innocence of their relationship was made? He could enjoy her friendship and laugh at her jokes without caring what anyone thought or said. Few of her jokes had he savoured more than the one he quoted to Montagu in May 1766:

> My Lady Shelburne has taken a house here, and it has produced a bon-mot from Mrs. Clive. You know my Lady Suffolk is *deaf*, and I have talked much of a charming old passion I have at Paris who is *blind*; 'Well,' said the Clive, 'if the new Countess is but *lame*, I shall have no chance of ever seeing you.'

This was the kind of raillery that Walpole found so refreshing in this candid friend who appeared to him, as he surveyed his circle at Twickenham, to be 'the only heroine among all us old dowagers'.

❧ 4 ❧

The 'charming old passion' at Paris was, of course, the Marquise du Deffand, the 'old blind *debauchée* of wit' whom Walpole first met in September 1765. He had gone to France in rather a disgruntled, not to say disillusioned, frame of mind, and was looking for distraction as well as diversion. He was suffering from bruised pride, feeling hurt at the conduct of his cousin Conway whom he felt had failed to appreciate the political help he had given him. He was in Paris only to avoid being in England, he wrote rather sulkily to Horace Mann, and was pretty indifferent as to how he passed his time: 'When I have broken from politics, and shown that I have, I shall return to my own chateau, and quiet.' Though he had set off without much enthusiasm, procrastinating (according to Gilly Williams) as much on the English side of the water as Lord March, who was then in France, did on the other, when he finally reached the French capital he arrived in some style, carrying recommendations from two previous French ambassadors to England, the Duc de Nivernois and the Comte de Guerchy, as well as from his friend George Selwyn who was already a seasoned *habitué* of the leading Parisian salons. In spite of Walpole's rather grim mood, the consciousness that his French was not perfect, and the inconvenience of a sudden attack of gout, French society took him to its heart and he scored something of a minor triumph. This soon had an exhilarating effect on his depressed spirits. He wrote to Conway:

> It would sound vain to tell you the honours and distinctions I receive, and how much I am in fashion, yet when they come from the handsomest women in France, and the most respectable in point of character, can one help being a little proud? If I was twenty years younger, I should wish they were not quite so respectable.

And to Selwyn he boasted: 'it is charming to totter into vogue.'

It was natural that Walpole should wish to penetrate the select society of the salons, for they were a peculiarly French institution that no other nation had quite succeeded in copying; they set the tone to the intellectual life of the capital simply by the quality of the conversation that flourished there. Here, in bursts of brilliant dialogue, were born the ideas that would soon shake the very foundations of French society, for in Paris at least they were about the only places, in a country without representative institutions, where men of genius could give vent to their ideas. People like d'Alembert, Diderot or Helvétius, who in England would probably have sat in the House of Commons, in France had to confine their flights of oratory to the drawing-rooms of Madame Geoffrin, Madame du Deffand or Mademoiselle de Lespinasse, each the centre of a dazzling coterie and all, for different reasons, bitter enemies of each other. In such circles Walpole would have been received with interest even before he made any impression on his own account for his reputation was not entirely unknown in France if only as his father's son, as first cousin to the British Ambassador Lord Hertford, and as the close friend of the Duke of Richmond who was about to succeed him. But his wit, his gaiety, and his conversational powers quickly gained him a general welcome everywhere because his vivacious personality seemed in such marked contrast to his hosts' preconceived idea of the silent, phlegmatic Englishman.

Walpole had first gone to Madame Geoffrin's after he reached Paris in September, having an introduction to her from his old friend Lady Hervey. He visited her several times and was impressed by her understanding and knowledge of the world, though he was still feeling a little unsure of expressing himself in French and was not fully in sympathy with the main topics of conversation. He reported to Montagu:

> The French affect philosophy, literature, and freethinking. The first never did, and never will possess me; of the two others I have long been tired. Freethinking is for one's self, surely not for society; besides one has settled one's way of thinking, or knows it cannot be settled, and for others I do not see why there is not as much bigotry in attempting conversions from any religion as to it.

To another friend he was more explicit:

> I assure you, you may come hither very safely, and be in no danger from mirth. Laughing is as much out of fashion as pantins or bilbouquets. Good folks, they have not time to laugh. There is God and the King to be pulled down first; and men and women, one and all, are devoutly employed in the demolition.

Perhaps some of his disapproval came from the growing lack of rapport with the mistress of the salon. Her opinions of people, he felt, were never favourable; she was 'an epitome of empire, subsisting by rewards and punishments'.

He began, after a while, to settle down and feel more at ease, and then very soon started to enjoy himself, though he continued to take exception to the views of the *philosophes* whose opinions he considered 'insupportable, superficial, overbearing, and fantastic'. He found, upon the whole, that he preferred the women he met to the men. If they were less gay than they used to be, they were better informed and delightful in conversation. After nearly a month in Paris, he told Conway:

> For so reasonable a person as I am, I have changed my mind very often about this country. The first days I was in violent spirits; then came a dismal cloud of whisk and literature, and I could not bear it. At present I begin, very *Englishly* indeed, to establish a right to my own way. I laugh, and talk nonsense, and make them hear me . . .

This letter was written in the first week of October, the day after he had dined at Madame du Deffand's. Supper was a very essential part in the art of conducting a salon. Here, round the supper table, the leading spirits of the place would gather. Madame Geoffrin provided splendid repasts, but whatever attracted people to Madame du Deffand's room in the Convent of St Joseph, it was not the food. The only difference, it was said, between her cook and a notorious poisoner was one of intention. What attracted people was her wit, which was famous, and her intelligence; for of what other women in Paris at that time could it be said that she corresponded with Voltaire on terms of equality?

Walpole's first encounter with Madame du Deffand took place on 17 September when he had supper with her after a visit to the opera. He found one or two Englishmen there, for she liked to entertain his fellow countrymen among whom, as we know, George Selwyn was a favourite. He also met the elderly and, by this time, rather decrepit Charles-Jean-François Hénault, President of the first Chamber of the Paris Parlement and member of the Académie Français, 'our ramshackle (*délabré*) President' as Voltaire called him, who many years before had been Madame du Deffand's lover and was now as deaf as his former mistress was blind. They must have appeared an

odd and slightly grotesque couple to Walpole at this first sight, the
marquise almost seventy and her ancient admirer even older, one
blind, the other deaf, and it was some time before he was able to see
them in a rational perspective and adjust himself to a conversational
style that occasionally took a scatological turn, especially when the
talk centred on the more disagreeable aspects of the dauphin's illness
which was just then entering its critical stage. It was only gradually
that he discovered those qualities of heart and mind that her old lover
had recorded in one of those character studies which the members of
her circle loved to write about each other. Hénault had written:

> Never did a woman have so many friends or better deserved them,
> friendship with her was such a passion that one forgave her
> exactions . . . Noble and generous, with a heart direct and sincere,
> she was unceasingly busy in being useful and devising ways in
> which she could help her friends. How many, and what important
> people might testify to this! She had a just intelligence, a vivid
> imagination and a rejuvenating gaiety (I speak of the past when her
> appearance was charming); a cultivated mind, of which she makes
> no boast, at a time when amusement is the only ambition.

The rooms in which Madame du Deffand lived in the secular wing
of the Convent of St Joseph had once been occupied by the convent's
foundress, Louis XIV's mistress the Marquise de Montespan, an
association that would at once have appealed to Walpole's strong
sense of the past. When he began to learn more about the present
tenant's earlier life his interest was excited yet further, for he
discovered that she too, like his friend Lady Suffolk, had enjoyed the
embrace of a royal prince. For her, however, there had been none of
the drudgery and squalid bickerings that had been the English
woman's lot for so many years; the scene of her brief romance could
hardly have differed more from the dreary and philistine Court of
George II. Her lover had been Philippe, Duke of Orléans, Regent of
France during the minority of Louis XV, a vital, cultivated and
debauched man whose mistresses came and went with such rapidity
that Madame du Deffand's reign, if such it can be called, lasted no
longer than a fortnight or three weeks at the most and might have
been lost to history altogether if Horace Walpole had not uncovered
this fascinating secret from her past.

She had known the somewhat tainted glories of the Palais Royal during its most brilliant and notorious period, but after the death of the regent had attached herself to the more elevated circle of the Duchesse du Maine, a granddaughter of the Grand Condé who had been married to Louis XIV's eldest bastard, the rather dim and colourless Duc du Maine whose futile and half-hearted attempt to gain political power after the old king's death had been quickly crushed by the regent. At Sceaux, just south of Paris on the road to Orleans, the duchesse established a court of her own where intellectual pursuits were cultivated, where Voltaire, the Abbé Prévost, and Fontenelle, the dates of whose births and deaths—1657 to 1757—now read like an epoch in history, were the honoured guests, and where men of a younger generation, later members of Madame du Deffand's salon, like d'Alembert, Marmontel, Grim and Helvétius, were no less welcomed and encouraged. It was at Sceaux that she had met the amiable President Hénault, an intelligent and learned hedonist, and their never very serious liaison had started. Here, more importantly, Madame du Deffand found a way of life she had been looking for which the regent's rakish Court had not provided; but it was here too that she had to face the great tragedy of her existence when in the early 1750s she realized that she was losing her sight.

It was after the death of the Duchesse du Maine in 1753 that Madame du Deffand moved into the Convent of St Joseph. The courageous way in which she coped with her blindness was recorded by Hénault in the portrait to which reference has already been made. He concluded:

> Who would believe that I am speaking of a woman who had lost her sight? This misfortune had no influence on her talk or her spirits—one would have said that sight was a superfluous sense. The sound of a voice called up a vision of the speaker, and she was as quick in the uptake as anyone with a pair of eyes.

Her situation was eased to some extent by the presence of a young relative, Julie de Lespinasse, the illegitimate daughter of her brother, whom she had befriended and rescued from a wretched existence. But shortly before Walpole's arrival in Paris there had been a tremendous drama when it was found that Julie had been in the habit of holding a sort of preliminary salon of her own in her rooms on the floor above those of her benefactress, where some of the younger and brighter stars had been accustomed to foregather before going down to the apartment of the marquise. When Madame du Deffand, hearing voices upstairs, at length discovered this deception (for such she considered it) a frightful scene ensued. Julie de Lespinasse was denounced as an ungrateful traitor and responded with shrill denunciations of her own. Of the members of the salon who were the astonished witnesses of the encounter, some supported one woman, some the other, and a rift was formed that failed to heal, leaving Madame du Deffand bitter and depressed and more a victim than ever before to the prevailing sense of ennui that affected her like some chronic disease.

She was still smarting from the disloyalty of her protégée and the defection of many of the younger members of her salon a year later, at the time of Walpole's visit. Life seemed to have lost its savour, and though she continued to visit the opera and theatre, to have all the latest books read to her and, after her guests had gone home, to be driven restlessly about Paris until the small hours of the morning as an antidote to insomnia, she remained profoundly unhappy and bored. It was a boredom, now almost habitual to her, of which she had once complained bitterly to Voltaire: 'For God's sake rescue me from my boredom. I can interest myself in nothing. Everything bores me to death: history, ethics, novels and plays.' Even her friends failed to interest her. 'Last night I had twelve at my table,' she told Voltaire on another occasion, 'all of them bores.' It was in this dark mood of depression that Walpole found her; but his presence, the charming nonsense he introduced into the conversation, the very sound of his voice with its slightly mispronounced French completely captivated her and she suddenly found herself, in her seventieth year, in love with a man twenty years her junior. Here at last was someone who could banish the tediousness and monotony of her existence and revive her dejected spirits.

Walpole was no less fascinated, but to a very different degree. What captivated him, as had been the case with Lady Suffolk, was her past, the memories she could so easily recall of a period that to him had all the glamour of the vanished age, the almost legendary figure of the Regent Orléans and the brilliant company at Sceaux. Writing to thank Selwyn for introducing her to him, he declared that he found her delicious—that is to say, as long as he could 'get her fifty years back'. This was not always easy, for she was as eager to talk about what happened every day as he was about the previous century. 'I sup there twice a week,' Selwyn was informed, 'and bear all her company for the sake of the Regent.' Soon he would be going to the Convent of St Joseph every day, and it was largely on account of this new friendship that his visit to Paris was extended until the beginning of April 1766. Yet he did not feel the same strong attachment for Madame du Deffand that she came so increasingly to feel for him; indeed he found her impetuous response to all situations, her loves and hatreds, a little alarming, for 'she is all love and hatred,' he confessed to Thomas Gray, 'passionate to her friends to enthusiasm, still anxious to be loved . . . and a vehement enemy, but openly.' To a man with Walpole's fear of emotional commitment all this was rather disquieting, and at the back of his mind was always the dread of ridicule, of the slightly absurd figure he might cut before the world if it became known that at the age of forty-eight he had become an object of devotion to a woman of seventy, to someone whose brief and disastrous marriage to her long-forgotten husband, the Marquis du Deffand, had taken place when he had been only a year old.

In spite of all this he came to be very fond of her. She was probably the only woman who ever managed to revive in him some of the love he had once felt for his mother, something Madame du Deffand herself instinctively felt when she wrote to him '*Je serais votre mère*'. He was much more ready to acknowledge the affection he felt for her to his friends than he was ever prepared to do to her, though she longed after his return to England, for some slight indication of warmth in his letters to her. But his fears still stood in the way of any free expression of love. It was a word he forbade her to use, most of all in the long correspondence that started between them after he left France. It was an imposition that his old friend found extremely inhibiting, and she sometimes rebelled against it only to receive a sharp rebuke. She had to fall back upon expressions like '*mon tuteur*' or '*mon gouverneur*', titles that implied a little flattery but behind which lay a silent supplication for something more intimate.

It was this unequal distribution of feeling between the two of them that made the relationship so poignant, all the more so when added to the already existing difference in their ages. Walpole's remark in his letter to John Craufurd, written during this visit to Paris, that he was not at all of Madame du Deffand's opinion that one might as well be dead as not love somebody, nicely sums up their different attitudes.

The marquise, whose heart had survived so many batterings, who had come through so much disillusionment, so many long years of boredom, was all devotion and possessiveness as though her youth had suddenly been renewed. She became quite infatuated with him, to her still young, whose face she would never see yet whose compelling personality had given her a thirst for life. She wanted to be with him all the time, talk to him, listen to him, share all her experiences with him. Walpole was flattered and intrigued but alarmed by the intensity of her feelings. He knew the limits of his own emotional nature: he could commune with her on an intellectual level as he could with Lady Suffolk or laugh with her as he did with Kitty Clive; but when she was in one of her introspective moods, when she wanted to indulge in one of those engrossing exercises in self-analysis, then he took fright and became the 'tutor' when she would have wished him to become the lover. She rebuked him for being stern; he chided her for being sentimental. Walpole has been blamed for cruelty in his treatment of her, but this is unfair. One cannot blame a person for the limitations of his basic character. He loved her in so far as he was able to love anybody; he esteemed her more than he did anyone else; and he never deceived her by pretending to be anything other than what he was.

Madame du Deffand found it difficult to understand the reservations in his nature. 'If you were French I should think you a big fop; as you are English you are only crazy [*un grand fou*],' she wrote to him while he was on his way back to England. Her own feelings for him were quite clear:

> Since no one is listening, I wish to tell you that no one can love more tenderly than I love you. I believe one gets what one deserves, and as I claim to possess a tender and sincere heart I am reaping my reward at the close of life. I will not allow myself to say all I think. In the pleasure you give me there is an element of sadness since you will be away for a long time, but I will not turn this letter into an elegy. I only ask you to keep your promise to write to me in full confidence and to believe that I belong more to you than to myself.

For Walpole such declarations were far from welcome and made him nervous and ill-tempered; he begged her to keep her comments to 'proper names' and not indulge in romantic flights. He dreaded what might happen if news of this curious affair was to find its way into the English newspapers where he would be mercilessly lampooned, for he knew that letters from abroad were often opened by the post office in England as they were by Louis XV's *cabinet noir* in France—and indeed fourteen of his letters were opened and copied by the secret police, thanks to which we can still read them, for all the rest were destroyed on his instructions after his death.

It was thus that the pattern of their long correspondence continued, with periodic outburst of affection on the part of Madame du Deffand receiving cross, often almost rude snubs from their over-anxious recipient. The letters alone might make it appear that Walpole was very lukewarm in his response to her feelings for him, which were as maternal as they were romantic, yet had it not been for her he would probably never have gone to France again. As it was, between this visit of 1765-6 and her death in 1780 he made four more crossings of the channel, in 1767, 1769, 1771 and 1775 for no other reason than to be reunited with his 'dear old woman' who he well knew, as he once confessed to Conway, 'loves me better than all France together'.

Following a custom that went back to her time at Sceaux, Madame du Deffand sent Walpole her 'portrait' of him, a verbal picture that shows how acute was this blind woman's observation:

> I know you are very intelligent and a very good sort. You have principles and courage. Your heart is good and your friendship reliable, though neither tender or easy. I do not know if you have any sentiment; if so you resist it as a weakness. You have one failing, which is unpardonable, to which you regulate your conduct—the fear of ridicule. You do good without ostentation or hope of reward. Finally your soul is both good and beautiful.

Walpole's reply was to send her a picture in verse. It began with the lines:

> Where do Wit and Memory dwell?
> Where is Fancy's favourite cell?
> Where does Judgement hold her court,
> And dictate laws to Mirth and Sport . . .?

It is not one of his best efforts, but the first line showed the qualities he most admired in his friend, the brilliant wit that Voltaire himself

had acknowledged when he said of her, 'you are the person of this age
the most in accord with my taste and with my heart'; and that clear
memory that could open the door to scenes that brought to
Walpole's imagination an imperishable impression of the past.

After Walpole's death a selection of Madame du Deffand's letters
to him were edited by Mary Berry and published in 1810. Only a few
excerpts of his replies were included and his side of the correspondence was then destroyed, presumably at his request, for he was
afraid that his French might not be perfect. The old fear of ridicule
that Madame du Deffand had found so unpardonable had followed
him to the grave. In making this request he probably did harm to his
reputation, for the accusation that he treated his French friend rather
shabbily is based on such few letters of his that have survived. If we
had both sides of the correspondence in full we might reach a
different conclusion, but as it is the case for Walpole's defence goes
by default because of his fear of being caught in a few grammatical
errors. His fear, ironically, would seem to have been groundless, for
Sainte-Beuve named Walpole with Anthony Hamilton and the Abbé
Galiani as the only three foreigners who wrote and spoke the French
language like natives. When the letters were issued in France two
years after they appeared in England, they caused quite a sensation.
After the upheavals of the Revolution and Empire Parisian society
found something charming in this picture of life under the *ancien
régime*. Napoleon himself read the book in proof on his way to the
Russian border, and in Paris, where curiosity was growing fast
among the younger generation as to how things had been before the
Revolution, the letters were eagerly read and discussed, though
Lytton Strachey's claim that in the sensation they caused 'the
excitement of the Russian campaign itself was half forgotten' is a
characteristic exaggeration.

Madame du Deffand never came to Strawberry Hill; age and
blindness made the journey impossible for her to undertake. But she
was very much there in spirit, and soon her portrait came to join
those of Lady Suffolk and other friends of Walpole whose pictures
adorned the walls. The painting by Carmontelle has disappeared but
fortunately engravings of it survive. It shows the marquise sitting in
her *tonneau*, the tub-like armchair designed to protect her from the
draught. Her face, with its closed sightless eyes, is almost hidden by a
close-fitting bonnet. She holds out thin, delicate hands to the

Duchesse de Choiseul who is offering her a puppet doll. Between them, asleep on a stool, is her pet dog Tonton who was to end his days in England in the house his mistress never visited. Walpole was delighted with the picture. He hung it in the Breakfast Room and wrote to tell his friend that he was now the happiest of men.

V

Thomas Gray and the
Republic of Letters

◆≫ 1 ≪◆

'Remember,' Walpole would say in his later years when the subject of poetry was under discussion, 'Remember, I have lived with Gray and seen Pope.' Whether he ever actually spoke to Pope is not clear; he never claimed to have done more than see him, and indeed Pope died three years before Walpole came to live near the former's famous villa at Twickenham. Gray, it would seem from a reference in one of his letters, met Pope at least once, but as the elder poet's last years coincided with the brief period of Walpole and Gray's estrangement, it is most unlikely that Walpole, who helped the other's literary career in so many ways, was responsible for this interesting encounter between the two greatest poetic figures of the age, one near the end of his life and crowned with glory and renown though only in his fifties, the other a youth in his twenties as yet unknown to fame. A book with Pope's autograph in it and Gray's name written below, with a date in Pope's lifetime, is a possible memento of this meeting.

Walpole's relationship with Gray began, as we have seen, in his school-days, in those happy years of the 'Quadruple Alliance', and continued while they were both up at Cambridge. It was here that Gray's character began to take on some of those peculiarities that were to mark him for life, in particular his taste for solitude and the melancholy, introspective turn that his retiring habits encouraged. He wrote to his friend West when he was only twenty-one:

> Low spirits are my true and faithful companions. They get up with me, go to bed with me, make journeys and returns as I do; nay, and pay visits, and will even effect to be jocose, and force a feeble laugh with me; but most commonly we sit alone together, and are the prettiest insipid company in the world.

It was probably the very contrast in their characters that made Walpole so attractive to him, for at this time the latter was all bubble, sparkle, vivacity, and high spirits. There can be little doubt that Gray, who was indifferent to the charms of the female sex and even shunned the company of his own except for a small circle of chosen friends, was in his schoolboy and undergraduate days somewhat infatuated with Walpole.

This feeling sprang from a genuine admiration that the shy often have for more extrovert people. Walpole was leading rather a giddy life just then which Gray could enjoy vicariously in his monk-like seclusion at Peterhouse. Walpole was his 'dear Damon', the type of the faithful friend, to whom Gray wrote from Cambridge in 1735: 'Thou dear envious Imp, to set me a longing with accounts of Plays and Operas, and Masquerades after hearing of which I can no more think of Logick and Stuff, than you could of Divinity at a Ball, or of Caudle and Carroway-Comfits after having been stuffed at a Christening . . .' Unlike the calculating Ashton, whose friendship for Walpole was to cool after his father's fall from office, Gray, though he appreciated the glamour that radiated from the son of the most powerful man in the kingdom, was completely disinterested in his attachment to this friend who lived so close to the source of patronage and preferment. He was totally unambitious in the worldly sense. He claimed to dislike Cambridge, where he considered the Fellows of his college 'sleepy, drunken, dull, illiterate Things', but there was something in the very dreariness of the place (as he saw it) that accorded with his own cautious and timid nature.

Gray had a fragile quality about him, a lack of adventurousness, a feminine fastidiousness that made him fill his rooms with vases of flowers and adopt an attitude that even those well disposed towards him found strangely wanting in robustness and to others appeared plainly epicene. William Cole, a slightly older friend at Eton and Cambridge, and a man who revered his qualities of mind, admitted to finding his manner from boyhood onwards as being 'disgustingly effeminate, finical and affected'. He never learnt to ride a horse and had a morbid fear of fire. These traits, added to his small delicate physique and his mincing gait made him an odd and rather isolated figure among the hard-drinking, noisy and boisterous young men who formed the bulk of his college contemporaries. This caused him to cling all the more to the friendships he had already made at Eton.

Richard West was the closest to him, sharing his love of poetry and recoiling with the same mild distaste from the prospect, which faced them both, of a career at the Bar; but West was now at Oxford and their opportunities for close communication, except by letter, were few. Ashton was at Cambridge, but he always had an eye to the main chance and could now be numbered among the undergraduates who came up, as Gray expressed it, 'to get good Learning that they may all be Archbishop of Canterbury'. And so when Walpole came to King's a year after Gray had entered Peterhouse, he was about the only real friend that Gray could count upon.

He was a natural scholar. He pursued learning for its own sake but with such scant respect for the requirements of the university that he never took a degree. As Dr Johnson was later to state in his rather ill-tempered life of Gray, he appeared to have been 'very little delighted with academic gratifications'. It was only later, when a legal career seemed at one moment almost inevitable, that he rather reluctantly took a bachelor's degree in law, but even then he did not bother to proceed to a doctorate which would then have qualified him to practise in the ecclesiastical courts. As things turned out, he always had just enough means, without ever being a rich man, to preclude any necessity to earn a living. This was a mixed blessing. His poetic output might have been larger had there been more incentive to publish, though it could be argued with equal force that the quality of his work might have suffered in consequence. As it was, he never showed any eagerness to publish his poetry and might indeed have remained unpublished altogether until after his death if his friends, and Walpole in particular, had not encouraged him to venture into print. He never expected any financial reward, and the forty guineas he received from Dodsley when his *Odes* appeared in 1757 seems to have been the only money he earned with his pen in the whole of his life.

His growing discontent with the way his life was going at Cambridge was summed up in a letter to West written in December 1736:

You must know that I do not take degrees, and, after this term, shall have nothing more of college impertinences to undergo . . . Must I plunge into metaphysics? Alas, I cannot see in the dark; nature has not furnished me with the optics of a cat. Must I pore upon mathematics? Alas, I cannot see in too much light; I am no eagle. It is very possible that two and two make four, but I would not give four farthings to demonstrate this ever so cleverly; and if these be the profits of life, give me the amusements of it. The people I behold all around me, it seems, know all this and more and yet I do not know one of them who inspires me with any ambition of being like him . . .

Cambridge was another Babylon which the prophet had given over to a 'pretty collection of desolate animals which is verified in this town to a tittle'. The alternative to Cambridge, however, was not much better. His London home in Cornhill was an unhappy place, and though he was now entered at the Inner Temple, he had no inclination at all for legal studies.

Gray's life had reached a kind of impasse when Walpole came forward with a suggestion that offered him a welcome form of escape. His friend now enjoyed a comfortable income from the sinecures his father had secured for him, and early in 1739 he decided to travel. What he now proposed was that Gray should accompany him to France and Italy. He offered to pay all the expenses of the journey though they would, of course, travel upon terms of complete equality and Gray would have all the independence he desired. To the latter, who was already steeped in classical learning, this chance to visit Italy was one that he could not otherwise have hoped for, and he accepted with alacrity. The proposal came at just the right moment for him, and Walpole made it with sufficient tact for Gray to be able to accept it without any feeling of dependence or hurt to his pride. It was a wonderful opportunity to make the Grand Tour in congenial company and the two friends set out under the happiest of auspices, having nothing worse to contend with than the hazards of the Channel crossing. In this, however, there was perhaps an omen of what was to come, for they left Dover (as Gray wrote to tell his mother) in a pretty brisk gale which pleased everybody very well except himself, who was extremely sick the whole time.

Walpole and Gray were to spend the next two years together in close proximity, which is testing for any friendship. What is surprising, considering their differences in wealth, in social background and in temperament, is not that they eventually quarrelled and parted from each other, but that they did not quarrel sooner.

Gray was not an easy person to get on with; his fits of melancholy and dislike of company, as well as his pride and touchiness, made him a difficult companion in the exacting circumstances of eighteenth-century travel. Walpole at this time was often self-willed and thoughtless, and had not as yet lost the arrogance of youth. He was mainly bent upon enjoying himself while his friend was more interested in opportunities for study and research. In particular Walpole had a gregarious nature, delighted in company and was eager to make new friends while Gray, in his own words to West, written while he was in Florence, suffered from 'a want of love for general society, indeed an inability to it'.

The growth of tension between them, however, was only gradual and did not begin to show itself until they had been for some time in Italy. In France all went well. They had left England towards the end of March and were in Paris by the first week of April, where they found Walpole's two cousins, Lord Conway (who later, as Earl of Hertford, was to be himself British Ambassador to Versailles) and his younger brother Henry. The novelty of foreign travel had proved a good antidote to Gray's low spirits and he joined in quite happily with the carefree mood of his aristocratic companions as they frisked about Paris seeing the sights, visiting the theatres and attending supper parties that lasted until the small hours of the morning. Here they met the Abbé Prévost d'Exiles, the author of *Manon Lescaut*, then in his late forties, and Marivaux, in his early fifties, whose *Vie de Marianne*, at that time still appearing in instalments, was rather surprisingly a favourite with Gray, who once admitted that if the Mohammedans' idea of paradise consisted in playing on the flute and lying with houris, his was to be able to read eternal new romances by Marivaux and Crébillon. They visited Versailles, the front of which, as approached from Paris, Gray considered no more than a 'huge heap of littleness', though when he saw the garden façade he agreed that nothing could be vaster or more magnificent. They walked in the gardens by moonlight where they heard 'ladies and nightingales sing', and next day, being Whitsunday, saw Louis XV install nine new knights of the order of the Saint-Esprit.

Their time in Paris had been spent so much in the company of their fellow countrymen that at the beginning of June they went with Henry Conway to Rheims with the object of improving their French. It was here that they took part in a sort of impromptu entertainment that reflected all the charm and gaiety of the *ancien régime*. Gray wrote to his mother on 21 June:

> The other evening, we happened to be got together in a company of eighteen people, men and women of the best fashion here, at a garden in the town to walk; when one of the ladies bethought herself of asking, Why should we not sup here? Immediately the cloth was laid by the side of a fountain under the trees, and a very elegant supper was served up; after which another said, Come, let us sing; and directly began herself. From singing we insensibly fell to dancing, and singing in a round; when somebody mentioned the violins, and immediately a company of them was ordered. Minuets were begun in the open air, and then came country-dances, which held till four o'clock next morning; at which hour the gayest lady proposed, that such as were weary should get into their coaches, and the rest of them should dance before them with music in the van; and in this manner we paraded through all the principal streets of the city, and waked everybody in it.

Walpole was so enchanted with this Watteauesque occasion that he thought of making a custom of it, but somehow the mood passed and their night of fête and dancing remained unique.

In September they began their journey south, travelling by easy stages towards Italy, visiting the Grande Chartreuse en route. Both Gray and Walpole were deeply impressed by the grandeur of the mountain scenery. For Gray, as he wrote in a letter to his mother, it was one of the most solemn, most romantic, and most astonishing scenes he had ever beheld. The same feelings were expressed in a letter to West sent from Turin on 16 November:

> In our little journey up to the Grande Chartreuse, I do not remember to have gone ten paces without an exclamation that there was no restraining. Not a precipice, not a torrent, not a cliff, but is pregnant with religion and poetry. There are certain scenes that would awe an atheist into belief without the help of other argument.

Mount Cénis, on the other hand, he considered carried 'the permission mountains have of being frightful rather too far', and it was not without relief that they found themselves surveying the more serene landscapes of Italy.

From Turin they travelled on to Genoa which quite delighted Gray. In another letter to West, he wrote:

> Only figure to yourself a vast semicircular basin, full of fine blue sea, and vessels of all sorts and sizes, some sailing out, some coming in, and others at anchor; and all around it palaces and churches peeping over one another's heads, gardens and marble terrases full of orange and cypress trees, fountains, and trellis-works covered with vines, which altogether compose the grandest of theatres.

They spent a week there before pressing on to Parma, then Modena ('an ill built melancholy place, all of brick') and Bologna, where they spent another twelve days seeing the sights—'churches, palaces, and pictures from morning to night'. By 16 December they had reached Florence where Horace Mann had sent his servant to meet them at the city gate and conduct them to his house. Gray took at once to the affable British minister whom he declared to be the best and most obliging person in the world.

The next day they were introduced to the Prince of Craon who was acting as viceroy for the absent Habsburg Grand Duke. Here Gray saw the advantage of travelling with so well-connected a companion. 'The princess and he were extremely civil to the name of Walpole,' he wrote home, 'so we were asked to stay to supper, which is as much as to say, you may come and sup here whenever you please, for after the first invitation this is always understood.' But these purely social formalities had no real appeal for him; he was at his happiest in the galleries where he could profitably have passed many months, and which he visited every day. When Walpole was presented to the widowed Electress Palatine, last survivor of the House of Medici who was then living in grand but sombre retirement in Florence, Gray did not go with him.

Early in February 1740 Pope Clement XII died at the advanced age of eighty-eight and the prospect of witnessing a conclave and papal coronation lured Walpole and Gray to Rome. The idea filled Walpole with excitement and he wrote in anticipation to Conway: 'Popes, Cardinals, adorations, coronations, St. Peter's! oh, what costly sounds!' They arrived in Rome late in March and found the city overflowing with visitors. Walpole wrote to West: 'Nations swarm here. You will have a great fat French Cardinal garnished with thirty abbés roll into the area of St. Peter's, gape, turn short, and talk of the chapel of Versailles.' His enthusiasm soon cooled, however, and he was shocked by the ignorance and poverty of the contemporary Romans, by the destitution of the noble families and the squalor and disrepair of their palaces where half the pictures were spoiled by damp. As the conclave continued to drag on in inconclusive session (it was to prove the longest of the century) he grew restless and decided to go to Naples. It was now that Gray began to experience slight irritation by his commitment to the other's whims. He would gladly have stayed longer in Rome where there was so much to learn and discover. He felt himself imbued with the antiquity of the place and wrote jokingly to West that he had just dined at Pompey's: 'We had the dugs of a pregnant sow, a peacock, a dish of thrushes, a noble scarus just fresh from the Tyrrhene, and some conchylia of the Lake with garum sauce. For my part I never eat better at Lucullus' table.' But he knew that he must submit to Walpole's plans, and to Naples they went, where some small consolation was gained by a visit to Herculaneum where new excavations had recently revealed more paintings and treasures from the past.

They spent most of June in Naples before returning to Rome where the conclave still laboured without producing a pope and the chances of being able to witness a coronation became more than ever remote; indeed, the way things were going it began to look to Walpole as though he might have to wait until he was old enough to be pope himself. Meanwhile the heat of July made the city unpleasant, and all who could left for the cooler climate of the *castelli Romani* in the Alban hills. Rumours of the unhealthy atmosphere, of 'a horrid thing called mal'aria that comes to Rome every summer and kills one' alarmed Walpole who did not wish, as he remarked with ironic Protestant fervour to Conway, to die 'so far from Christian burial', and he decided to return to Florence. Once again Gray had to sacrifice his own inclinations to his friend's impulse. He had no particular regrets about missing a papal coronation, but, as he told his father in a letter written after they were back in Florence, 'the city itself I do not part with so easily, which alone has amusements for whole years.' He began to take a more jaundiced view of what he considered to be Walpole's slightly frivolous attitude, while Walpole himself began to find Gray's more serious interests to be verging on the pedantic and becoming rather tedious.

Their encounter with Chute and Whithed in Florence caused a welcome diversion and probably prevented their final quarrel from coming earlier than it did. Gray and Chute became close friends; they had a common interest in music, for Gray was spending much of his time transcribing musical manuscripts as well as in writing a poem in Latin hexameters based on the philosophy of Locke which he called *De Principiis Cogitandi*. Walpole was also busily composing a long poem, a Whiggish commentary on English history for the benefit of their friend Ashton who had recently been appointed tutor to the Earl of Plymouth. This exercise was partly prompted by a twinge of conscience, for he realized that he was wasting a lot of time on mere frivolities:

> What time fair Florence on her peaceful shore,
> Free from the din of war and battle's roar,
> Has lap'd me trifler in inglorious ease,
> Modelling precepts that may serve and please;
> Yours is the task—and glorious in the plan,
> To build the Free, the Sensible, Good Man.

The reference in the last two lines was to Ashton and his important young charge, but one can also find in the lines a hint of Walpole's slightly embarrassed awareness that while he was enjoying the pleasures of Florence to the full, Gray was putting his time to more studious and recondite pursuits. They both began to behave rather pettishly: Gray wished to visit Pisa and other neighbouring cities but Walpole was sated with sightseeing and told him he could have the carriage and go on his own; Gray took offence at this and refused the offer. Gray, too, was no doubt hitting out at Walpole when he described Florence quite unjustly as 'an excellent place to employ all one's animal sensations in, but utterly contrary to one's rational powers'. This remark was probably inspired by the fact that Walpole had embarked on an amorous skirmish with the beautiful Marchesa Elisabetta Grifoni who, however deep his feelings for her may have been (and they were possibly not very profound), undoubtedly fell very much in love with him. This was an added mortification for Gray. There was an element of homosexuality in his character, probably unconscious and certainly deeply repressed, that made this little affair of Walpole's, for whom, in spite of their growing differences, he still felt a strong attachment, seem an act of unkind disloyalty, an added injury to his already sadly wounded pride.

It now needed very little to precipitate an open quarrel. On 24 April 1741 they left for Venice at the beginning of what was to be a leisurely progress back to England. There is a note of rather bored resignation in Gray's last letter to West from Florence: 'Well; next to Venice by the 11th May, there to see the old Doge wed the Adriatic Whore. Then to Verona, so to Milan, so to Marseilles, so to Lyons, so to Paris, so to West, &c in saeculorum. Amen.' In the same letter he complained of a 'reasonable quantity of dullness, a great deal of silence, and something that rather resembles, than is, thinking'. The spirit of melancholy was setting on him again with its cruel tendency to distort his emotional responses.

Their route took them through Reggio in Emilia which they found given over to the enjoyment of its annual fair. The temptation of the masquerades and balls, of listening to the opera from the Duchess of Modena's box, was too much for Walpole and he decided to stay for a few days. To Gray this was the last straw. He was wrought up to a high nervous pitch; Walpole too, though he did not know it, was on the verge of a serious illness. Both were tense and the storm which had been hovering over them at last broke out. They had a most tremendous row and parted company. Gray went on to Venice with Chute and Whithed in a state of near collapse; Walpole was soon laid low with a violent fever and inflamation of the throat from which he very nearly died. What actually sparked off their quarrel has never been entirely clear. It seems that Gray had written to Ashton complaining of Walpole's conduct and Ashton, ever the toady, had mischievously passed on the information to Walpole. But the immediate cause of the rupture is not important. There were more serious, long suppressed differences and misunderstandings that now suddenly came to the surface.

After Gray's death, Walpole was to take all the blame for their quarrel upon himself:

I was too young, too fond of my own diversions, nay, I do not doubt, too much intoxicated by indulgence, vanity, and the insolence of my situation as a Prime Minister's son, not to have been inattentive and insensible to the feelings of one I thought below me; of one, I blush to say it, that I knew was obliged to me

. . . I treated him insolently; he loved me, and I did not think he did. I reproached him with the difference between us, when he acted from conviction of knowing he was my superior.

All Walpole would say against Gray was that his temper was not conciliating and that he freely told him his faults. But clearly there were faults on both sides. Gray was not the most tolerant of men and made few attempts to accommodate himself to the other's point of view; he was also quick to find fault and to harbour what he considered to be slights, a situation that was not made easier by the difference in their circumstances which all the goodwill in the world could not completely hide. He had a way, as Dr Johnson put it, of watching his own dignity 'with troublesome and punctilious jealousy', and given Walpole's often thoughtless and arrogant behaviour at this period of his life, trouble was bound to follow.

Mann and Chute, both older and more mature men, were deeply distressed by this breach between their young friends. Mann wrote to Walpole, reminding him of Gray's fundamental affection for him: 'I am convinced of his regard for you, nay I have been witness to his uneasiness and tears when he suspected you had less confidence in him than his inward and real friendship for you made him think he deserved.' Walpole, as he recovered from his illness, was even ready for a reconciliation, and Mann arranged a meeting, knowing the despair Gray was in; but when they met again at Reggio, Gray's pride once more got the better of him and he rejected Walpole's peaceful overtures with indignation and scorn. His feelings were too deeply hurt to be cured so quickly. He left again for Venice and from there returned to England on his own. Without his knowledge, Walpole arranged for money to be advanced to him through the agency of Mann and Joseph Smith, the British consul in Venice, knowing that Gray would have rejected it outright if he had known it came from Walpole himself. Nor was Gray ever to discover that before they left England Walpole had made a will in his favour.

⋙ 2 ⋘

They were, of course, reconciled. The restoration of harmony between them did not occur for some years, however, partly because Chute and Mann, who were both still in Italy and too far away from their young friends, had now returned to England; and partly because Gray and Walpole themselves were almost immediately involved in family affairs that kept them both fully occupied with their own concerns. Walpole had been returned to Parliament while he was still in Italy. When he got back to London in September 1741, he found his father under serious attack in the House of Commons and his long period of power nearing its end. In the debates before and just after his father's fall from office, Horace Walpole had his first experience of parliamentary affairs, and delivered his maiden speech in opposition to the motion to set up a commission of inquiry into the last ten years of his father's administration, a speech that drew from William Pitt the mixed compliment that while it was becoming in him to remember that he was the child of the fallen Prime Minister, the House must not forget that they were the children of their country.

Sir Robert Walpole's dismissal had been wrung from a reluctant George II who parted from his favourite minister with many embraces, with tears, with the offer of a substantial pension and with the title of Earl of Orford. Horace Walpole drew much closer to his father during these last years of his life and would even abandon the pleasures of the town for what to him was the boredom of country life, and pay long visits to the old statesman at Houghton, though these rustic sojourns made him feel, as he confessed to Chute, as though he had murdered a man whose name was Ennui, for his ghost was ever before him. His consolation was Lord Orford's great collection of pictures, and he spent his time in compiling a catalogue of them which he called *Aedes Walpolianae*, giving a brief description of all the various canvases, showing the rather bizarre and idiosyncratic nature of his taste, ranking Raphael, Guido and Annibale Caracci as the only masters in whom all the qualities of a perfect painter could be found while the entire Dutch school was dismissed and such other masters as Andrea del Sarto, Titian and Poussin were all in some quality or other found wanting. He had previously composed a sermon on painting, a parody of contemporary pulpit oratory based on the Houghton collection, and preached before Lord Orford in a mock ceremony by his chaplain.

As a child, Walpole had been very much a mother's boy; his earliest visit to his father's country house did not take place until he was at Cambridge. But it was now, in these last few years before his father's death that a strong attachment grew up between them. The younger man had been shocked by the way some of his father's old political colleagues had turned against him at the end, prompted by ambition, opportunism, malice or sheer ingratitude. It was a lesson for him in the realities of political morality. He was also moved by the courage and fighting spirit of the beleaguered old minister when his friends began to desert him and he saw his political power slipping away. The son was never to forgive the men whose plotting he considered to have encompassed his father's fall and he was to use much ink on their ridicule and vilification in the years to come. He remained at his father's side during his last illness and was with him when he died at his London house in Arlington Street on 18 March 1745.

Gray had returned to England shortly before Walpole, revisiting the Grande Chartreuse on his way back. It was on this occasion that he composed the Latin ode that he inscribed in the visitors' book kept by the fathers of the monastery, with its plea for deliverance from the tumult of the crowd and the cares of mankind, a theme that he would later develop in his famous *Elegy*. His return to London in fact plunged him into the very cares he had prayed to avoid, for he found his father on the point of death. The loss of a parent for whom he had felt no love and who had treated him with cruelty and indifference as a child was no great burden to bear; what worried him was the discovery that his father had been squandering his fortune on the building of a country house at Wanstead and that his mother and aunt were likely to suffer some financial inconvenience as a result of this unnecessary extravagance. It was eventually decided that they should join another sister, recently widowed, at Stoke Poges in Bucking-hamshire, and there the three elderly women settled, and there from time to time he would join them, using their house as a country retreat. Meanwhile, when not in London, he re-established himself at Peterhouse in Cambridge, taking his degree in civil law in 1743. It was the nearest he ever got to following a regular profession.

In London he had been joined again by West but was shocked to find his friend in seriously declining health. To West's physical sufferings was now added the mental strain of the discovery (which he confided to Gray) of his mother's liaison with her late husband's former secretary, a relationship which he may have guessed at before but which was confirmed when the man went out of his way to poison Mrs West's mind against her son, depriving him of her affection in what were to prove his last months on earth. In March 1742 he moved into the country, hoping that the purer air might strengthen a frame already wasted by the ravages of consumption. From here (he was staying with friends at Popes, near Hatfield) he continued to correspond with Gray on common literary interests, exchanging and criticizing each other's poems and discussing their various readings in verse and prose. His letters were much as they had always been and Gray clearly did not realize how very ill his friend had now become, so much so that he was puzzled rather than alarmed when a letter was returned unopened. It was only a few days later that the truth was suddenly revealed to him when he chanced to read in a newspaper some verses written in memory of his friend who had died on 1 June 1742 in his twenty-sixth year. The lines, as he quickly guessed, were in fact written by Ashton, who rather strangely had not informed Gray of this sad news which so closely concerned them both, but when the latter wrote to Ashton for more detailed information, he only blamed the heartlessness of West's friends in Hertfordshire for their want of feeling in return-ing his letter without giving him any hint of the reason. He told Ashton:

> The stupid people had put it [in] no cover, nor thought it worth while to write one line to inform me of the reason, tho' by knowing how to direct, they must imagine I was a friend. I was a fool indeed to be surpriz'd at meeting with Brutishness or want of Thought among mankind . . .

Ashton's own remissness in failing to communicate the news of their mutual friend's death he passed over in silence, merely congratulat-ing the ambitious clergyman on a recent valuable preferment.

West was now dead, he had quarrelled with Walpole, he had no real rapport with Ashton; at this moment in his life Gray must have felt sadly dejected and alone. He had to guard against that 'black melancholy', about which he had written to West less than a month before the latter's death, a melancholy that was

> black indeed, which I have now and then felt, that has somewhat in it like Tertullian's rule of faith, *Credo quia impossibile est*, for it believes, nay, it is sure of everything that is unlikely, so it be but

frightful; and on the other hand, excludes and shuts its eyes to the most possible hopes, and every thing that is pleasurable.

One way of combating these dark moods was to lose himself in study. As Sir Edmund Gosse was to observe: 'From this time forward we find his ailments, his melancholy, his reserve, and his habit of drowning consciousness in perpetual study, have taken firm hold upon him, and he begins to plunge into an excess of reading, treating the acquisition of knowledge as a narcotic.' He did, of course, have some friends at Cambridge, but they were not many in number and were to be found not so much at his own college as at Pembroke just across the road. In London he seems to have had few friends at all. If ever there was a time for him to make up his quarrel with Walpole, it was now.

Walpole himself, who had nothing of the solitary in his character and who was never short of friends, would have felt less need to restore their old happy relationship, but the fact that he had shown himself ready for a reconciliation while they were still in Italy, while the angry words they had exchanged were fresh in his memory, should have made Gray realize that a friendly approach on his side would not have been rejected. Walpole might possibly have made some such move himself but for his recollection of Gray's scornful response to the overtures made at Reggio. What was needed was some mutual friend who could bring them together again, and towards the end of 1745 just such a mediator appeared. Who it was remains a mystery. According to Walpole it was 'a lady, who wished well to them both'. It has been suggested that this lady was Mrs Francis Chute, John Chute's sister-in-law, and there is much to support this supposition. Chute himself did not return from Italy for another year, but he was on good terms with his sister-in-law and no doubt corresponded with her. He of all people was anxious that his two friends should make up their quarrel as he was devoted to both of them, and would wish to have them united again when he eventually came home. He already knew from Horace Mann that Walpole was not undisposed to a reconciliation; all that was needed was to persuade Gray to swallow his pride. What could be more likely than that Chute should encourage his sister-in-law to undertake this peaceful mission?

Whoever the mysterious lady was, her efforts were rewarded with success. It would not have been difficult to get Walpole to write to Gray; it was Gray's reaction that was in doubt. But all went well. Gray accepted the olive branch, albeit somewhat cautiously and sullenly to begin with, finding Walpole's determination to act as though almost nothing had happened between them rather disconcerting. He was, as he wrote to his Cambridge friend Thomas Wharton, 'something abashed' by Walpole's confidence when their meeting took place at the latter's London house:

> he came to meet me, kiss'd me on both sides with all the Ease of one who receives an Acquaintance just come out of the Country, squatted me into a Fauteuil, began to talk of the Town and this and that and t'other, and continued with Little Interruption for three hours, when I took my leave very indifferent pleased, but treated with wonderous Good-breeding.

In fact Walpole had adopted the best course to cover the inevitable embarrassment which such a delicate situation entailed, even though it left Gray slightly bewildered.

The next evening they had supper together. Something of the original cause of the trouble was indicated by Ashton's presence at this second reunion. His formalities, Gray informed Wharton,

> tickled me inwardly, for he I found was to be angry about the letter I had wrote him. However in going home together our Hackney-Coach jumbled us into a Sort of Reconciliation: he hammer'd out somewhat like an Excuse; and I received it very readily, because I cared not two pence, whether it were true or not.

Shortly after this Walpole and Gray had breakfast alone together when, as Gray put it, 'we had all the Eclaircissment I ever expected, and I left him far better satisfied than I had been hitherto. When I return, I shall see him again.' The breach between them was healed, not least by Walpole's tact in leading his touchy friend by easy stages to this agreeable conclusion.

So the three surviving members of the old 'Quadruple Alliance' were reunited, though Ashton soon faded out of the picture. The friendship between Walpole and Gray was to continue without further disruption, until the latter's death, though something of the former warmth and spontaneity was lacking. This was mainly due to Gray's reserve, which became more marked as he grew older. If

Chute had indeed been at work behind the scenes in attempting to resolve the discord between his two friends, then he must have been well satisfied with the letter he received from Gray in October 1746. 'I find Mr. Walpole then made some mention of me to you,' Gray wrote to the returned wanderer who had just been visiting Walpole.

> Yes, we are together again. It is about a year I believe since he wrote to me to offer it, and there has been (particularly of late) in appearance the same kindness and confidence almost as of old. What were his motives I cannot guess; what were mine, you will imagine, and perhaps blame me. However as yet I neither repent nor rejoice over much: But I am pleased. He is full, I assure you, of your panegyric, never anybody had half so much wit as Mr. Chute (which is saying everything with him, you know), and Mr. Whithed is the finest young man that ever was imported.

Gray's guarded accounts of the reconciliation, his refusal to admit without reserve that he was satisfied with the situation or that he could wholly condone Walpole's easy, man-of-the-world attitude, was simply the last concession he made to his pride and to his stubborn spirit of independence. He was clearly glad and relieved that their quarrel was over at last, but felt that he must show that he had accepted the restoration of friendship on equal terms and had not come running back at Walpole's bidding. They were soon meeting regularly, and while Walpole had his house at Windsor and Gray was at Stoke Poges near by, they dined together at least once a week. More significantly, he now began to send copies of his poems to Walpole as he had once sent them to Richard West.

⇾ 3 ⇽

Walpole's greatest service to Gray lay, as we have already seen, in his ability to persuade this shy and reticent poet to allow his work to appear in print. Gray wrote for his own amusement and to entertain his friends, and if left to himself might never have published anything at all, partly from a want of ambition and partly, it had to be admitted, from sheer inertia. Walpole was one of the first people to recognize Gray's genius; he was certainly the first person to champion him in public and to promote his work in literary circles, and for this cause alone posterity has reason to be thankful that reconciliation took place between the two men after their estrangement in Italy. Gray's poems would undoubtedly have become known in due course through the efforts of his Cambridge friends, but his fame might have been adversely affected if they had not appeared until after his death when literary taste had changed; certainly his influence would not have been so great. Walpole was ideally placed to recommend his friend's work. By 1745 he was sufficiently well known for publishers to listen to what he had to say and to be ready and eager to please him.

Publishing at this time was still in the hands of booksellers. In the mid-eighteenth century two of the leading publishers of books in London were Robert Dodsley and John Newbery, both of whom had risen from comparatively humble origins, the latter specializing in children's books while the former was more of what today would be called a general publisher. As a youth he had been apprenticed to a stocking weaver but had broken his apprenticeship and become a footman. He devoted such leisure as he had to reading and in 1729, at about the age of twenty-five, he published *Servitude, a Poem*. More verse and some plays followed. In 1735 his dramatic piece *The Toy Shop* was acted with sufficient success at the Covent Garden Theatre for him to be able to set up as a bookseller on his profits, helped by the gift of £100 from Alexander Pope. As well as Pope, he published works by Johnson and Goldsmith and had soon established a flourishing business in which he was later joined by his younger brother. Dodsley maintained a refreshing frankness about his obscure beginnings. When Johnson once mentioned to him a certain 'modern epicure' named Darteneuf, Dodsley replied: 'I knew Darteneuf well, for I was once his footman.'

In 1748, Dodsley decided to bring out an anthology of contemporary verse in three volumes to be called *A Collection of Poems by Several Hands*. The name of Walpole, as Gray had witnessed at Florence, was still powerful even though Sir Robert was now dead and his youngest son only started on his career of fame, and Dodsley was eager for a contribution from him. Three poems by Walpole were included, the long historical poem he had written in Italy and dedicated to Ashton, an epilogue to *Tamerlane* which the actress Mrs Pritchard had spoken after a performance at Covent Garden on 4 November 1746, and his poem *The Beauties*, a celebration of various young ladies of his acquaintance but in particular of Lady Caroline Lennox, wife of his friend Henry Fox, and her sister Lady Emily, daughters of the Duke of Richmond. It was a light affair addressed to the German-born portrait painter Ecchardt, urging him to abandon classical models and studies from the great Continental masters but instead 'in Britain's isle observe the Fair'. In following this advice, the artist was assured, he would discover

> Such patterns as shall raise your name
> To rival sweet Correggio's fame.

Both *The Beauties* and Walpole's epilogue to *Tamerlane*, a patriotic blast to applaud the victorious suppression of the Rebellion of 1745, had been published before by Dodsley as broadsheets, and Walpole was able to use his good standing with the publisher to urge him to include some poems by Gray in his collection. He already had some to hand which he could produce as evidence of his friend's talent. Early in the year 1747 there had been a minor domestic tragedy in his household when his cat had drowned in a tub of goldfish, an event that produced from Gray a tender letter of condolence: 'Then as to your "handsome cat", the name you distinguish her by, I am no less at a loss, as well knowing one's handsome cat is always the cat one loves best.' Was it Zara or Selima, he asked, or was Selima in fact called Fatima? He enclosed with these inquiries the lines now known as the *Ode on the Death of a Favourite Cat*. This charming poem, with the *Ode on a Distant Prospect of Eton College*, the moving evocation of Gray's school-days, and the *Ode to Spring*, were shown to Dodsley who agreed to include them in his collection. They appeared in the second volume, but though he was now in print Gray still had a reluctance to sign his work, and the poems were published as being by 'Mr ———'.

The publication of these anonymous pieces in January 1748 made no great stir. Over two years later, on 12 June 1750, Walpole received a letter from Stoke Poges where Gray was staying with his mother. 'I have been here at Stoke a few days (where I shall continue a good part of the summer),' he wrote, 'and having put an end to a thing, whose beginning you have seen long ago, I immediately send it you.' The 'thing' to which he had now put an end was the *Elegy written in a Country Churchyard* which Walpole now saw for the first time in its completed form though Gray had been working away at it for some years, inspired perhaps originally (though this is not certain) by the death of Richard West in 1742. Walpole at once recognized its genius and could not resist showing it to his friends, who themselves could not resist taking copies. The copies began to circulate and the fame of the poem gradually spread. By the beginning of the following year, an obscure periodical got hold of it and wrote to inform the author that they were about to print it. Gray was naturally indignant that his poem should appear in an unauthorized edition, and blaming Walpole for the awkward situation in which he found himself, wrote to him in February 1751, pointing out that he had only one way of escaping the 'honour' they would inflict on him and that was for Walpole to make Dodsley print the poem immediately from his own copy. It was to be printed, he insisted, 'without my Name, in what Form is most convenient for him, but in his best Paper and Character.'

Did Walpole, it is fair to ask, circulate his friend's poem in this rather careless manner in order to force him to publish it? Knowing, as he did, Gray's staunch reluctance to print, it is possible to believe that this was indeed the case. Certainly he lost no time in seeing the poem through the press, adding at Gray's request a brief introductory note explaining how it came to be printed. Its success was immediate. The first printing sold out and several others were called for, but Gray was unable to keep the secret of his authorship. On 16 February, the day after Dodsley's edition came out, the pirated version made its appearance, full of errors but boldly announcing the poem as being the work of 'Mr Gray of Peterhouse, Cambridge'.

Gray accepted the situation in a meek enough spirit and bore Walpole no grudge for the fame he had brought him. 'You have indeed conducted with great decency my little *misfortune*,' he wrote to him on 20 February, which turned out rather appropriately for his mood to be Ash Wednesday,

you have taken a paternal care of it, and expressed much more kindness than could have been expressed from so near a relation. But we are all frail; and I hope to do as much for you another time. Nurse Dodsley has given it a pinch or two in the cradle, that (I doubt) it will bear the marks of as long as it lives . . . I thank you for your advertisement, which saves my honour, and in a manner *bien flatteuse pour moi*, who should be put to it even to make myself a compliment in good English.

If Gray had now to acknowledge that he was the father of what would soon be regarded as one of the greatest poems in the English language, Walpole could claim with good reason to having been its godfather.

About the same time, Gray was enjoying another success with his poem *A Long Story*, written in a light, mocking vein in marked contrast to the style of the *Elegy*, though the latter poem was responsible for the other being composed. One of the early privately circulated copies of the *Elegy* had found its way to the manor house at Stoke Poges where it was read by the dowager Lady Cobham who was intrigued to learn that the author was staying in the same parish. She determined to meet him and at once dispatched her niece, Henrietta Speed, and a Lady Schaub who was also staying at the manor, to call upon Mrs Gray. Gray himself was so alarmed when he saw this female invasion bearing down on the house to threaten his seclusion that he ran into the garden to hide until their visit was over, but he later plucked up courage to return the call, and indeed discovered in Miss Speed one of the few young women for whom he could feel any sort of warm regard. He was soon a regular caller at Lady Cobham's house. The poem, which in fact is not long at all (Dr Johnson was to dismiss it summarily as 'an odd composition') was written as a light-hearted account of how they all came to meet, and not least of how on their first appearance the poet had fled in confusion with the result that

> On the first marching of the troops
> The Muses hopeless of his pardon,
> Convey'd him underneath their hoops
> To a small closet in the garden.

The success of this poem and of the *Elegy* decided Walpole to bring out an edition of Gray's poems, again using Dodsley as his publisher. Knowing well the timidity and qualms of the author he provided a bait by suggesting that Richard Bentley should decorate the volume, for Gray held Bentley's work in high esteem and was even to write a poem in his honour claiming that the poet's 'tardy Rhymes' would 'catch a lustre from his genuine flame'. Gray's poetic output was never very prolific, and only six poems were included in this edition, three of which had already been printed in Dodsley's *Poems by Several Hands* and two others, *A Long Story* and the *Elegy* were well known. The sixth poem was the *Hymn to Adversity* whose sombre lines, as Gray admitted when he sent the work to Walpole, presented some difficulty to the artist who had to provide it with a head and tailpiece. The qualms that Walpole had anticipated were not yet entirely banished. Gray complained to Dodsley that he would appear 'very justly ridiculous' if a book containing only six poems—'half a dozen little matters'—was to come out under the pompous title of a 'Collection of Poems', and indeed he had a point here, for Dr Johnson again, whose comments on Gray always betray an uncharacteristic sneer, was later to remark that when the volume was issued, only one side of each leaf was printed 'that they might in some form or other make a book'. To meet Gray's objection, Dodsley agreed that the title should be changed to 'Designs by Mr. R. Bentley for six poems by Mr. T. Gray,' and it was in this way, with the poet modestly taking second place to the designer, that the book appeared in March 1753.

It was a most attractive volume. Bentley provided a plate to illustrate each poem as well as a head and tailpiece in his fragile combination of gothic and rococo which had about it something of the airiness and fantasy of Chippendale's 'Chinese' designs. Gray was delighted with Bentley's work, but he very nearly had another major row with Walpole when he learnt that Dodsley planned to have a portrait of the author by way of a frontispiece. Walpole had commissioned a picture of Gray from Ecchardt based, according to the fashion of the day, on the portrait of a musician by Van Dyck from the Duke of Grafton's collection. It hung in the Blue Bedchamber at Strawberry Hill and it was this offending work that the publisher was having engraved. Gray wrote to Walpole on 13 February:

> Sure you are out of your Wits! This I know, if you suffer my Head to be printed, you infallibly will put me out of mine. I conjure you immediately to put a stop to any such design . . . The thing, as it was, I know will make me ridiculous enough; but to appear in proper Person at the head of my works, consisting of half a dozen Ballads in 30 pages, would seem worse than the Pillory. I do assure

you, if I had received such a Book with such a frontispiece without any warning, I believe, it would have given me a Palsy.

He was extremely in earnest, he concluded, declaring that he could not bear even the idea. Walpole quickly set him at ease; the picture would not appear. Gray was right in his judgement on this occasion. A portrait would have been out of place in so slender and delicate a volume.

His insistence, on the other hand, that he and Bentley should feature as 'Mr. R Bentley' and 'Mr. T. Gray' on the title-page of *Six Poems* is more difficult to understand. He wished to be so described because he thought that to omit the 'Mr' would make him appear 'a classic'. Walpole thought his reason quite absurd. 'Without ranging myself among the classics,' he replied, 'I assure you, were I to print anything with my name, it should be plain Horace Walpole: *Mr* is one of the Gothicisms I abominate.' Gray, as we have seen, had his way and the strangely awkward title was printed as he wished. In spite of the apparent self-effacement of Gray's newly arranged title-page, it screened what one can only call a kind of inverted vanity not unlike the inverted snobbery of certain modern peers who like to pass without their titles but at the same time have no real wish to be mistaken for commoners. For all his shyness, his love of solitude and his gentle melancholy there was also a hint of arrogance in Gray that matched his equally unexpected pride. There was also in this modest backing from the limelight a form of self-protection against the possibility of failure. Gray's fear of ridicule was something that Walpole should have appreciated, for it was a failing that he shared with his friend, and in his own works when they were published, he developed the habit of introducing some comment that was clearly designed to forestall criticism.

Walpole had enjoyed the business of seeing *Six Poems* through the press, acting as a sort of impresario for his two talented friends. The experience was one of the causes that led him in the summer of 1757 to set up his own printing press at Strawberry Hill. It was the first private press to be established in England, and it meant that he was now free from the commercial printers and could publish whatever he wanted in as many copies as he wished. He had no intention of rivalling such men as Dodsley and Newbery, indeed, the first edition to be struck from the press was printed for Dodsley, who had also been invited as one of the guests when the press was opened. Walpole's editions were usually quite small, were often given away to his friends or when sold were usually done so for the benefit of the author alone. To inaugurate his new press, he again chose two poems by Gray, the *Progress of Poesy* and *The Bard*, as he explained in a letter to John Chute. He had met the poet in London: 'He had brought his two Odes to be printed. I snatched them out of Dodsley's hands and they are to be the first-fruits of my press.' The printing press was first erected in a small outbuilding in the garden on 25 June (it later had to be moved when the Cloisters and Gallery were built); printing began on 16 July, and on 3 August the first thousand copies of *Odes by Mr. Gray* were ready for Dodsley to sell at the price of one shilling each. The next day, Walpole wrote to Mann with great satisfaction:

> 'My abbey is a perfect college or academy. I keep a painter [Müntz] in the house, and a printer—not to mention Mr. Bentley, who is an academy himself. I send you two copies . . . of a very honourable opening of my press—two Odes of Mr. Gray; they are Greek, they are Pindaric, they are sublime—consequently I fear a little obscure . . .

On this last point, though on few others, Walpole might have agreed with Dr Johnson who held that in all Gray's odes there was 'a kind of cumbrous splendour which we wish away'.

The decade from 1758 to 1768 was to be a period of great literary activity for Walpole. In these ten years he was to issue his *Catalogue of Royal and Noble Authors* as well as his collection of *Fugitive Pieces in Verse and Prose* in 1758; his 'gothic' novel *The Castle of Otranto* came out in 1765, *Historic Doubts on the Life and Reign of King Richard III* in 1768, and his verse tragedy *The Mysterious Mother* in the same year. In 1762, the first two volumes of *Anecdotes of Painting in England* made their appearance and were followed two years later by a third volume and the *Catalogue of Engravers*. As the historical memoirs and correspondence were not to be known until after his death, it was upon these works that his literary reputation during his lifetime was based and by which his contemporaries judged him as a man of letters. Though Walpole's art and mastery as a letter-writer now overshadows everything else that he wrote, it is not without interest to note that *The Castle of Otranto* has never been out of print since its first publication, that *Historic Doubts* was reprinted as recently as 1965, and that the volumes of the *Anecdotes of Painting* (of which a fifth and final volume, finished in 1771 but not then published, came out in 1780) remains an invaluable source of reference for the history of art in Britain and has earned for its author the reputation of being the first English Vasari. If none of Walpole's letters had survived and he had never bothered to record his political reminiscences, he would still have had a small but not entirely insignificant place in the history of literature. As Lord Byron was to write in 1820, twenty-three years after Walpole's death, in what must be one of the greatest compliments ever paid by one writer to another:

> It is the fashion to under-rate Horace Walpole; firstly, because he was a nobleman, and secondly, because he was a gentleman; but, to say nothing of the composition of his incomparable letters, and of *The Castle of Otranto*, he is the 'Ultimus Romanorum', the author of *The Mysterious Mother*, a tragedy of the highest order, and not a puling love-play. He is the father of the first romance and of the last tragedy in our language, and surely worthy of a higher place than any living writer, be he who he may.

Not many people today would endorse Byron's opinion of *The Mysterious Mother* beyond agreeing that it was no love play, though it has some strong passages and good scenes. With its theme of incest, there is no doubt that a psychoanalyst could elaborate very convincingly why such a subject should appeal both to Byron and to Walpole, but to a modern reader its rather clumsy mechanism no longer carries conviction. Even the author himself never expected, or indeed wanted, to see it performed. 'The subject', he admitted, 'is more truly horrid than even that of Oedipus.' *The Castle of Otranto*, on the other hand, for all its now rather false-seeming gothicism and contrived horror, has a place in the history of literature if only for the long line of 'gothic' novels of which it was the first, a line that includes Mrs Radcliffe, Beckford and 'Monk' Lewis, and takes us by way of Mary Shelley and Bram Stoker writing at opposite ends of the nineteenth century to the 'horror movies' of today. It was praised by Walter Scott not only for the wild interest of the story, but 'as the first modern attempt to found a tale of amusing fiction upon the basis of the ancient romance of chivalry'.

It will be recalled that Walpole described his villa at Strawberry

Hill as 'a very proper habitation of, as it was the scene that inspired, the author of *The Castle of Otranto*'. His novel and his house were, indeed, all of a piece in their romantic and self-consciously gloomy conception of the medieval past. He started to write his novel after a curious dream in which he found himself in an ancient castle where he saw on the uppermost banister of the staircase, a gigantic hand in armour—'a very natural dream', as he wrote in explanation to his friend William Cole, 'for a head filled like mine with gothic story'. The next day he sat down and began to write, allowing the story, as he put it, to grow on his hands, and so he went on in one continuous creative urge until he had finished it in less than two months. One evening, as he told Cole, 'I wrote from the time I had drunk my tea, about six o'clock till half an hour after one in the morning, when my hand and fingers were so weary, that I could not hold the pen to finish the sentence, but left Maltida and Isabella talking, in the middle of a paragraph.' He made use of rooms in his own house, vague memories of the medieval courts of Cambridge colleges, and impressions of 'gothic' grandeur going back to the days of his Grand Tour when he had written to West of the horrors of waterfalls, chasms and precipices in the wild Alpine scenery. It is a curious fact that Strawberry Hill, Fonthill Abbey, *The Castle of Otranto* and *Vathek* all owe a debt to the Grande Chartreuse.

When the story was finished, he showed it to Gray who encouraged him to publish it. With some nervousness as to its reception, not unlike Gray's over the publication of *Six Poems*, he hid his authorship, in the first edition, behind the fiction that the work was translated from the original Italian of a rather improbable canon of Otranto called Onuphrio Muralto, but reassured by its instant success he allowed his name to appear in later editions. From Cambridge, Gray wrote when the book came out: 'I have received the C. of O. and return you my thanks for it. It engages our attention here, makes some of us cry a little, and all in general afraid to go bed o'nights.' Compliments came to him from all sides, and in the *St James's Chronicle* an anonymous admirer hailed him in verses that began

> Thou sweet Enchanter! at whose nod
> The aery train of phantoms rise:
> Who dost but wave thy potent Rod,
> And marble bleeds and canvas sighs.

There was something in this tale of supernatural happenings, of ghosts, and figures that step out of pictures, that appealed to a world that was growing weary of Augustan propriety and well ordered classicism; like Walpole himself, it was ready to 'live back into centuries that cannot disappoint one'. Only one comment was heard in opposition to the general chorus of praise, and it came from the irreverent pen of Gilly Williams. What, he asked George Selwyn, had their old friend Horry Walpole been up to? 'How do you think he has employed that leisure which his political frenzy has allowed of? In writing a novel that no boarding-school Miss of thirteen could get half through without yawning . . . He says it was a dream, and I fancy one when he had some feverish disposition in him.' But Walpole had no need to worry. By the end of the century his book had gone through twenty-one editions, and translations had appeared in Paris, Amsterdam, Berlin and Parma. It is still being printed and only recently came out in a large edition in Russia.

✦ 4 ✦

Gray's growing fame as a poet did not make him any more relaxed or easy in company. At the time Dodsley published his first poems, Walpole had remarked in a letter to Montagu:

> I agree with you most absolutely in your opinion about Gray; he is the worst company in the world—from a melancholy turn, from living reclusely, and from a little too much dignity, he never converses easily—all his words are measured, and chosen, and formed into sentences; his writings are admirable; he himself is not agreeable.

This lack of social address could have a damping effect on others. In the summer of 1760 Lady Ailesbury, the wife of Walpole's favourite cousin Henry Conway, invited Gray to stay at Park Place near Henley for a visit that included his friend Henrietta Speed and Lady Carlisle among the guests. They were a merry group and did their best to entertain the morose poet, but it was uphill work. One day when they went on a picnic and the ladies of the party were full of laughter and fun, the only remark they could coax out of Gray was 'Yes, my Lady, I believe so', in answer to a question from his hostess.

Gray himself once admitted that he preferred a situation where he could 'sit still, and be alone with pleasure' rather than to have to contend with 'company and cards at home, parties by land and water abroad, and what they call *doing something*, that is, racketing from morning to night'. No wonder that Dr Johnson (who in fact never met Gray) should pronounce upon his reputation for dullness to Boswell and even use it for another unjustified attack on his poetry: 'Sir, he was dull in company, dull in his closet, dull everywhere. He was dull in a new way, and that made many people think him *great*. He was a mechanical poet.'

The terror of fire that always haunted Gray was increased when his London property in Cornhill, which he had inherited from his father, was burnt down in March 1748. Not only was the house in which he had been born destroyed but, as he had failed to insure it fully, he suffered financial loss as well. He felt no safer in Cambridge than in London, though the danger was less there. He was constantly worried by the thought of candles being knocked over by rowdy or drunken undergraduates and his staircase being consumed by flames. As a precaution he bought a rope ladder which he kept in his rooms, and had an iron bar fixed outside his window to which he could attach it in case of emergency. Both Gray's fear and his precaution against it were well known in the college. In February 1756 some of the wilder elements there, who took a perverse delight in tormenting Gray, raised a cry of fire one night in the hopes of seeing the rope ladder put to use.

All that in fact happened (according to an account given at the time) was that a 'delicate white night-cap' was seen to pop out of a window and was as quickly withdrawn when it was seen that the alarm was a false one. It was not a very dramatic result. The idea of Gray descending his ladder in a night-shirt like a character from one of the bawdy tales in Chaucer was too good a story to be denied through any mere want of fact, and soon a detailed version of the event was circulating in which Gray not only climbed down his ladder but landed in a tub of water that had been placed at the bottom specially to receive him. The story, which has even found its way in this form into some lives of the poet, is not supported by any contemporary testimony. The only positive result of this rather silly but ineffective game at Gray's expense was that he decided to transfer himself to Pembroke College on the other side of the road where he had many friends, and where he was to live unmolested for the remainder of his life.

In January 1759, the British Museum was first opened to the public, an event that brought a novel interest into the lives of Walpole and Gray who were both enthusiastic supporters of the new institution. Walpole himself was one of the first trustees; he looked forward to what he described as 'a new era for *virtù*' resulting from its opening, and hoped that a British Academy of Arts might develop if the Museum proved successful. Gray was one of the first people to make regular use of the reading-room which was a narrow, rather dark place in the 'base story' of the building. The Museum was, he told a friend in that August, 'my favourite domain, where I often pass four hours in the day in the stillness and solitude of the reading-room'. Here he could work without interruption at his historical research or the study of Icelandic and Celtic verse, an interest of his for which Walpole had very little sympathy, disturbed only by the occasional appearances of Dr Stukeley, the antiquarian, who bustled in from time to time 'to talk nonsense and coffee-house news'.

Gray's interest in ancient verse had been encouraged by the so-called translations of James Macpherson when they came out as *Fragments of Ancient Poetry* in 1760. Like many other people in the British Isles and Europe he found something in the Ossian legend that strongly appealed to his imagination. 'I continue to think them genuine,' he wrote to his friend and subsequent biographer William Mason on 7 August, 'though my reasons for believing the contrary are rather stronger than ever: but I will have them antique, for I never knew a Scotchman of my own time that could read, much less write, poetry; and such poetry too!' He was relieved when David Hume assured him that similar poems were in everybody's mouth in the Highlands, and had been handed down from father to son. The future author of *The Castle of Otranto*, on the other hand, was rather suprisingly completely sceptical when *Fingal* made its appearance in 1762. Here was something gothic that for once made no appeal to him. He wrote to Montagu:

> I will trust you with a secret, but you must not disclose it; I should be ruined with my Scotch friends. In short, I cannot believe it genuine. I cannot believe a regular poem of six books has been

preserved, uncorrupted by oral tradition, from times before Christianity was introduced into this island. What! Preserved unadulterated by savages dispersed among mountains, and so often driven from their dens—so wasted by wars civil and foreign? Has one man ever got all by heart? I doubt it. Were parts preserved by some, other parts by others? Mighty lucky, that the tradition was never interrupted, nor any part lost—not a verse, not a measure, not the sense! Luckier and luckier!

Walpole was more interested in Gray's general historical research than in his preoccupation with ancient Welsh and Norse poetry, studies that were to result in *The Descent of Odin* and *The Fatal Sisters*. In 1768, the year these poems first appeared, Walpole published the result of some of his own historical research in the book he called *Historic Doubts on the Life and Reign of King Richard III*, a work that sought to exonerate the king from some of the crimes attributed to him by Tudor propaganda and to question the villainous character presented in Shakespeare's play, based as it was upon the only source known to the poet of the same tainted origin. Walpole had relied on Gray for some help in his researches, but the general conception and form of the book was entirely his own.

It is perhaps unfortunate that he did not submit more of his work to Gray's scrutiny before publication, for Gray was an exact and meticulous scholar while Walpole, with his dilettante approach, held what he considered to be mere pedantry in contempt and had altogether too gentlemanly and easygoing an attitude to his studies. The result, of course, was that while he provoked a general interest by taking a new and original look at the accepted view of Richard's reign, many aspects of which he validly criticized, his slipshod and careless scholarship laid him open to dangerous attack from the very pedants he claimed to despise. Even Gray himself was a little guarded in his response to the book when his copy reached him, and congratulated the author with more tact than enthusiasm. From Cambridge he wrote to Walpole:

> Certain it is, that you are universally read here, but what *we* think, is not so easy to come at. We stay as usual to see the success, to learn the judgment of the town, to be directed in our opinions by those of more competent judges. If they like you, we shall; if anyone of name write against you, we give you up: for we are

modest and diffident of ourselves, and not without reason. History in particular is not our *fort*; for (the truth is) we read only modern books and the pamphlets of the day.

The initial success of the book with the general public was considerable, and it immediately went into a second edition; but when the tiresome pedants began to question some of his doubts as being not quite so historically accurate as they might have been, or pointed out errors in his use of source material, a few of his friends began to reserve their judgement in the manner of the Cambridge dons. Lady Mary Coke was uncertain from the start. 'The style and language are admirable, as everything that he writes is,' she noted in her diary on 29 January, 'but he has not made it appear (at least to me) that Richard was innocent of many of the crimes laid to his charge by former historians.' She read one of the attacks on the book and acknowledged that though it was 'much inferior to his style, and even vulgar in many places' she none the less found herself in agreement with the author's argument against Walpole's position. A month later, she recorded a remark of George Selwyn's: he hoped that Richard III might rise again and give the world his historic doubts on Horace Walpole. Selwyn's young friend Lord Carlisle was ready with his witticism before he had even read the book. 'The Emperor Nero's character wants a little white-washing,' he observed, 'and so does Mrs. Brownrigg's who was hanged for the murder of her apprentice the other day. I hope he will undertake them next, as they seem, next to his hero, to want it most.'

Walpole could accept the quips of his friends in good part, but he was irritated and hurt by the attacks of certain scholars, especially one launched by Dr Jeremiah Milles, Dean of Exeter and President of the Society of Antiquaries, a body of which Walpole had been for many years a distinguished and respected member. The Dean, in his attack, had referred to the contrast between 'ridiculous traditions' and true history, a rebuke that touched Walpole on his most sensitive spot. Not long afterwards he resigned from the Society in something of a huff, only waiting for a suitable opportunity. This came his way when the Antiquaries turned their attention to a study of the history of Dick Whittington and his cat, a subject that made him feel that he could return the charge of ridicule to the president and make his departure with dignity. If this was something in the nature of an over-reaction, it was in character with his acute sensitivity to any criticism of his published works. When his *Catalogue of Royal and Noble Authors* came out in 1759 he wrote to a friend: 'I am sick of the character of author; I am sick of the consequences of it; I am tired with reading foolish criticisms on me, and as foolish defences of me; and I trust my friends will be so good as to let the last abuse of me pass unanswered.' He now complained in a similar tone to Gray. 'Pray do not be out of humour,' his friend replied. 'When you first commenced as an author, you exposed yourself to pit, box and gallery. Any coxcomb in the world may come in and hiss, if he pleases; aye, and (what is almost as bad) clap too, and you cannot hinder him.' This was sound and sensible advice coming, as it did, from someone who would himself probably never have 'commenced as author' but for Walpole's encouragement and help.

Gray's life after he settled down at Pembroke College was that of a man of growing national fame but still one who liked to live as much retired from the world as possible with his books, his harpsichord, and a small circle of friends mostly connected in one way or another with the university. In 1757, when Colley Cibber died, Gray was offered the post of Poet Laureate. Cibber had held the office since 1730, and is now remembered as a dramatist and actor but forgotten as a poet; his predecessor in office, Laurence Eusden, is remembered for having held the post but not for anything else, least of all for anything he might have written. He had been appointed in 1718, almost forty years before the offer was made to Gray. During that long period very little lustre had been shed on this ancient appointment and Gray saw no reason for accepting something that he looked upon as more of a burden than an honour. He declined the nomination, writing to William Mason:

> The office itself has always humbled the professor hitherto (even in an age when Kings were somebody), if he were a poor writer by making him more conspicuous, and if he were a good one by setting him at war with the little fry of his profession, for there are poets little enough to envy even a poet laureate.

The post was then offered to William Whitehead, who had written a play or two and was secretary to the Order of the Bath. He was to hold it until his death in 1785, continuing the tradition of dullness that Eusden's appointment had initiated sixty-seven years before.

There was only one public post that Gray coveted and that was the professorship of Modern History at Cambridge, which at that period was also associated with modern languages. It had been established in 1724 by George I when he also founded a similar chair at Oxford. The duties were not arduous; the incumbent was expected to lecture at least once a term, but no one so far had regarded this obligation as a duty—indeed, the first three professors to occupy the chair had been notable only for their silence. The professor was also required to appoint two deputies to teach French and Italian and to pay them out of his stipend of £400 a year. Gray had hoped to be appointed in 1762 when the second of the three mute oracles had departed to the realm of eternal silence. As soon as he had heard of the professor's death, he wrote to Chute saying that it was probably already too late to start asking for it but added: 'we had (if you remember) some conversation on that Head at Twickenham; and as you have probably found some Opportunity to mention it to Mr. Walpole since, I would gladly know his Thoughts about it.' It was too late; the post had already been given to Laurence Brockett, an intemperate clergyman who might well have outlived Gray had he not fallen off his horse and broken his neck in a drunken fit six years after his appointment.

This time the professorship was offered to Gray by the Duke of Grafton in very flattering terms, and on 29 July 1768 he was able to write to his niece Mary Antrobus that

> this day, hot as it is, I kissed the King's hand; that my warrant was signed by him last night; that on Wednesday I received a very honourable letter from the D. of Grafton, acquainting me that his majesty had ordered him to offer me the Professorship, and much more, which does me too much credit by half for me to mention it.

He was particularly pleased that the appointment had come to him without any intrigue or pleading on his behalf by his influential friends. Walpole, as is clear from a letter he wrote to Conway on 9 August, had had no hand in it, though he was delighted that 'my Gray, Gray the poet' had achieved this ambition at last.

Gray entered on his duties full of enthusiasm. He was determined that the old days when the professorship had been treated as a sinecure were to end. He gave a great deal of thought to possible courses of study and wrote lengthy memoranda suggesting numerous reforms, among them being the proposal that the professor should give private lectures to his students at short and regular intervals as well as his statutory lecture once a term, which so far none of his predecessors had bothered to deliver. He also planned to give an inaugural lecture in Latin. But somehow none of these laudable intentions was translated into fact. His natural timidity made him dread the thought of lecturing in public and the curious inability he had to bring certain things to a proper conclusion frustrated his other schemes for amendment. When Gray died three years after his appointment, he had still not finished the composition of his inaugural lecture. It remained for his successor to introduce the reforms.

The habit that Walpole had described as 'living reclusely' grew more marked as Gray got older. His lapses into silence when in company became so frequent that they gained him a gratuitous reputation for profundity. In the combination-room of his college he rarely spoke unless spoken to, and then as often as not made only the briefest reply, a mere word of agreement or disagreement. It was only with young people that he was able to unbend and talk more freely; there was something in the tribute they paid him as a famous poet that thawed his reserve and made him communicative and relaxed in their society as he never was with his contemporaries. It was in this way that he met an undergraduate of Trinity Hall in the summer of 1762 who quite simply thought of him as 'one of the greatest Men who ever existed in the World'. This was Norton Nicholls, twenty-six years junior to Gray, who was to become a close friend of the poet in his final years, sharing, among other things, his love of music and the passion for botany and natural history that now occupied much of Gray's time. Nicholls was later to take Holy Orders, though his interests were almost entirely literary and social, giving Walpole so much the impression of one of the worldly courtier-priests he had known in Paris and Versailles that he would often refer to him in his letters as the Abbé Nicholls.

It was to Nicholls that Gray owed an introduction that was to transform his life and rescue him, at least for some months, from the somewhat slothful atmosphere that characterized his retired existence in Cambridge. In November 1769, Nicholls had been in Bath where he met Charles-Victor de Bonstetten, an attractive young Swiss then twenty-four years old, the son of a prominent citizen of

Berne. Bonstetten was what is known as a charmer; he had all the graces, physical, intellectual and social, and was at this moment passing through a romantic phase, having recently fallen in and out of love and toyed, not very seriously, with the idea of suicide. He was handsome, highly intelligent, lively and affectionate, but in his father's opinion too ardent and inconsistent, too eager for new but transitory experiences, and had been sent to pursue his studies in Holland and England in the hope that these stolidly Protestant countries would have a sobering influence on his volatile spirits. He captivated Nicholls by his enthusiastic talk of the mountainous scenery of the homeland, of pine forests that grew darker as one penetrated their depth, 'the cries of eagles and other birds of prey adding to the horror'. Such a person, it at once occurred to Nicholls, was ideally suited to be presented to the author of the *Elegy written in a Country Churchyard* whom Bonstetten already revered as the premier writer and premier poet in England. A letter of introduction was written and Gray, intrigued by Nicholls's eulogy, went up to London to meet this paragon.

The meeting was a great success. Gray at once fell captive to Bonstetten's infectious charm and found himself infatuated as he had been only once before, many years ago, when he had succumbed to the equally compelling fascination of the young Horace Walpole. There was this difference, however, that at the age of fifty-five and with an established literary reputation, there was none of the feeling of insecurity on his side that had marred his early relations with Walpole. Any suffering that this new relationship caused would be of a different sort. Bonstetten was invited to Cambridge for the Christmas of 1769, intending to stay only a couple of weeks. 'I never saw such a boy: our breed is not made on this model,' Gray wrote to Nicholls on 6 January 1770. 'He is busy from morning to night, has no other amusement than that of changing one study for another, likes nobody that he sees here, and yet wishes to stay longer, tho' he has passed a whole fortnight with us already.' He was in fact to remain in Cambridge until the following March dashing in and out of Gray's rooms at all hours so that there was no time for melancholy or introspection, and so the days passed happily away, Gray touched and his heart strangely warmed by the young man's homage and friendship, Bonstetten flattered and proud to be on such intimate terms with so celebrated a person. He wrote to his mother on 6

February: 'I eat every day in his rooms. He lives in great retirement, and is so kind as to show pleasure in seeing me. I call on him at any hour, he reads with me what I wish ...' As one week followed another in this agreeable association, Gray became more and more dependent on the company of this charming young friend and admirer.

The advent of Bonstetten in Gray's life came as a sort of Indian summer, all too brief and sudden for comfort, reviving sentiments and sensations that had long seemed withered away, if not actually dead. It is doubtful whether the young man himself ever knew or suspected the tumult he had caused in the other's heart; like many people who exercise unusual physical magnetism, he was not always conscious of the havoc he was producing. But there can be no doubt that Gray had fallen in love with him, half-unconsciously perhaps, certainly innocently, but in a way that awakened deeply suppressed longings yet at the same time dangerously disturbed that essential calm of his whole existence which he had spent the greater part of his life in cultivating and protecting. He was both grateful for this new and unfamiliar warmth and sunshine that had come to him so unexpectedly, and fearful of the shattering effect it had had on his tranquillity and peace. It was a situation with which his past life had not equipped him to deal, and his happiness was uneasily mixed with fear.

If Gray had felt some alarm at the growing intensity of his feelings, it was only when he realized that Bonstetten's visit must come to an end, when the news reached him of the anxiety of the young man's parents for their son's return, that the full anguish of his situation dawned upon him. On 20 March he wrote to Nicholls:

On Wednesday next, I go (for a few days) with Monsieur de Bonstetten to London. His cursed Father will have him home in the autumn, and he must pass through France to improve his talents and morals. He goes for Dover on Friday ... He gives me too much pleasure, and at least *an equal share* of inquietude. You do not understand him so well as I do, but I leave my meaning imperfect, till we meet. I have never met with so extraordinary a Person. God bless him! I am unable to talk to you about anything else, I think.

The void left by his young friend's departure served only to emphasize how solitary and desolate his life had now become, and he waited to hear from him with all the anxiety of a deserted lover. At last a letter came, 'and here am I again,' he wrote to Nicholls, to whom alone he could confide his feelings,

> to pass my solitary evenings which hung much lighter on my hands, before I knew him. This is your fault! Pray let the next you send me be halt and blind, dull, unapprehensive, and wrong-headed. For this (as Lady Constance says) *Was ever such a creature born*! and yet—but no matter . . . You will think I have caught madness from him (for he is certainly mad) and perhaps you will be right. Oh! what things are Fathers and Mothers! I thought they were to be found only in England, but you see.

He ended his letter on a sad, almost desperate note: 'This place never appeared so horrible to me as it does now. Could not you come for a week or fortnight? It would be sunshine to me in a dark night.'

It was agony for him to think of Bonstetten confronted by all the temptations of Paris, 'the allurements of painted women *comme il faut*, or the vulgar caresses of prostitute beauty', as his distraught imagination saw it, and his letters were awaited with apprehension. 'I did not conceive till now, I own, what it was to lose you,' he wrote from Cambridge on 12 April when another letter at last arrived, 'nor felt the solitude and insipidity of my own condition before I possessed the happiness of your friendship.' He heaped advice on Bonstetten, ending on a touching but rather forlorn note—his friend's letter had proved that in the midst of his new gaieties he still held some place in his memory: 'Go on, my best and amiable friend, to shew me your heart simply and without the shadow of disguise, and leave me to weep over it, as I do now, no matter whether from joy or sorrow.'

Gray had just over a year to live when he wrote this letter. Bonstetten had appeared in his life just as it was about to close, awakening long suppressed or abandoned hopes for love, friendship and human companionship. The experience had been both exhilarating and deeply disturbing to one who had for so long renounced all intimate human contacts that in any way involved his deep affections, and the experience left him shaken and emotionally prostrated. He continued to hear from Bonstetten and sent him affectionate letters in return though he felt unable to make the journey to Switzerland to meet his friend again as the latter had hoped. He must depend instead upon his memories. 'My life now is but a conversation with your shadow,' he wrote later in the same month, 'the known sound of your voice still rings in my ears—there, on the corner of the fender, you are standing, or tinkling on the piano-forte, or stretched at length on the sofa.' These recollections he could carry always in his mind unclouded by any quarrels such as had impaired his youthful friendship with Walpole or by the possibility of disappointment that a further encounter might have entailed. His friendship for Bonstetten, for all that it emphasized by contrast the emotional aridity of his life both before and after he met him, had at least brought some warmth and feeling into an otherwise withdrawn and lonely existence. He had taken a risk that Walpole would never have permitted himself to take.

Gray's health had never been robust and he was now, though only in his mid-fifties, subject to increasing bouts of illness. His small and fragile frame was not built to withstand a long period of ill-health and his will to live was not strong. In the summer of 1771, just before Walpole left for Paris, he and Gray were together for what was to prove to be their last meeting. Gray complained of gout and various other aches and pains. Walpole found him changed and ill-looking but never for a moment considered him in any danger. He left for Paris confident that he would be seeing his friend again after his return. He was to learn of Gray's death in much the same way that Gray himself had learnt of the death of West nearly thirty years before, by reading of it in a newspaper. 'I started up from my chair when I read the paragraph,' Walpole told Chute in a letter of 12 August, 'a cannon-ball would not have surprised me more.'

It was a double shock for Walpole, for not only had he lost a friend whom he had known for so many years and whose genius he had consistently admired and championed, but for the first time he suffered the loss of someone who was almost his exact contemporary. He wrote to Chute:

As self lies so rooted in self, no doubt the nearness of our ages made the stroke recoil to my own breast; and having so little expected his death, it is plain how little I expect my own. Yet to you, who of all men living are the most forgiving, I need not excuse the concern I feel.

In much the same strain, he wrote to Henry Conway, who had also known Gray since their school-days together: 'It seemed more a corporal than a mental blow; and yet I am exceedingly concerned for him, and everybody must be so for the loss of such a genius.'

Reference has already been made to the portrait of Gray painted by Ecchardt in the manner of Van Dyck that hung in the Blue Bedchamber at Strawberry Hill. At some time after Gray's death, Walpole received the gift of a picture from his brother Edward which was suitably gothic in its subject and treatment to grace the walls of his crenellated villa. He placed it in the Breakfast Room, and in his guide to the house and collection, he described it as 'a view of the church at Stoke Poges, the moon shining on Mr. Gray's tomb in the churchyard; by Baron: a present from Sir Edward Walpole'. It was a fitting tribute to the memory of the man whose famous *Churchyard Elegy* he had been so instrumental in bringing before the public, and whose friendship, after their early misunderstandings had been resolved, he had always been so proud to own.

VI
Politics and the Conways

Walpole had been born into a family that stood at the very centre of British politics. His father, his uncle, and his cousins were all one way or another involved in the political life of the nation. The rise and fall of ministers, the making and un-making of cabinets, the fortunes of parties, political factions and cabals had been topics he had heard discussed from his earliest days. He had entered Parliament as a matter of course in 1741 at the age of twenty-four and had remained in the House of Commons, except for one very brief interlude, until 1768, a period of twenty-seven years. All the constituencies he represented, in those days before parliamentary reform, came under the influence of his family: first Callington in Cornwall, controlled by his sister-in-law, Lady Walpole (his eldest brother had been created a baron in 1723); then Castle Rising in Norfolk whose twenty-odd electors were all in the pocket of the Walpole family; and finally King's Lynn, vacated when his uncle Horace also went to the House of Lords, with a somewhat larger and more independent electorate, but one that could be relied upon to vote in the Walpole interest. He rarely had to contest an election, and when he did so was never in any real danger of being defeated. He hardly ever visited his constituents, but when he was compelled to do so, as was the case when the citizens of King's Lynn presented him with the freedom of the town after the election of 1761, he found the experience far from agreeable. 'Think of me,' he wrote with a slight shudder to Montagu,

the subject of a mob, who was scarce ever before in a mob, addressing them in the town hall, riding at the head of two thousand people through such a town as Lynn, dining with above two hundred of them, amid bumpers, huzzas, songs, and tobacco, and finishing with country dancing at a ball and sixpenny whisk!

He bore his ordeal with cheerfulness, but clearly had no wish to repeat it.

The business of politics was for a long time the breath of life to him, though he would eventually tire of it. He did not often intervene in debates in the House of Commons for his voice was not strong and he had no talent for oratory, but his connections were such that he became an influential back-bencher whose opinions were listened to with respect and whose reputation as a power behind the scenes was not insignificant. In spite of this he had a certain contempt for the whole parliamentary scene, which came perhaps from too much familiarity and the fact that he had never had to strive for position. His disdain was reserved especially for political fortune-hunters and place-seekers, and he despised all cliques and factions most of which he considered disruptive and evil, and incapable of achieving any public good.

He liked to think of himself as the enemy of arbitrary government in all its forms and as 'the only unadulterated Whig left in England'. The strength of the British constitution, he believed, lay in the check which the King, the Lords, and the Commons each had over the other. He wrote in his *Journal of the Reign of George III*:

> But it must be remembered, at the same time, that while any two are checking, the third is naturally aiming at extending and aggrandizing its power. The House of Commons has not seldom made this attempt, like the rest. The Lords, as permanent and as a proud body, more constantly aim at it: the Crown always.

His liberal attitude to such issues as slavery, which he abominated, was extended to his passionate dislike of war and bloodshed and the strong sympathy he felt for the cause of the Americans in their struggle with the home government that led to their ultimate independence. He confessed to being something of a rebel himself. He considered that 'soldiers and sailors who are knocked on the head, and peasants plundered or butchered are to my eyes as valuable, as a lazy luxurious set of men, who hire others to acquire riches for them; who would embroil all the earth, that they may heap or squander.'

Yet these fine sentiments, sincerely held as they were, did not leave Walpole entirely uncorrupted. Politics, which tend to bring out the worst in most people, made no special exception in his case and his political writings are spiced with a malice and lack of charity we do not find anywhere else in his correspondence or other published works. It enlivens, but at the same time weakens in authority, the narrative of his memoirs, in particular the often vicious portraits of these whom he considered to be enemies of the true Whig cause. The surviving opponents of his father came in for the worst abuse, especially the 'burlesque' Duke of Newcastle and William Pulteney, Earl of Bath. Sometimes he was able to bring both down with a single shot as when he wrote of Pulteney:

> Who does not know that he had not judgment or resolution enough to engross the power, which he had forfeited his credit and character to obtain? and who does not know that his ambition, treachery, irresolution, timidity, and want of judgment were baffled and made advantage of by a man who had all those vices and indeficiencies in a stronger proportion—for who does not know the Duke of Newcastle?

In the same scurrilous spirit, he dismisses Lord Chancellor Hardwicke as 'a man of low birth and of lower principles', the Duke of Devonshire as being a man whose 'outside was unpolished, his inside unpolishable', and wrote of Lord North, 'two large prominent eyes that rolled about to no purpose (for he was utterly short-sighted), a wide mouth, thick lips and inflated visage, gave him the air of a blind trumpeter,' a description that hardly predisposes one to accept the later comment that 'within that rude casket were enclosed many useful talents.' In such shafts as these Walpole displayed a deadly mastery in the art of character assassination.

What source fed this fountain of malice that flows so constantly yet uncharacteristically in Walpole's political memoirs? Revenge for his father's betrayal was one obvious source, but he was quite capable of employing cruel and biting epithets at the expense of people who were too young to have had any part in his father's fall. It sprang also from an unconscious resentment that anyone, howsoever able, should dare to aspire to the place of eminence that Sir Robert had once occupied with such majesty and power. It was also, possibly, fed by a sense of inadequacy or frustration that he himself, who always boasted so proudly of his relationship to the great minister, did not possess the qualities needed to excel in the same manner as his father had done before him. For this reason he never expressed a wish to hold office, indeed, he went out of his way to declare his unwillingness to do so, but there may have been a subconscious feeling of guilt that he could not follow in his father's footsteps and a desire to punish those who possessed the ability which he so conspicuously lacked. As a result, these rather crude and often malicious attacks on certain personalities that he seemed compelled by some hidden urge to bring into his narrative tended to introduce a disenchanted, jarring note that greatly shocked his readers when the memoirs were first published twenty-five years after his death. They were one of the reasons for the slump in his reputation that came in the nineteenth century. One must remember, however, that Walpole was writing in an age when polemicists were accustomed to dip their pens in gall. The offending passages belong more to the world of James Gillray and the distortion of political caricature than to the serious business of historical portraiture and have tended to detract from the great historical value of his memoirs as a whole.

Walpole's awareness of his own inadequacy as a candidate for high office made him all the more enthusiastic in promoting the claims of his cousin Henry Seymour Conway who had entered Parliament for the first time in the same year as himself. Conway was his favourite cousin. It was a relationship all the more precious to him in that it came from his mother's side of the family, for Henry Conway was the second son of Charlotte Shorter, sister to Lady Walpole. She had married the first Lord Conway in 1718 and her younger son was born three years later and was thus some four years younger than his cousin Horace. Walpole himself, by so much the youngest son of his own family and having in his youth such bad relations with his brothers, always looked upon Conway more as a younger brother than a cousin, all the dearer to him in that they shared the blood of his beloved mother's family. He felt a protective affection for him that went with an almost uncritical admiration: in his eyes this man would ever be 'Harry Conway, whom nature always designed for a hero of romance'.

An opportunity came for Walpole to show his affection for Conway in a concrete way when the latter fell in love with Lady Caroline Fitzroy in 1744, but was unable to marry her because of his lack of income at the time. Walpole immediately offered to share his own income with his cousin so that the marriage, of which he privately disapproved, could take place. Conway declined the offer;

the marriage in fact never took place and Conway later married very happily elsewhere, but the letter Walpole wrote on 20 July gives some indication of his feelings:

> I must talk of myself to prove to you that it will be right for you to accept it. I am sensible of having more follies and weaknesses, and fewer real good qualities, than most men. I sometimes reflect on this, though I own too seldom. I always want to begin acting like a man, and a sensible one, which I think I might be if I would. Can I begin better, than by taking care of my fortune for one I love? You have seen (I have seen you have) that I am fickle and foolishly fond of twenty new people; but I don't really love them—I have always loved you constantly: I am willing to convince you and the world, what I have always told you, that I loved you better than anybody. If I ever felt much for anything, (which I know may be questioned), it was certainly for my mother. I look on you as my nearest relation by her, and I think I can never do enough to show my gratitude and affection to her. For these reasons don't deny me what I have set my heart on—the making your fortune easy to you.

Conway had many natural advantages; he was handsome, courageous, incorruptible and had a gracious if rather aloof manner and a voice that his contemporaries described as 'sweet'. What Walpole termed 'the beauty of his person, and the harmony of his voice' made a remarkable contribution to the debates in the House of Commons. In the opinion of David Hume, who was for a while his secretary, he was 'the most reasonable, equal-tempered, and gentlemanlike man imaginable'. No man of his time, it was said, was so generally liked, but while he had the gift of achieving popularity he was deficient in some valuable qualities. He lacked decisiveness, both as a soldier and a politician, and was easily led by other people upon whose advice he too readily relied. He was also wanting in imagination and perception, and in spite of his easygoing friendliness was at heart rather a cold, withdrawn man who found it difficult to respond to the warmth of Walpole's attachment, for all that he was genuinely fond of him and very dependent on his counsel in his political career. He shared with his cousin a lifelong love of the arts especially the theatre. He was fond of amateur theatricals, like Walpole wrote one or two prologues for plays, and in his retirement adapted Louis de Boissey's *Dehors Trompeurs* for the English stage as *False Appearances*. It was acted privately in 1788 at Richmond House and the following year was given a professional production at Drury Lane.

Conway's career had been divided between the army, which he entered at an early age, and his duties in Parliament. His military career was distinguished. He had fought with bravery at Dettingen and Fontenoy and had commanded a regiment of foot at the bloody battle of Culloden where the army of Prince Charles Edward Stuart had been defeated by the Duke of Cumberland. Conway had previously been aide-de-camp to Cumberland with whom he was later also to have political associations. With the old system of purchasing commissions still in operation, he attained the rank of lieutenant-colonel as early as 1741 when he was only twenty, and was a major-general by the age of thirty-six. At the same time he was appointed Groom of the Bedchamber to George II, a Court appointment that he continued to hold into the next reign.

In 1747 Henry Conway married Lady Caroline Campbell, daughter of the Duke of Argyll and of the charming Mary Bellenden, a companion of Lady Suffolk at the Court of George II, whose pretty face had first excited the king's amorous attention before she managed to escape his unwanted embraces by accepting the hand of Colonel John Campbell. The colonel had later become a lieutenant-general and later still succeeded his kinsman as fourth Duke of Argyll. Lady Caroline had been married to Charles, third Earl of Ailesbury, a man very much older than herself who had already been married twice before, and had borne him a daughter. When Conway married her on 19 December she had been a widow for about a year. According to the custom then prevailing, she continued to be known as Lady Ailesbury after her second marriage. Conway had returned to England from Flanders just before his marriage as something of a hero. In the previous July, he had been wounded and very nearly killed at the battle of Laffelt in circumstances dramatically described by Walpole in a letter to Montagu, telling how his cousin

> was overpowered and flung down, when one French hussar held him by the hair, while another was going to stab him: at that instant an English serjeant with a soldier came up, and killed the latter; but was instantly killed himself; the soldier attacked the other, and Mr. Conway escaped; but he was afterwards taken

prisoner; is since released on parole, and may come home to console his fair widow . . .

Console he did; his marriage was to prove supremely happy.

If Walpole had had his doubts about the suitability of Lady Caroline Fitzroy as a wife for his cousin, he had nothing but praise for the other Caroline whom Conway had now married. Lady Ailesbury was soon a close friend, and their daughter Anne, the only child of the marriage, born in 1749, took the place of a favourite niece in his life. When her parents were in Ireland in 1751–3 and again in 1754 when Conway was appointed secretary to the Lord-Lieutenant, Lord Hartington, Anne came to live with him at Strawberry Hill. A picture of the Conway family was soon added to his collection in the Blue Bedchamber. Like all the portraits in this room it was by Ecchardt, and following the convention that had made him paint Gray in the manner of Van Dyck, and Walpole's sister Lady Mary Churchill and her husband after Rubens, he depicted Conway and Lady Ailesbury (as Walpole described it) in 'attitudes and dresses taken from Watteau'. The attitudes are, in fact, a little stiff and formal and Lady Ailesbury is shown standing perilously close to a fountain that might at any moment drench her silken mantle, but her face is very handsome and her husband looks at her with eyes full of uxorious devotion. Beside them on the ground squats the sturdy little Anne playing with a puppy. She was to grow up into a no less sturdy and rather formidable woman, winning renown under her married name of Mrs Damer as an accomplished sculptress.

Walpole's attachment to Conway, dating as it did from his childhood, was the strongest family tie he was to acknowledge, certainly stronger than such feelings as he may have had for any other member of his family since his mother's death, and he quickly adopted Lady Ailesbury as a sort of honorary sister-in-law. With Conway he also shared many other friendships going back to their Eton days, for his cousin was an admirer of Gray whom he had known at school and in France during their Grand Tour, and had been a contemporary at Eton with Selwyn and Edgcumbe, both later to sit in Parliament with him. Parliament was the scene of the cousins' closest association, for while Walpole was an adept in the art of manoeuvre, putting in a word at a party at Devonshire House or dropping a hint at the card table in some minister's drawing-room—'lost in loo and politics,' as Gilly Williams said, 'it is this day Conway, and the next Chatham, and he is behind them both alternately at the Opera'—Conway, for his part, could hold the attention of the House of Commons in a way that was beyond Walpole's power. 'Mr Conway soothed and persuaded . . .' Walpole declared of his cousin's prowess in the House, he 'seemed to speak only because he thought his opinions might be of service.' In this way they could complement each other's skills and form between them a valuable partnership.

This was seen at its most effective, though with unexpectedly unfortunate results for Conway, in the rumpus stirred up after the Government had decided to prosecute John Wilkes, the radical Member of Parliament for Aylesbury, for his attacks in the *North Briton*, especially after the publication of the notorious number forty-five which had contained a strongly worded criticism of the speech from the throne at the proroguing of Parliament on 19 April 1763, as a result of which Wilkes was arrested by the issue of a general warrant and confined in the Tower of London. He was soon released on the order of the Lord Chief Justice on the ground of a breach of parliamentary privilege, and the whole question of the constitutional legality of general warrants became a matter of urgent debate. The Government defended their action; the King strongly supported them; but many members of Parliament, including Walpole, believed that an important principle of liberty was at stake and determined to vote against the Government. Conway was at first undecided and his brother Lord Hertford, who was about to leave for Paris as ambassador, advised caution. As soon as Hertford had left for his post, however, Walpole had little difficulty in winning Conway over to his point of view. Here was indeed a case of the Crown 'aiming at extending and aggrandizing its power' in a way he had always pledged himself to oppose, and in the debates on 15 and 24 November both he and Conway voted with the minority against the ministry.

Walpole was satisfied by the stand he and his cousin had taken even though they had not been able to muster enough support to defeat the Government. 'It has been hard service,' he reported to Lord Hertford, 'and nothing but a Whig point of this magnitude could easily have carried me to the House at all, of which I have so long been sick.' He had not foreseen, however, the effect that Conway's vote against the administration would have upon the king. George III, who looked upon Wilkes's attack on his ministers as an attack upon himself, was incensed that a general officer in his army and a man holding a Court appointment should have presumed to vote in opposition to his sovereign's known wishes. He told his chief minister George Grenville that he could not tust his army to the hands of those who were against his measures and demanded that Conway should be deprived of his command and his Court post.

When the news of the king's angry reaction reached Walpole, he was mortified to think that he had been responsible for his cousin's impending disgrace and rushed about trying to use such influence as he had to persuade ministers to placate the royal wrath. At the same time, he was himself angry at what he considered to be yet another example of the abuse of the royal prerogative and a vindictive one at that, for it was clear that Conway alone had been singled out for punishment even though other officers had voted with him when the House divided. George Grenville himself was a little shocked at the extent of the king's displeasure and tried to ward off the blow; he was only able to delay it, however, and in April 1764, five months after the fatal vote, it was announced that General Conway was relieved of the command of his regiment of dragoons and dismissed from the post of Groom of the Bedchamber.

Walpole was furious, and felt compelled to retire to Strawberry Hill until he had sufficiently regained his composure. He immediately offered Conway £6,000, all of his invested capital, to compensate him for his loss of income, and when this was declined he flung himself with energy into the battle of pamphlets that ensued, attacking and counter-attacking those who dared to criticize his cousin's stand against arbitrary power. Conway bore his public rebuke with stoic calm, rising grandly above the dust and storm of controversy. His cold and disdainful disregard for the machinations of Court and Government left Walpole spellbound with admiration. Two days after the royal edict had been proclaimed, he wrote on 24 April:

I rejoice that you feel your loss so little. That you act with dignity and propriety does not surprise me. To have you behave in character and with character, is my first of all wishes; for then it will not be in the power of man to make you unhappy. Ask yourself—Is there a man in England with whom you would change character? Is there a man in England who would not change with you? Then think how little they have taken away!

To Horace Mann in Florence he wrote extolling his cousin's courage in misfortune, declaring his temper, patience and resignation as being beyond example: 'His calmness and content prove how much his mind is at ease. He would not bear his sufferings with such fortitude if his conduct had not been as pure as virtue itself.' Never had he held his cousin in such esteem; never had his hero-worship seemed so justified.

⇥ 2 ⇤

They were soon to have their revenge on the unfortunate ministers, and it was to bring to Walpole his greatest political triumph and his greatest personal disillusionment. Very soon the Government was itself in serious trouble with the king. George III's illness in 1765 had shown the need for a regency bill and the necessary legislation was laid before Parliament. But by some series of misunderstandings the Government, in drafting the bill, had omitted the name of the Princess Augusta, dowager princess of Wales and mother of the king. What led to this miscalculation does not concern us here, but it resulted in the king's loss of confidence in his ministers, and it soon became clear to the opposition groupings that the days of the Grenville administration were numbered.

Walpole now threw himself into the complicated business of trying to weld the various divergent elements opposed to the Government into something resembling a party that could take its place. Rarely had he exerted himself so hard in any political undertaking, often frustrated by the indecision he met with and the apparent inability of 'any three to assemble and enter into concert'. It was tiring and unrewarding work, especially when his 'political frenzy' often met with so little response. He was even compelled to swallow his pride and make friends with the Duke of Newcastle, a man he had ridiculed for years. It was not a very enlivening experience. 'With regard to the Duke of Newcastle,' he wrote in his *Memoirs*, 'whom I had always despised, and with whom a common cause had obliged me to act, I did find how well grounded my contempt of him had been, and to how little purpose it was to act with him.' He met with no more encouragement from many of the people he was trying to help than he had received from the duke, and even Conway contrived to snub him when he attempted to establish an alliance between his cousin and William Pitt.

When the Government at length fell in July 1765, and the final discussions and negotiations were taking place for the formation of a new administration Walpole, exhausted by his exertions was laid up with a severe attack of gout and had withdrawn again to Strawberry Hill. Grenville resigned on 16 July and the Marquess of Rockingham was invited to form a government. The moment of triumph for Walpole's friends had come at last, but the coalition that Rockingham led was of such fragile construction that at first Walpole almost felt it his duty to warn Conway against taking office. He was at least able to dissuade him from accepting the post of Chancellor of the Exchequer when it was offered to him, and approved when Conway refused it 'with a vehemence much beyond his natural temper'. On the other hand, he quite agreed that his cousin was 'excellently fitted' for the office of Secretary of State, a post that was then divided between the southern and the northern departments. With Conway's appointment as Secretary of State for the southern department (which at that time embraced many of the duties now undertaken by the Foreign Secretary) Walpole had the satisfaction of seeing his cousin officially restored to royal favour and placed in a position of prestige and power. He was, for the moment, thoroughly content with the situation and felt that he could congratulate himself upon the part he had played in bringing it about. His sense of satisfaction was soon to be shattered, however, and his previously unquestioning devotion to Henry Conway was to receive a severe blow.

Walpole had always maintained his independence of close political alliances, and beyond proclaiming himself a firm and redoubtable Whig liked to enjoy what he described to Lord Holland as the liberty of pleasing himself without being tied to party. With this went his known unwillingness to hold a Cabinet office, a disinclination he had often expressed. But as he lay at Strawberry Hill in July 1765 suffering the agonies of gout—'I have been extremely ill for these last sixteen days,' he wrote to Mann, 'with the gout all over me, in head, stomach, and both feet . . . Oh! it is a venemous devil!'—he consoled himself with the thought that the offer of some post, 'some considerable employment', would be made to him by the administration. He was in no doubt but that he would refuse any such proposal, yet after all the work he had done in the past months in undermining Grenville's power and in organizing an effective alternative party, he considered that some sort of token offer was the very least that was due to him. He could, he felt absolutely sure, rely upon Conway to see that this was done. He did not covet office but, as he quite frankly confessed in his *Memoirs*, his vanity would have been gratified in refusing it. The extent of his mortification can only be guessed when he discovered not only that no offer of any sort would be made to him, but that in the discussions that had taken place when the new ministry was being formed, his name had not been so much as mentioned.

What made the new Government's neglect all the more humiliating was the fact that Conway had known quite well what Walpole wanted but had been too lacking in gratitude or imagination to do anything about it. It now became clear to Walpole that Conway had all along taken his friendship and devotion for granted. He had inflicted this deep wound to Walpole's feelings not from any malice or ill will but from sheer thoughtlessness and lack of perception. It was not just the question of a 'place' or office; Walpole had another grievance that he had hoped the new ministers would redress. In the past both Henry Fox (who claimed to be his friend) and George Grenville had made a habit of delaying the payments due to him as Usher of the Exchequer as a means of putting political pressure on him or punishing him for lack of parliamentary support, which was mortifying to someone who prided himself on the fact that he owed no debt to any party or faction. He now expected Conway to ensure that his payments might be secured in such a way that, as he put it, he would not be exposed to the 'caprice or wanton tyranny of every succeeding Minister'. He had mentioned this to his cousin when they were both in opposition, hoping that something would be done when their political fortunes changed for the better. Conway had received his complaints in silence and now, when it was in his power to relieve his anxiety, did nothing. It was not, as Walpole knew, in his own nature to repeat such a hint. He had to accept his neglect in indignant silence while he watched Conway scheming to have his brother appointed Lord-Lieutenant of Ireland in order that the Paris embassy could go to the Duke of Richmond who had married Lady Ailesbury's daughter by her first marriage. It was plain from the way he helped his brother and his Campbell relations that it was from no scrupulous principle that Conway had failed to remember his cousin Horace. 'Such failure of friendship,' Walpole lamented, 'or, call it by its truer name, such insensibility, could not but shock a heart at once so tender and so proud as mine.'

He was determined, in so far as his public demeanour was concerned, that he would give no indication of how deeply he was offended and hurt; and he also resolved that he would say nothing in private to his cousin who was completely unaware of the distress he had caused. But though he had sufficient command over himself to appear before the world with his 'wonted cheerfulness', as though nothing had disturbed the calm tranquillity of his existence, in the seclusion of his study, as he toiled at the pages of the memoirs that no eye but his would see until after his death, he poured out his feelings without restraint. He did not blame the other members of the Government. Why should the Duke of Cumberland whom he had never courted, or the Duke of Newcastle whom he had constantly ridiculed, or Rockingham whom he had treated 'with a very moderate share of regard' be concerned to recognize his claims when no demand was made on his behalf by his own intimate friend and near relation? He wrote:

> He must be supposed to know my mind best, if he was silent, what called on them to be more solicitous for my interest? But what could excuse this neglect in Mr. Conway? For him I had sacrificed everything; for him I had been injured, oppressed, calumniated. The foundation of his own fortune, and almost every step of his fortune, he owed solely to me. How thoroughly soever he knew my sentiments, was a compliment at least not due to me? Whatever was due to me, much or little, he totally forgot it; and so far from once endeavouring to secure my independence, in his whole life after he never once mentioned it.

It is never very pleasant to discover that one's idol has feet of clay, and Walpole was now going through this disagreeable process. Conway, in fact, had a very literal mind. He knew that Walpole had never sought office; he presumed that if he had changed his mind he would say so; he lacked the mental finesse to see that someone could want what they did not ask for and be flattered by having the opportunity to decline what they did not want. All this was too subtle for his cut and dried military approach. But he could appreciate straightforward acts of kindness and in fact was not ungrateful for the help he had received. When Walpole offered him financial assistance after he had been dismissed his regiment, though refusing the help he told his brother that 'Horace Walpole has on this occasion, shown the warmth of friendship that you know him capable of, so strongly that I want words to express it.' Conway has been described somewhat unkindly as having been 'a better soldier than he was a general, a better general than a statesman'. If Walpole had elevated him into a hero of romance and was now disappointed when he failed to live up to this dream, the fault was not Conway's. Yet even in the bitterness of his distress, Walpole could not fail to respect the other's solid if unimaginative qualities. 'His temper hurt me,' he concluded, 'but I forgave his virtue, of which I am confident, and know it was superior to my own.'

Walpole's way of showing his displeasure was to leave for Paris as soon as his health had sufficiently recovered and he felt fit enough to undertake the journey. The only favour he asked of Conway was on behalf of his old friend Horace Mann, for as Secretary of State for the southern department his cousin had responsibility for all foreign missions. Walpole asked that Mann should be promoted to the rank of envoy and the request was granted. He also secured a promise from Conway that Mann's name would be submitted for the Order of the Bath when the next red ribbon was bestowed, but this request could not be gratified at once as several other people had prior claims.

Just how little Conway realized that he had offended his cousin is shown by the annoyance and slight peevishness he displayed when he heard of the other's plan for an extended visit to the French capital. He was so used to coming to Walpole for advice that he felt quite lost without it, especially now that he had the responsibility of office. In his memoirs Walpole recorded:

He no sooner discovered that my intention was to remain in France much longer than he expected, than he broke out into complaints, entreaties, and reproaches: and, as if he had satisfied all the duties of friendship, and I had violated them, he tried with angry words to divert me from my purpose, urged the occasion he should have for my advice, and called my retreat a desertion of friends.

Walpole almost enjoyed the irony of the situation. He treated the matter 'lightly, civilly, and desultorily' (which must have annoyed Conway even more) and reminded his cousin that he had always meant to quit the political scene as soon as their party was successful, a fact that the other could not deny. He then added 'with a little mixture of conscious scorn' that he knew the obligations the party had to him but of none he owed to them. With that he left for France with 'inflexible, and consequently mysterious cheerfulness', leaving the ingenuous and uncomplicated Conway utterly bewildered and decidedly disgruntled.

The quarrel or misunderstanding (for it never developed into an open quarrel) between the cousins lost much of its bitterness for Walpole after the soothing experience of his reception in Paris where he was soon to meet Madame du Deffand and enjoy the stimulating sensation of 'tottering into vogue'. When he came back to England in April 1766 the friendship with Conway was resumed, though Walpole could no longer regard himself as the other's political mentor. He had, in any case, finally decided to retire from the House of Commons and at the next general election he did not offer himself again to the loyal citizens of King's Lynn. His interest in politics remained and he continued to regale Mann with bulletins of political news and gossip, but he had lost his desire to be an active participant. Conway remained in office until 1768 when he decided to return to military life. He had continued to serve under Chatham and the Duke of Grafton after Rockingham's dismissal in July 1766, when he remained in the Cabinet as a Secretary of State but was transferred to the northern department. His period in power was not noted for any particularly dramatic measures, but he showed a consistently lenient attitude to the aspirations of the American colonists which resulted in the people of Boston asking for his portrait and in new settlements being named after him in Massachusetts and New Hampshire, a fairly unique distinction for a British minister at that period.

❖ 3 ❖

If Conway was rather dull and plodding in his public character, he came into his own in the setting of his private life which was happy and secure. In 1751, he had bought Park Place at Henley-on-Thames, and this remained his country house for the rest of his life. Lady Mary Coke describes a visit there in July 1768 when Walpole and David Hume were also of the party. One needed to be a good walker, she complained, to keep company with the General and Lady Ailesbury, but she found it a delightful place even though the hills were steep to someone who preferred a game of cards to a country walk. 'After taking a very long walk, we play'd at Bowls,' she wrote in her diary. 'It is a great while since I play'd, yet I think they agree I was one of the best of the Party. When it grew dark, we came in and finished the Evening with Pope Joan. I won eighteen shillings.' One day, after a number of visits and excursions in the neighbourhood, the party returned to Park Place with 'a very good stomach' for their dinner. Walpole had just finished writing his play *The Mysterious Mother* and it was on this occasion that he had quoted some passages to Lady Mary. Talk about the drama seemed to be a theme of the day, which would not have been unusual at the Conways'. Over the meal they all launched into an attack on the unfortunate David Hume who had admitted that he did not like Shakespeare. 'Wou'd you have thought it possible,' Lady Mary asks, 'that a Man of Genius shou'd not be able to discover the Beauties of that admirable Writer?'

Nearly twenty years later Hannah More, the religious writer and poet, a very different character from the somewhat worldly Lady Mary, visited the Conways and gave another picture of life as it continued in their circle. 'I spent a day at Lady Ailesbury's,' the pious authoress of *The Religion of the Fashionable World* wrote in 1787.

> In the evening there was a concert; it was quite 'le temple des beaux arts'. Lady Ailesbury works portraits as Raphael paints; and there was Mrs. Damer to remind us of her famous dogs of exquisite sculpture, and there was my Lord Derby to talk about his company of Richmond House Comedians, and there was General Conway, poet of the ducal theatre.

Between them, Conway and his wife had established quite a reputation as patrons of the arts. Sir Joshua Reynolds was a close friend and the portrait painter Angelica Kauffmann owed to them her first introduction to London society. One altogether more curious foreigner who was sometimes to be seen with them was that strange transvestite the Chevalier d'Eon or, if one preferred it, Mademoiselle d'Eon, for at this period he appeared in London in the character of a woman and was generally thought to be one, though many people had their doubts. Among the latter was the Earl of Mount Edgcumbe, brother of Walpole's friend Dick Edgcumbe, who declared, when asked his opinion on the tantalizing question of her sex, that Mademoiselle d'Eon was her own widow.

It was in this cultivated and urbane atmosphere, with its cosmopolitan background, that the Conways' daughter Anne grew to womanhood, occasionally, as we have seen, exchanging Park Place for Strawberry Hill when her parents were abroad. She had shown her gift for modelling quite early in life. David Hume, so the story goes, had rebuked the child for laughing at the rather poor work of an itinerant Italian sculptor: her reply was to model a head in wax just to show that she could do as well, if not better, than the artist whose work she had criticized. Her parents encouraged the talent. She studied under John Bacon, sculptor of Dr Johnson's statue in St Paul's Cathedral, and later under Joseph Ceracchi, an Italian artist roughly her contemporary in age who was in London between 1773 and 1791 and who himself carved a statue of her as the muse of sculpture. This was presumably after her husband's death when she took up her art more seriously and established her fame for rather sentimental animal studies as well as portrait busts. Her skill was sufficiently professional for her enemies to spread the report that she was helped in her work by 'ghosts', but there is no evidence that this was so.

Her marriage in 1767 to the wealthy and profligate John Damer, son and heir to the first Lord Milton, later Earl of Dorchester, had been unhappy from the start and ended in tragedy. Neither party was particularly well suited for marriage. Anne Seymour Conway was a handsome but rather masculine woman; the artist Joseph Farington was later to recall seeing her wearing a man's hat, jacket and shoes. Her emotional tendency lay in the direction of intense relationships with other women, and after becoming a widow when only twenty-seven, she gave no inclination of ever wishing to remarry. The marriage was entirely one of convenience; there seems to have been little if any love or affection between the couple, and there were no children in the nine years it lasted. Her husband was wild, dissipated and improvident. Though heir to an annual income of £30,000 he managed, with the inordinate capacity of young eighteenth-century aristocrats for irresponsible extravagance, to run into debt to the extent of £70,000 by the age of thirty-two. It is true that he was assisted in his folly by his two young brothers, but even so there was almost an epic quality in the scale of his ability for self-inflicted ruin. By August 1776, his affairs had reached a crisis. His marriage had virtually broken down and his father, unexpectedly apprised of his son's burden of debt, had flatly refused to pay it. On 15 August, his brothers having fled to France, Damer solved his problems in his own way as Walpole described five days later in a letter to Horace Mann:

> On Thursday, Mr. Damer supped at the Bedford Arms in Covent Garden, with four common women, a blind fiddler, and no other man. At three in the morning he dismissed his seraglio, bidding each receive her guinea at the bar, and ordering Orpheus to come up again in half an hour. When he returned, he found a dead silence, and smelt gunpowder. He called, the master of the house came up, and found Mr. Damer sitting in his chair, dead, with a pistol by him, and another in his pocket! The ball had not gone through his head, nor made any report. On the table lay a scrap of paper with these words, 'The people of the house are not to blame for what has happened, which was my own act.' This was the sole tribute he paid to justice and decency!

The immediate effect upon the young widow, whose heart was quite obviously not broken by the tragedy, was that she had to sell all her jewels, which Walpole described as being magnificent, to help discharge the debt. Her father-in-law not only continued in his refusal to help but turned his fury on the innocent survivor, an injustice which she bore without resentment. The suicide, meanwhile, became a fascinating topic among Walpole's friends. Lord Carlisle wrote to George Selwyn, that connoisseur of the macabre:

> What were Mr. Damer's motives for so dreadful an action? There was no man more indifferent to me, but the account shocked me extremely. It is a bad example to others in misery. It makes people

think of having recourse to that method of finishing their calamities, without which, perhaps, it had never entered their heads. If it were not so selfish an action, it would be difficult, I think, to condemn it in some cases. There never appeared anything like madness in him, yet the company he kept seemed indeed but a bad preparation for eternity!

In spite of her husband's pile of debts and the loss of her jewellery, Anne Damer remained in quite comfortable circumstances. As Walpole, with his sharp eye for the practical, pointed out to Mann, Lord Milton could make no more demands on her after the jewels were gone: 'This is all the hurt he can do her; she must have her jointure of 2,500*l* a-year.' Her husband's wardrobe had meanwhile been sold. It raised the sum of £15,000, a quite extraordinary amount which would have to be multiplied very many times to represent its value in present-day terms. It helps to give some idea of the extravagant scale of John Damer's life, a life upon which his widow now resolutely turned her back as she reached for the sculptor's apron and chisel which, as she directed, would one day be buried with her.

She now had her own house in town, and divided her time between London and her parents' place at Henley. She also became an indefatigable traveller, once even being captured by French privateers, paying visits to France and Italy. Introducing her to Horace Mann before a projected visit to Florence, Walpole wrote: 'In Italy she will be a prodigy. She models like Bernini, has excelled the moderns in the similitudes of her busts and has lately begun one in marble.' It was typical of the overpraise he always lavished on the artistic efforts of his friends, as when, in his *Anecdotes of Painting*, he claimed that her work was 'not inferior to the antique'. It was a fault of generosity rather than taste, and one that was not altogether unique to Walpole. When considering late nineteenth- and early twentieth-century sculptors the name of Violet, Duchess of Rutland, does not immediately spring to mind, for all that she was not without talent; yet Rodin compared her to Donatello and G. F. Watts to Holbein. Even when his opinions were sometimes rather silly, Walpole usually found himself in good company.

His exaggerated praise for Anne Damer's work sprang from the fact that she was the daughter of the cousin he could not cease to

admire even after the disillusioning experience at the time of the
Rockingham ministry. She was, indeed, almost like a daughter to
him. He was blind to the harsher side of her character and showed his
affection for her by leaving her a life interest in his house and
collection at Strawberry Hill. But not everyone saw her with such
uncritical eyes. We get a more independent view of her character
from a contemporary, Lady Sarah Lennox, writing in 1778, two
years after her husband's death, when the slight slur of scandal caused
by that event had not quite subsided.

> Upon the whole [Lady Sarah wrote], I think she is a sensible
> woman without sensibility, a pretty one without pleasing, a
> prudent one without conduct, and I believe nobody will have a
> *right* to tax her with any fault, yet she will be abused, which I take
> to be owing to a want of sweetness in her disposition; she is too
> *strictly right* even to be beloved.

Towards the end of Walpole's life one begins to detect a slight note
of impatience in some of Anne Damer's references to him which
suggest that the affection he felt for her was not always reciprocated
to the same degree. Her brisk, masculine mind was not of the kind to
sympathize with the infirmities and occasional querulousness of old
age in others. There was, in addition, another more subtle and
unexpressed reason for the spasmodic irritation that appears in some
of her remarks about him in her letters, comments that fall just short
of hostility as when, after one of his illnesses, she wrote unkindly to
Mary Berry: 'I am sure, when I think of *what* his dinners are, and
how he eats them, I wonder he and his cat are not sick together every
day for their desert.' These outbursts sprang from a hidden jealousy
of which Walpole was completely unaware and to which Mrs Damer
could make no open reference: they were both in love with the same
person.

Walpole's deep affection for Mary Berry, which warmed the last
years of his life, will be dealt with at a later stage; what concerns us
here is the fact that Mrs Damer had also fallen under the spell of that
charming young lady. Miss Berry had an extremely sympathetic
personality and in her Anne Damer found someone to whom she
could pour out her troubles and offer affection as she could to few
other people. They soon became fast friends after Walpole

introduced them to each other, though the passion was all on Mrs Damer's side. In October 1793 she wrote to Mary Berry:

> I am just come in late from my walk . . . but I find that I can settle to nothing till I have thanked you, dear kind soul, for your letter which I received this morning, for writing to me oftener than I could expect, which, besides the gratification of hearing from you, of reading your letters, so well assures me that you know how I feel the comfort I receive from them. I write to you about my head-aches and about my finger-aches, because you encourage me, and there is nothing I would not wish to hear from you: however trifling it may appear to yourself, to me it can not.

The following December she wrote expressing the need she felt for her friend's company. She began, 'I feel uncomfortable when more than a day or two passes without writing to you . . .' and ended:

> When you can say in truth, that I in any degree contribute to your comfort or composure of mind, can I hear it too often! It is, Heaven is my judge! my first wish, and my mind is too apt to run to the painful idea of adding to your anxieties. How then must I feel the thousand kind methods your friendship takes to smooth the melancholy you *know* I must at times suffer from.

That Walpole should act possessively over Mary Berry, as he very often did, provoked the other woman's anger and resentment; she was irritated when he read her passages from Miss Berry's letters yet showed no interest when she offered to read him extracts from the letters written to herself, and she made rather cruel fun of him when he boasted 'with all the insolence of a lover' over three letters he had just received, writing in a conspiratorial way to the object of their joint affection: 'I am sometimes diverted with this, and shall (I hope) one day laugh at him about it with you. Sometimes I do not half like it; when occupied with one subject, he talks to me with his life and quickness, of another.' Both of them, it must be admitted, acted a little pettishly where Miss Berry was concerned, as another example from Mrs Damer's correspondence shows. Walpole was very concerned, as well he might have been, when the Berry sisters made a journey through France in the ominous, revolutionary year of 1791. Anne Damer was with him at Strawberry Hill with a friend named simply as Louisa, whose presence clearly constrained Walpole when he wished to give vent to his anxiety. 'The tea over Louisa went to her room,' Mrs Damer wrote to the innocent cause of his distress.

> I saw that he was all impatience and bursting with something he wanted to say to me. She had scarcely shut the door when his face changed, and with an expression of much concern he told me that you was to come through France. On my trying to comfort him, and saying what I really *now* in a great measure think, he quite hurt me by suddenly checking himself and saying 'that one had better keep one's ideas and anxieties to oneself' or to that effect. I am sure if partaking them gives a right I have as good a right as himself.

There can be no doubt that Walpole was quite unaware of this undercurrent of emotional jealousy, this sub-plot, as it were, to his romantic friendship for Mary Berry. His regard for Mrs Damer did not diminish in any way as he reached the end of his life. How strong Mary Berry's feelings were for Anne Damer we cannot say beyond the fact that a very close friendship existed between them. After Walpole's death they travelled together both on the Continent and in England, and Miss Berry took part in the amateur theatricals that Mrs Damer organized at Strawberry Hill after it came into her possession; but it seems unlikely from what we know of her character that there was the same intensity of feeling on her side, though the friendship endured until Mrs Damer's death. The devotion Mary Berry showed to Walpole's memory after his death, the untiring work she put into the editing of his papers, and the vigour with which she countered Macaulay's attack on him in the *Edinburgh Review* all point to the fact that there were no reservations in the sincerity of her feelings for him. Mrs Damer, on the other hand, was one of the few of Walpole's correspondents who gave orders for the destruction of all the letters she had received from him, and they were burned with her other papers after her death. Whether she ordered this from mere indifference or was inspired by some obscure motive of revenge, it was at least an indication that she did not hold his memory in any very great respect.

❈❈❈ 4 ❈❈❈

General Conway was to hold office again in 1782 when the Marquess of Rockingham returned briefly to power in March and remained in

office until the marquess's unexpected and premature death the
following July. It was, however, more a military than a political post
that Conway filled for he was appointed commander-in-chief of the
army with a seat in the Cabinet. The ministry of 1782 was also the
first one in which Charles James Fox was to hold Cabinet office as
Secretary of State. As the son of his old, if somewhat unreliable,
friend Henry Fox, first Lord Holland, Walpole was delighted with
the appointment, and coupled it with his cousin's promotion in his
letter of 5 May to Horace Mann:

> Perhaps I am partial to Charles Fox because he resembles my
> father in good sense—I wish he had his excellent constitution too;
> yet his application to business may preserve his life, which his
> former dissipation constantly endangered. Another advantage we
> have is in Mr. Conway's being at the head of the Army. With him
> nobody stands in competition. His military knowledge is
> unquestionably without a rival.

There is something of the old hero-worshipping in the tone of
Walpole's reference to his cousin's military renown, though whether
his opinion would have been endorsed in the same uncritical way by
Conway's brother officers is another matter.

Before his appointment as commander-in-chief Conway had been
Governor of Jersey which had been a post of some danger after
France had declared her support for the American colonies in 1778
and joined in the war against England. It was in the following year
that Anne Damer had her brush with the French privateer. In those
days, independent travellers were not in the habit of allowing
anything so inconvenient as a war to divert their plans, and Mrs
Damer had set out for France on the Dover packet with the Duchess
of Leinster and Lady William Campbell just as calmly as they would
have done in the time of peace. Adventure soon overtook them,
however, as Walpole first heard from Lady Ailesbury when she came
to see him at Strawberry Hill, 'all terror and distress' at her
daughter's fate. 'Her daughter was really taken prisoner, and she had
been told her husband and his island were captive too,' he informed
Lady Ossory on 20 June. Fortunately, the situation was not quite so
black as Lady Ailesbury had first thought, though the packet had
been engaged in a running fight for several hours. The captain of the
French ship, it seemed, was 'a Paladin in disguise' and behaved with

exemplary courtesy. He not only treated his prisoners 'with the continence of Scipio, but with disinterest, a virtue still more rare in a freebooter'. Instead of demanding a ransom he would not touch a pin, so Walpole was told. The ladies were informed that they could go wherever they pleased, and Mrs Damer was soon reunited with her father on the island of Jersey which had not, after all, been invaded by the enemy.

In spite of the slight anticlimax to the story, Walpole was immensely proud of the valour shown by Anne Damer, and indeed she was probably in her element in such a situation of danger. She was certainly not the kind of woman who would have flinched or swooned away as the guns began to fire. Hearing of the safe outcome of the affray, Walpole wrote to Lady Ailesbury:

> I am not at all surprised, my dear Madam, at the intrepidity of Mrs. Damer, she always was the heroic daughter of a hero. Her sense and coolness never forsake her. I, who am not so firm, shuddered at your Ladyship's account. Now that she has stood fire for four hours, I hope she will give as clear proofs of her understanding, of which I have as high opinion as of her courage, and not return in any danger.

For a man like Walpole, who instinctively shuddered at the horrors of war, the fact that General Conway could turn his hand to a set of verses or adapt a play from the French was a matter for congratulation as well as praise. The art-loving side of Conway's nature was always there and was not to be suppressed even on purely military occasions. When Frederick II of Prussia, the greatest soldier of the age, received him in audience at Berlin in 1774, the English general admired the splendid first battalion of foot guards, 'so well dressed, such men, and so punctual in all they did', but also noticed and recorded with equal interest how music still occupied much of that warlike monarch's time, observing in his room about twenty boxes with a German flute in each one.

When he retired from active military command, he was at last able to indulge his talent for prose and verse, and though the result has been described as 'correct and unreadable', it at least inspired some lines of panegyric from Walpole in celebration of his cousin's ability at 'writing so well in various ways which you never practised when you was much younger'. The six lines were dispatched to Conway in

September 1789 in return for a tale which the admiring recipient described as 'very pretty and easy and genteel':

> The Muse, most wont to fire a youthful heart,
> To gild *your* setting sun reserves his art;
> To crown a life in virtuous labours pass'd,
> Bestow'd her numbers, and her wit at last;
> And, when your strength and eloquence retire,
> Your voice in notes harmonious shall expire.

'The *swan* was too common a thought to be directly specified, and, perhaps, even alluded to,' the poet modestly added when he sent the lines to his old friend, 'no matter, such a trifle is below criticism.'

Private theatricals, in which all the Conway family delighted, had become something of a craze at this period in which both children and adults indulged themselves. The setting for the production of Conway's *False Appearances* was Richmond House, the London home of Lady Ailesbury's son-in-law, where a company of amateurs headed by Lord Derby put on a series of entertainments. After seeing a performance, Walpole wrote to Lord Stafford on 17 June 1788:

> Mr. Conway's play, of which your Lordship has seen some account in the papers, has succeeded delightfully, both in representation and applause. The language is most genteel, though translated from verse; and both prologue and epilogue are charming. The former was delivered most justly and admirably by Lord Derby, and the latter with inimitable spirit and grace by Mrs. Damer.

The juxtaposition of the names of Lord Derby and Mrs Damer was to occur again as a result of this play in circumstances rather embarrassing to the latter, but in such a way as to show that her attachments to other women were no great secret. When the play received its professional production in the following year, the cast was graced by Elizabeth Farren, with whom Lord Derby was in love. This well-known fact, however, did not protect her from certain sneers later appearing in print to suggest that the real object of her affections was Anne Damer. Hinting that Lord Derby would marry her when he was free to do so, as indeed he did, a malicious publication called *The Whig Club, or a Sketch of Modern Patriotism* declared of Miss Farren that 'superior to the influence of MEN, she is

supposed to feel more exquisite delight from the touch of the cheek
of Mrs D—r than the fancy of any *novelties* which the wedding night
can promise with such a partner as his lordship.' Elizabeth Farren
was certainly a friend of Anne Damer's and was an occasional guest at
Park Place, but apart from this there seems to have been no ground
for bringing this particular accusation against her, and her name was
probably only used as a means of attacking Mrs Damer, whose Whig
sentiments were as loudly proclaimed as any less acceptable
proclivities might be whispered.

It was due to the Conways, or more particularly to Lady
Ailesbury, that Walpole was able to clap eyes on someone who had
long been an object of his curiosity. This was Princess Louise of
Stolberg-Gedern, known as the Countess of Albany, the widow of
Prince Charles Edward Stuart. Walpole had always shown an interest
in the rather pathetic shadow court that the 'young Pretender'
maintained, first in Florence and then in Rome, and had treasured
any morsel of gossip that Sir Horace Mann, the nearest British
representative to the exiled royal family, could pass on to him.
Politically, of course, he had never entertained a shred of sympathy
for the Stuarts; their interest for him was now purely historical. He
saw them, ever since the disaster of 1745, as belonging entirely to the
past, and prefaced a request for news about Prince Charles, in a letter
to Mann, with the phrase: 'I interest myself little in novelties, but I
own I have some remains of curiosity from ancient impressions.'
When the prince married in 1772, rather late in life for someone
whose main duty was to perpetuate a dynasty, Walpole was eager to
learn all he could about the young woman he termed the
'Pretendress', whom he believed to be 'but sixteen and a Lutheran'
though in fact she was twenty and a Catholic. When, eight years later,
the marriage broke up and Louise ran off with the poet Vittorio
Alfieri, the scandal fascinated him and he wrote a slightly garbled
account of the whole *opera buffa* episode to Lady Ossory, laying
more stress on the drunken behaviour of the Prince than on the frail
morality of his wife.

The Countess of Albany's grandmother, who had married a prince
of Hornes, was the daughter of a former earl of Ailesbury, which
gave her a connection with the family of Caroline Ailesbury's first
husband, and so made the Countess a distant kinswoman of General
Conway's wife, a point of natural interest to anyone so genealogi-

cally minded as Walpole. That the Countess should visit England at all was rather extraordinary, but that she should also (with an eye on a pension) curry favour with the reigning Hanoverian dynasty, showed a lack of sensitivity that was characteristic of her. To Walpole, who had witnessed the state trials of the rebel lords after the insurrection of 1745 and had recorded their brave deportment on the scaffold, there was something piquantly ironic in the thought of the 'Pretender's Queen' being received by the family of George III. But the time of her arrival, May 1791, when the French Revolution was beginning to take a more ugly turn and English society was accustoming itself to the presence of distinguished *émigrés* from across the Channel, gave her a measure of excuse, especially as she came to London directly from Paris.

It was on 19 May that Walpole wrote to Mary Berry telling her of the interesting foreigner's arrival:

> The Countess of Albany is not only in England, in London, but at this very moment, I believe, in the palace of St. James's—not restored by as rapid a revolution as the French, but, as was observed last night at supper at Lady Mount Edgcumbe's, by that topsy-turvy-hood that characterises the present age.

The 'young' Countess of Ailesbury, wife of the successor to the other Lady Ailesbury's first husband, was, so he heard, to present her relative at Court. Walpole was both fascinated and at the same time slightly shocked. He could appreciate the Countess's curiosity to visit England, and realized that she could have had little love for her husband, indeed that she had probably abhorred him, yet all the same he thought her behaviour neither very sensible, nor very well bred to her former husband's family. Her brother-in-law, the Cardinal of York, was, after all, still living in Italy and had not in any way abandoned his family's royal claims. Walpole could not wait, however, to add a postscript to his letter that evening describing the encounter at St James's Palace:

> Well! I have had an exact account of the interview of the two Queens, from one who stood close to them. The Dowager was announced as Princess of Stolberg. She was well dressed, and not at all embarrassed. The King talked to her a good deal; but about her passage, the sea, and general topics: the Queen in the same way,

but less ... The Queen looked at her earnestly. To add to the singularity of the day, it is the Queen's birthday.

When Walpole finally saw the 'Pretendress', he was rather disappointed. He was invited to a 'small assemblage' to meet her, and went with General Conway, Lady Ailesbury and some other friends who had all breakfasted with him the same day at Strawberry Hill. 'Well! I have seen Madame d'Albany, who has not a rag of royalty about her,' he wrote to the Berry sisters on 2 June. 'She has good eyes and teeth; but I think can have had no more beauty than remains, except youth. She is civil and easy, but German and ordinary.' His disappointment gave way to distaste when he learnt that on 10 June, the day when the Jacobites celebrated the 'old Pretender's' birth as White Rose Day, the Countess chose to watch George III in his crown and royal robes proroguing Parliament in the House of Lords. 'What an odd *rencontre*!' he commented. 'Was it philosophy or insensibility?'

Before the Countess of Albany left England, Lady Ailesbury asked her down to Park Place, but some complications arose in which the actress Elizabeth Farren again played an unconscious role. It involved an obscure point of etiquette of importance only to royal personages, but all the more delicate when the royalty in question was of the insubstantial variety enjoyed by the Countess. A letter from Mrs Damer to Edward Jerningham, a friend of hers and of Walpole's, gives some impression of the problem at issue but leaves us in doubt as to whether the intended visit was ever actually made.

My mother is in one of her grand distresses about Mme. D'Albany [Mrs Damer wrote], and if you can assist, it will be most acceptable and gratefully received by her. Mme. D'Albany was to have come today, and to have stayed two nights. Miss Farren has been appointed, and was fixed on next Wednesday. To-day Mad. D'Albany writes me word that one of her horses is lame, and that she can not come today, but will the first day her horse is well, or take post. Now she may not quite like Miss Farren, who, you know, does not speak French well; and it would not be the thing, and *de plus* the house would be very full. That however might be arranged. What I wish you to do is, if you can, to hasten her coming, that she may go on Wednesday; or, if that can not be, to *convey* to her *Royal* comprehension whom she will find here, so that she may not be surprised. But all this must come *purely* from yourself; as the least hint from *us* would be like wishing her not to come, and have an appearance of the *comédienne's* not giving way to the *Queen*—which is not the true state of the case. Do the best you can, and let me know.

Whether Jerningham, whose talents lay in the direction of sentimental poetry rather than drawing-room diplomacy, was able to sort out this little problem does not transpire. Walpole, one feels sure, would have succeeded.

The shadow of the French Revolution, of which the Countess of Albany's temporary presence in England was a very minor consequence, cast a gloom over the final years of General Conway, or Field-Marshal as he became in 1793. Both he and Walpole had friends in France whose fate was to cause them much anxiety. As lifelong Whigs, they had at first entertained some rather faint hopes that there might be a real birth of liberty in France, but the excesses of the revolutionary parties soon made them despair. As early as 15 July 1789, when only vague rumours of rioting in Paris had reached London and the fall of the Bastille the previous day was not yet known, Walpole wrote to Conway deploring the opportunities wasted by the States-General. 'They might have obtained many capital points, and removed great oppression,' he maintained. 'No French monarch will ever summon *états* again, if this moment has been thrown away.'

They were both now too old to experience the *frisson* of expectancy that the events in Paris had given to men of the younger generation like their friend Charles James Fox. Though they believed themselves devoted to the idea of liberty, to them equality was by definition incompatible with it and fraternity little more than a sentimental abstraction. To Walpole, the Revolution appeared as a profanation of true liberty which he could not conceive of as existing without order and justice. The very reasons that had made him support the American revolution now turned him against the French. 'How franticly have the French acted, and how rationally the Americans!' he wrote to his cousin in July 1790. 'But Franklin and Washington were great men. None have appeared yet in France; and Necker has only returned to make a wretched figure.' Even so, his reaction to the mounting horrors daily reported from France did not have the effect of throwing him completely into the opposite political camp; he did not lose the sense of balance that he had always prized as a quality of any civilized mind. He could still feel disgust at the sight of some of his own compatriots as they plotted and schemed for what he described to Conway in June 1793 as 'titles, ribands, offices of no business, which anybody can fill, and must be given to many'. It was, in his opinion, no better than being a footman waiting behind a chair. 'The outrageous proceedings of the French republicans have wounded the cause of liberty, and will, I fear, have shaken it for centuries . . .' he continued, 'but I do not see why detestation of anarchy and assassination must immediately make one fall in love with garters and seals.'

Meanwhile, nearer home, there had been poignant reminders of the tragedies that had overtaken some of his friends. In 1787, and again in 1791, the Princesse de Lamballe had visited England and formed a friendship with Lady Ailesbury, on the first occasion going on various sightseeing expeditions with her and, no doubt through Conway's influence, visiting the Royal Military Academy and witnessing a field-day of the Royal Artillery. Walpole had not met her on that occasion, and little guessing the fate in store for her, had written to Lord Strafford: 'I have no particular *penchant* for sterling princes and princesses, much less for those of French plate.' The second visit had occurred in the wake of the flight of the French royal family to Varennes, but after the failure of that desperate attempt at escape, she had bravely returned to Paris despite the Queen's plea for her to remain in the safety of England. Her death at the hands of the mob took place a year later during the September massacres.

When Conway died in 1795, the state of confusion into which the French Revolution had thrown the whole of Europe was still unresolved. Three years before, Walpole had written to the man whose political career he had once championed so ardently expressing his now almost complete sense of disillusionment at the political state of the world. To Conway, who was then still reading all the newspapers from France, Walpole wrote:

I read none, as they have long put me out of all patience: and besides, I hear so much of their horrific proceedings, that they quite disturb me, and have given me what I call the French disease; that is, a barbarity that I abhor, for I cannot help wishing destruction to thousands of human creatures whom I never saw. But when men have worked themselves up into tigers and hyaenas, and labour to communicate their appetite for blood, what signifies whether they walk on two legs or four, or whether they dwell in cities or in forests and dens?

It was a far cry from the time when they had both first taken their seats in the House of Commons in 1741 in the early days of the Enlightenment, when men could still believe that they had just entered into an Age of Reason.

VII
William Cole and
Lady Diana Beauclerk:
Antiquaries, Artists and Collectors

⋙ 1 ⋘

When Walpole set out for France in the autumn of 1765, still smarting from the blow to his pride inflicted by Conway's ingratitude and the indifference of the new administration to his claims for recompense for the services he had done them, he could console himself with the thought that he would be meeting in Paris an old friend who could be relied upon to distract his mind from all things political. This was the Reverend William Cole, a retiring but erudite clergyman who shared with Walpole the background, common to so many of his friends, of Eton and Cambridge, and who was his chief correspondent in all that pertained to his antiquarian and scholarly pursuits. Cole had told him that he was planning to visit France just as Walpole was about to set out himself, and he quickly replied to his friend that the news was most opportune. To think that they might meet on the other side of the Channel was highly agreeable. 'Why should you not advance your journey?' he asked. 'Why defer it till the Winter is coming on? It would make me quite happy to visit churches and convents with you: but they are not comfortable in cold weather. Do, I beseech you, follow me as soon as possible.'

The man to whom this plea was sent had only recently re-established relations with Walpole. They had been friends at school, for all that Cole was three years older (he was born on 3 August 1714) and had occasionally visited Walpole during the holidays at Chelsea, remembering his father Sir Robert as 'a very corpulent, lusty man', and Lady Walpole as being also a 'very lusty well-looking woman' which made him wonder why their youngest son should have had such a 'meagre frame' and been so generally delicate in health. He had already developed an interest in antiquity as a schoolboy and it was this that brought the two friends together. Like Gray, Cole came from comparatively humble origins when compared, at least, with Walpole's aristocratic connections, his father having been a well-to-do Cambridgeshire yeoman farmer who was chiefly remarkable for the fact that he had led four wives to the altar, the second of whom was his senior by twenty-one years. William Cole's mother was the third wife, described as being a cultured woman, but she died when he was only eleven years old, and as his father's fourth marriage was stormy and ended in a separation, the young boy was brought up without the maternal influence which had been such a strong element in Walpole's own childhood.

Unlike the members of the 'Quadruple Alliance', Cole had not been particularly happy at Eton where he later confessed that he had been good for nothing. He fell victim to the brutal system of the day when corporal punishment, even for mere trifles, was the common lot of most of the boys, and on one occasion ran away from school. It is strange to think that this unhappy and inept pupil should have developed into an exceptionally learned and devout priest, but much of his misery and failure to conform during his schooldays can no doubt be attributed to the sense of loss and isolation he felt as a result of his mother's death.

In 1733 he went up to Clare Hall at Cambridge, but instead of entering him as a pensioner or fellow-commoner, as he could well afford to have done, his father had him admitted as a sizar, that is to say as one who depended upon financial help from the foundation for his studies, in order, so the father maintained, to punish his son for his idleness at school. What Eton had failed to do, however, Cambridge succeeded in accomplishing, and it is from this period that Cole's reputation as an authority upon the antiquities of Cambridge and the surrounding parishes was gradually established. In 1735, his father died, leaving him in comfortable circumstances and he was at last able to exchange the somewhat humiliating status of sizar for that of fellow-commoner, and in the following year to migrate from Clare to King's College with its close association with his old school, and where Walpole had already been in residence for a year.

Cole never belonged to the great world of politics or to the exclusive social set, aristocratic and Whig, from among whom most of Walpole's friends were drawn. Though he would have known Selwyn, Edgcumbe and the two Conway brothers at Eton, the only schoolfriend apart from Walpole with whom he kept in touch was Gray, chiefly because the latter lived in Cambridge and Cole himself was never very far away from it. They were, however, more acquaintances than friends, for though Cole admired Gray's genius as a poet and respected his learning, he found his effeminate ways disagreeable and affected. Furthermore Gray, like Walpole, was a staunch Whig, while Cole was a High Church Tory. In this he was unique among the intimate friends who visited Strawberry Hill. What brought Walpole and Cole together was their common interest in antiquity, especially in the 'gothic antiquities' of the medieval world that Walpole found such a source of inspiration; politics they rarely discussed, and when they did they had to agree to differ. As Walpole wrote to him later in life,

> You and I differ radically in our principles, and yet in forty years they have never cast a gloom over our friendship. We could give the world a reason that it would not like. We have both been sincere, have both been consistent and neither adopted our principles nor have varied them for our interest.

They also differed very profoundly in religious matters. Cole was a High Church Anglican who looked back with nostalgia to the days of Archbishop Laud, and had much sympathy with the non-juror bishops who had refused to take the oath to William III. He had an exalted view of the priesthood, did not believe that the clergy should marry, and had a hankering for the monastic life. Living as he did before the revival of monasticism in the Anglican Church, these religious inclinations made him warm towards the Roman Catholic Church, another trait in his character that Walpole could not condone, for to him Rome was synonymous with tyranny and superstition. He could only appreciate the Church of Rome in the same way that he could appreciate a medieval statue or a gothic tomb: something that might stimulate romantic fantasies or provide the model for a stucco chimney-piece. He wrote to Cole:

> I like Popery as well as you and have shown that I do. I like it as I like chivalry and romance. They all furnish one with ideas and

visions, which Presbyterianism does not. A gothic church or a
convent fills one with romantic dreams—but for the mysterious,
the Church in the abstract, it is a jargon that means nothing, or a
great deal too much, and I reject it and its apostles, from
Athanasius to Bishop Ken.

Such views on Walpole's part caused his friend much distress.

He had visions of retiring to the Continent and living in the
neighbourhood of some monastic institution, and even asked
Walpole to look out for a suitable place on his behalf when he first
heard in the summer of 1764 of his friend's plans for a possible visit to
France. Walpole's rather discouraging reply was typical of the
distrust he felt for Cole's religious 'enthusiasm' and of the affection
in which he held him personally: 'If I make any stay in France . . .
you shall certainly hear from me, but I am a bad commissioner in
searching you out a hermitage. It is too much against my interest: and
I had much rather find you one in the neighbourhood of Strawberry.'
He also warned Cole that if he died in France his property would be
forfeit under the *droit d'aubaine*, a law which decreed that the
possessions of foreigners dying in his territories should pass into the
hands of the king. This would mean that Cole's precious collection of
ancient deeds, medieval charters, diocesan registers and armorial
achievements that he had laboriously copied out and planned to leave
to the British Museum—having decided that to leave them to his old
college would be 'to throw them into a horse pond'—would be lost.
The task of copying manuscripts had been his life's work; his
completed collection filled over a hundred volumes, it was to him, he
maintained, what a wife and family was to other people. The thought
of all this mass of historical material relating mostly to his native
Cambridgeshire gathering dust in the French royal archives after his
death was too much for him, and his vision of ending his days near
some religious house not far from Paris quickly faded, for all that he
had believed, as he confessed to his diary in an unmonastic moment,
that the French way of life 'as to Eatables and Drinkables' and the
mild climate might well agree with a man turned fifty, 'as the Wine
also might be cordial to that age'.

Walpole and Cole had kept up no more than an intermittent
acquaintance until the publication in 1762 of the first two volumes of
Walpole's *Anecdotes of Painting in England*. This was undoubtedly

his most important scholarly work. It was based on a mass of confused and disordered records and jottings collected in some forty notebooks by the engraver George Vertue concerning the lives and works of all the painters, sculptors, architects and engravers who had ever worked in England. Walpole had bought these manuscript notes from Vertue's widow in 1758. He found them in a hopelessly chaotic and confused state, for Vertue had had no sense of order or arrangement but had simply collected his notes at random in the hope of one day writing a history of the arts in England himself. Walpole set to work on sorting out the papers at the beginning of 1760. A severe attack of the gout made any other activity impossible and enabled him to concentrate on the job of sorting, cataloguing and editing. It was the only time his gout had been of any service to him, and as a result he had organized the papers into a lucid and coherent chronicle in a remarkably short time, adding information of his own to Vertue's material. In his Preface to the first volume, where his debt to Vertue was acknowledged on the title-page, he observed:

> Whenever I have added to the compiler's stores, I have generally taken care to quote as religiously the source of my intelligence. Here and there I have tried to enliven the dryness of the subject by inserting facts not totally foreign to it. Yet upon the whole I despair of affording much entertainment. The public have a title to whatever was designed for them: I offer this to them as a debt—nobody will suspect that I should have chosen such a subject for fame.

The disclaimer was typical of Walpole's insurance against adverse criticism. He need not have worried; if most of the source material was Vertue's, the style and presentation was entirely his own and has all the charm and vivacity, as well as the occasional foibles, that characterizes his best work.

One immediate result of the publication of the *Anecdotes* was that Walpole received a long, enthusiastic and detailed letter from William Cole, dated 16 May 1762. It began with praise and congratulations. Here was just the sort of work that Cole delighted in; the book was 'a continual feast from one end to the other'. But ever the exact scholar, he could not help pointing out 'two or three trifling observations' and proceeded to cover page after page with them. Walpole welcomed the praise and took the criticism in good part, recognizing in Cole an antiquary of formidable authority. Four days later, he replied:

> You have sent me the most kind and obliging letter in the world, and I cannot sufficiently thank you for it . . . I am glad my books amuse you; yet you, who are so much deeper an antiquarian, must have found more faults and omissions, I fear, than your politeness suffers you to reprehend, yet you will, I trust, be a little more severe. We both labour, I will not say for the public (for the public troubles its head very little about our labours), but for the few of posterity that shall be curious; and therefore, for their sake, you must assist me in making my works as complete as possible. This sounds ungrateful, after all the trouble you have given yourself; but I say it to prove my gratitude, and to show you how fond I am of being corrected.

It was not a fondness that Walpole was always so willing to show, but it was clearly genuinely meant, for from this moment their friendship entered a new and more intimate phase that was to last until Cole's death twenty years later.

Letters were now regularly exchanged on matters of common interest which, with two such professed antiquaries, could only mean things from the distant past. 'I have nothing new, that is, nothing old to tell you,' Walpole wrote in January 1764. 'You care not about the present world, and are the only real philosopher I know.' They sent each other details of their discoveries and purchases, Walpole boasting on having conveniently met with a 'very large lot of English heads, chiefly of the reign of James I', that just about completed his collection. Cole sent him presents of engraved portraits for the same collection and copied out epitaphs that might be of interest to him. He was soon invited to Strawberry Hill and liked it so much that a second visit was almost immediately proposed. As a result of these visits, he was able to record an intimate glimpse of his friend and his rather spartan mode of life:

> I have seen him at this house at Strawberry Hill . . . in the months of October and November, when the Dew was quite wet upon the Grass, within these 2 or 3 years, go out into his Garden, and all over the Grass, without so much as an Hat on his Head, a Light Silk Waistcoat, and thin Slippers, not thicker than good substantial

brown Paper, to feed his Poultry of all Sorts, after his Breakfast: and all this without the least inconvenience, when I have been muffled up in a cloak and forced to change my Shoes as soon as I got into the House.

It was most unfair, he thought, that such a man should suffer from the gout, for he had done nothing to deserve it. Tea and bread and butter, he declared, formed half his subsistence; he rarely ate coarse meat or anything salted, while water mixed with a very little wine was his 'constant and habitual Beverage'. 'With such a regular Way of Life,' he asked, 'could one have conceived that the Gout, which loves good Nourishment of both Eatables and Drinkables, would have condescended to have been acquainted? Yet such was its whim . . .'

Cole conceived a great admiration for Walpole, but was not blind to his faults, as a passage in one of his notebooks makes clear. He had presumably been discussing their mutual friend with his Cambridge neighbour Thomas Gray, a man who also had some reservations about Walpole and had never wholly forgotten the causes of their quarrel in Italy, when he made this assessment of his character:

> Mr. Walpole is one of the best writers, an admirable poet, and one of the most lively, ingenious, and witty persons of the age; but a great share of vanity, eagerness of adulation, as Mr. Gray observed to me, a violence and warmth in party matters, and lately even to enthusiasm, abates, and takes off from, many of his shining qualities.

Had Walpole's violence and warmth in party matters been for the Church and the Tories, Cole might have found it more excusable. He always deplored his friend's attitude to religion and had been surprised, while they were in Paris, to find him defending established religion against the theories of Jean-Jacques Rousseau if only because it tended to promote virtue and all the benefits of civil life. 'I was not a little pleased,' he wrote in his journal, 'to hear my friend argue so warmly in Defence of Religion; and should have been completely so had it proceeded . . . from a Conviction of the Truth of Revelation, than merely from Political Consideration.'

These few reservations quickly evaporated or were forgotten when he found himself in the company of his friend, when the liveliness, ingenuity and wit were there to be shared and enjoyed. Even political prejudice could be set aside under Walpole's seductive influence and Cole could find himself praising the memory of Sir Robert. Of the church of St Thomas du Louvre this usually pious Tory wrote:

> The middle chapel is quite taken up by a vast large Monument to the late Cardinal Fleury, Prime Minister of France at the Time when the great Sir Robert Walpole, afterwards Earl of Orford, was in the same station in England, during whose good (in Comparison of later Administrations) and happy Administration, tho' maligned and railed against, England knew and enjoyed Peace: since which Time we have been in constant Fraction and eternal Wars.

This eulogy to the memory of Sir Robert was a tribute to the persuasive influence of his son's presence as well as to the fairness and generosity of Cole's judgement.

✦✦✦ 2 ✦✦✦

Walpole's hope of visiting some churches and convents with Cole while they were in Paris was to some extent frustrated by the very severe attack of gout that had temporarily incapacitated him shortly after his arrival there. Cole, reaching the French capital in October 1765, a month after Walpole, found him very lame from this cause and consequently restricted in his movements, but they were able to take an airing in Walpole's coach, the latter having his legs wrapped in flannel and having to be helped in and out of the vehicle, a *vis-à-vis* or 'half-coach' as Cole described it, where the two passengers sat facing each other. In this small but elegant contraption the two tourists trotted round the faubourg St Germain, 'the politest part of the town,' as Cole noted, 'where all the Hôtels of any Consequence are situated, and where all the Foreigners of any Distinction are lodged', and then crossed the river to see the place Vendôme and other sights of interest, all without alighting from their coach as Walpole was too lame to walk. They twice stopped in the faubourg St Germain, first that Walpole might send his compliments to the Duc de Nivernois, until recently the French ambassador to the Court of St James's, and secondly to perform the same courtesy at the door of John Wilkes who, as Cole recorded in slightly shocked tones, was then 'in Banishment for seditious and blasphemous Writings', but who had called on his friend at his lodgings and thus necessitated this reciprocal exercise in good manners.

When Walpole had recovered the use of his legs, they were able to make some more adventurous excursions together. On 22 November, they visited the abbey of St Denis which contained the burial vaults of the French royal family, but were disappointed when the monk who had been deputed to conduct them round the church hurried them over the tombs, which was what they most wanted to inspect. Fortunately, Walpole remembered having been told that the treasury of the abbey contained wax figures of some of the later kings, and asked if they could see them. As a result, four cupboards were opened, and inside were discovered eight ragged figures of former monarchs up to Louis XIII. The faces, they were told, were made from wax impressions taken after death, and the absence of Louis XIV's effigy was explained by the fact (as Cole's journal records) that 'his face was so excessively wrinkled, that it was impossible to take one off from him'. They did, however, see Louis XIV's coffin covered by a large pall, a sight more to the taste of George Selwyn than to Walpole or Cole. The coffin, according to the custom of the French royal house, would not be buried until that of the late King's successor was ready to take its place.

The two men must have seemed a rather unusual couple as they pottered about Paris together. Cole in middle age was a very fat man, weighing as much as 15 stone, and always dressed in sober clerical black; Walpole, on the other hand, was slight and thin and though usually plain and simple in his dress, had taken the opportunity while in Paris to trick himself out in the latest fashions, Lady Hertford, wife of his cousin the British Ambassador, having (as he wrote to tell Lady Hervey) 'cut me to pieces, and thrown me into a caldron with tailors, periwig-makers, snuff-box-wrights, milliners, etc. . . . and I am come out quite new, with everything but youth'. Cole must have appeared very large, black and ponderous in his priestly garments while his companion darted about (when his gout allowed him) with that curious gait which an observer described as 'knees bent, and the feet on tip-toe, as if afraid of a wet floor', while to another his quick bird-like movements made him seem to run like a peewit.

When not visiting churches with his friend, Cole would accompany him to the porcelain shops where Walpole made several purchases. His reputation as a collector not only of *virtù* but of

almost anything had by this time become something of a legend, so
that James Boswell could solemnly report having heard that 'the
Honourable Horace Walpole has a collection of *Bon Mots* by persons
who have never said but one'. There was no exaggeration, however,
about his collection of china. After a later visit to Paris, in 1771,
complaining that there was nothing new in the shops, he told
Conway 'I knew the faces of every snuff-box and every tea-cup as
well as those of Madame du Lac and Monsieur Porier', the two
leading porcelain dealers of the day. On the present visit, at Porier's,
Cole watched while his friend bought 'a single Coffee-Cup, Saucer,
and a little square sort of *soucoupe* or under-saucer, to set them on'
for the price of ten louis. They were, he wrote, things to be admired
and looked at but never to be used for fear of breaking. From
Porier's, they went to Madame du Lac's where Walpole bought
presents for members of his family while Cole himself purchased one
or two things at the lowest price he could meet with at this
'extravagant and tempting shop'. Not the least of the temptations, it
would appear, was the mistress of the shop, whom Cole found quite
delightful, declaring gallantly that a younger man might be in danger
of losing 'what is of more Value than Money' unless he was much on
his guard. No wonder, he thought, that the shop was so thronged
with customers.

They were to visit both shops again when, at Madame du Lac's,
Walpole bought three vases, *garniture de cheminée*, for John Chute,
and at Porier's, an ormolu tripod incense burner 'in an antique
fashion'. Cole also bought a few things at Madame du Lac's, but still
guiltily smitten by the charms of the amiable proprietress was
relieved to quit 'this dangerous shop' for the safer store of Monsieur
Porier where he expended twelve livres (about half a guinea) on a
coffee cup and saucer. But more exciting for two such connoisseurs
was their inspection of the great art collection of the Comte de
Caylus, traveller, archaeologist and patron of the arts, a large part of
which was to be sold in consequence of the count's death the
previous September. Caylus had bequeathed his collection of Roman
antiquities to the Crown, but the remainder, including his pictures
and miniatures, was to be sold by auction and Walpole, who had a
particular interest in miniatures, was anxious to acquire some items
for his own collection at Strawberry Hill.

Cole found a certain morbid fascination in the fact that they began by examining some seals and rings in the very room in which the Count had died only two months before, the deathbed itself, 'a neat Canopy Bed of flowered silk', still standing there. They then went through several small chambers looking at the pictures and antiques that were being offered for sale, Cole, at Walpole's request, jotting down in his pocket-book the items that caught his friend's eye. An important sale is always a challenge to a dedicated collector and Walpole was evidently satisfied with his success when the auction later took place. 'I am over head and ears at Count Caylus's auction,' he wrote to Conway on 29 November, 'and have bought half of it for a song—but I am still in great felicity and luck, having discovered, by mere accident, a portrait of Count Grammont, after having been in search of one of these fifteen years, and assured that there was no such thing.' There was, perhaps, a little boasting in the first part of this claim with regard to the Caylus sale, for Walpole complained to Cole that in so far as the miniatures were concerned, a rich financier had bespoken all of them and was determined to outbid all competition. In spite of this formidable threat, however, at least three of the miniatures that Cole had noted down for him were later to be seen in the Breakfast Room at Strawberry Hill, portraits of the Duc de Vendôme, the Princess Palatine and the Duchesse de Montpensier, while in the Star Chamber was a vase of 'false porphyry', bronze bas-reliefs of Anne of Bretagne and Louis XII in the Great North Bedchamber, a bronze inkstand 'in good taste' in the Little Library, and nine objects in glass or ceramics in the Tribune, all from the same collection.

Even the garden at Strawberry Hill was to be embellished as a result of this visit to Paris, for while walking in the Jardin des Tuileries, Cole and Walpole were impressed by the effect of what Cole described as 'Arbours, and other Ornaments called Trellis-Work, made of thin pieces of wood crossing each other and painted green'. Both men were experienced gardeners (gardening was a subject upon which Walpole was to write an important monograph), and it seems rather surprising that the sight was a novelty to Cole as trelliswork had existed since long before the eighteenth century. 'Mr. Walpole,' he continues, 'designs to have some of the same sort of work at his Country House at Strawberry Hill near London: but I much question whether an English hand will be able to do it in the way they are finished at Paris.' Walpole was certainly aware of the existence of trelliswork before he went to France, but in a letter to

Cole written the previous March, it would appear that even he was not very familiar with the effect it produced:

> My bower is determined, but not at all what it is to be. Though I write romances, I cannot tell how to build all that belongs to them. Madame Danois, in the Fairy Tales, used to *tapestry* them with *jonquils*; but as that furniture will not last above a fortnight in the year, I shall prefer something more huckaback. I have decided that the outside shall be of *treillage*, which, however, I shall not commence till I have again seen some of old Louis's old-fashioned *Galanteries* at Versailles.

Trellis can be seen used to good effect in a drawing of the garden at Little Strawberry Hill made late in Walpole's life in 1791.

Cole's time with Walpole in Paris was not, of course, confined only to sightseeing and the purchase of *objets-d'art*; he also met many of Walpole's friends though not, it would seem, the chief of them, Madame du Deffand, a circumstance that was possibly fortunate as his clerical soul had been deeply shocked by reports of the 'nasty ideas' that were occasionally discussed at her table. He did meet her rival Madame Geoffrin, whom he described as 'an elderly French Lady of about 60 years of Age', though in fact she was nearer sixty-six. He found her behaviour rather free (to be expected, perhaps, in a notorious 'Bel-Esprit' or 'Free-Thinker') as she flung herself into an elbow chair 'with one leg thrown over the knee of the other', and he could not help observing that she was not wearing any stays, which gave her the appearance, to his eyes, of some one just out of bed and still in a nightgown rather than a lady dressed for an evening visit. He had to admit, in spite of her unconventional behaviour, that her company was very entertaining and her conversation 'spirited and agreeable'. The impression she made on him, however, had cooled somewhat by the time he had returned to the quiet of his country parish. When he read in the newspapers in October 1766 of her journey to Warsaw, he made the laconic comment in his journal: 'If I had not happened to have seen this celebrated Lady, I should certainly have conceived her to have been something more extraordinary.'

The time in Paris was the longest period that Cole and Walpole had spent in each other's company, dining together frequently and sharing various expeditions, and it confirmed the friendship that had been resumed three years before when Walpole's *Anecdotes of Painting* first appeared. When Cole returned to England early in December, he took up again the quiet life of scholarly research and simple parish duties that his visit to France had interrupted. On the first Sunday in January 1766, the old routine was resumed. After conducting morning service, followed by a baptism and churching, he sat down to dinner with seven of his neighbours in the parlour while William Woods, his parish clerk, Thomas Tansley, his gardener, and three labourers were similarly entertained in the kitchen. This was his usual Sunday custom. His life in Paris must now have seemed infinitely remote, but an occasional letter from his friend would remind him of it, as he noted in his journal for 7 March:

> Letter from Mr. Walpole at Paris . . . He wrote to me that he had bought me also 4 cups and saucers of the Sèvres or St. Cloud China Manufacture at 19 Livres each: and also some Incense or *Pastilles à brûler*, which they use in their Churches and are very agreeable to burn, a little at a time, in one's Parlour, immediately after Dinner is removed, to take away the Scent of the Victuals: and is a Piece of Luxury I learned with him at Paris.

When Walpole himself returned, their correspondence resumed the old familiar antiquarian themes, Walpole confiding in his friend various ideas he had for books and other projects. In April 1768, he wrote:

> I have long had thoughts of drawing up something for London like St. Foix's *Rues de Paris*, and have made some collections. I wish you would be so good, in the course of your reading, to mark down any passage to that end: as to where any great houses of the nobility were situated; or in what street any memorable event happened.

The project unfortunately came to nothing as did his more ambitious scheme for a history of Gothic architecture. He informed Cole:

> With regard to a history of Gothic Architecture . . . The plan, I think, should lie in a very simple compass. Was I to execute it, it would be thus: I would give a series of plates, even from the conclusion of Saxon architecture, beginning with the round Roman arch, and going on to show how they plaistered and

zigzagged it, and then how better ornaments crept in, till the beautiful Gothic arrived at its perfection: then how it decreased in Henry the Eighth's reign—Archbishop Warham's tomb at Canterbury being, I believe, the last example of unbastardized Gothic.

Cole, he hoped, would undertake to 'ascertain the chronologic period of each building; and not only of each building, but of each tomb, that shall be exhibited . . .' The letter, written in August 1769, reached Cole at an awkward moment in his life, usually so smooth and uneventful. He had not long before resigned his living at Bletchley and moved first to Waterbeach and then to Milton near Cambridge, and the letter caught him while he was still involved in these unsettling moves and therefore unable to give it much attention. The scheme came to nothing, even though as late as January 1771, Walpole was writing to suggest that it might receive the patronage of the king, a proposal that was somewhat damped when he added discouragingly: 'I own I do not know how to get it laid before him.'

More successful was their collaboration in the spring of the same year when Walpole wrote to say that he had just obtained the loan of seven manuscript letters from Edward VI to Barnaby Fitzpatrick. Fitzpatrick, who had been brought up with the king, had been a member of the family into which Walpole's friend Lady Ossory had married, and it was she who had lent these rare and valuable letters to him. He was anxious that they should not be damaged or rubbed by his printer and asked Cole if he would transcribe them. 'I need not desire your particular care,' he wrote on 29 May, 'for you value these things as much as I do, and will be able to make them out better than I can do, from being so much versed in old writing.' The letters were to be published by his own press at Strawberry Hill; two hundred copies were struck off by the printer, six of which were duly dispatched to Cole on 7 July 1772.

Though Cole accepted the living of Burnham in Buckinghamshire in 1774, he continued to live at Milton, installing a curate to carry out the duties of his new parish. When he occasionally complained of fevers or rheumatism, he got little sympathy from his fellow sufferer at Strawberry Hill. What did he expect, living in so damp and exposed a place? 'I am sorry for the fever you have had,' he was told, 'but, Goodman Frog, if you will live in the fens, do not expect to be as healthy as if you were a fat Dominican at Naples.' He needed little encouragement to come and visit his friend by the Thames, and the inducements that Walpole sometimes offered to tempt him there were hardly necessary. When the splendid shrine that had once adorned the church of Santa Maria Maggiore in Rome was about to be set up in the chapel in the woods at Strawberry Hill, Walpole wrote to him:

> My Chapel is finished, and the shrine will actually be placed in less than a fortnight. My father is said to have said, that every man has his price. You are a *Beatus*, indeed, if you resist a shrine. Why should not you add to your claustral virtues that of a peregrination to Strawberry? You will find me quite alone in July. Consider, Strawberry is almost the last monastery left, at least in England.

Walpole's light-hearted description of his friend as a *beatus* was not entirely inapt. Cole certainly had some of the shortcomings common to the eighteenth-century clergy. He was an absentee incumbent in so far as his last cure at Burnham was concerned, and he undoubtedly enjoyed the pleasures of what he called, with a certain relish, 'Eatables and Drinkables', his lavish use of capital letters making them seem all the more appetizing. But he had very many good qualities as well and they easily predominated over his few minor faults. Not least among these amiable traits was his warm benevolence and tolerant understanding of human frailty and folly, especially among the simple, unsophisticated folk who formed the bulk of his country neighbours and former parishioners. There was an innocence about him that was unusual in that age of worldly priests and political bishops. His quiet piety stands out among the deists and 'free-thinkers' who so epitomized the age in which he lived; it was a quality that Walpole himself recognized and may well have had in mind when he wrote to his old friend at a time when he thought that his life was in danger, referring to him as 'you who are full of nothing but gentle and generous sentiments'. It was this gentleness, and the quiet unambitious serenity of his life, that made him one of the most attractive members of Walpole's circle.

⋙ 3 ⋘

The trophies of Walpole's various trips to Paris, as had also been the case with his earlier visits to Florence, Rome and Naples as a young man, were to be seen in many items in his ever growing collection, from the Boccapadugli eagle that followed him to England after his Grand Tour of 1739–41, to the spoils of the Caylus sale that returned to Strawberry Hill with him in 1766, or the suit of armour of Francis I of France that he purchased in 1771. ('It is gilt in relief,' he informed Cole, 'and is very rich and beautiful. It comes from the Crozat Collection.') But in spite of these and many other items of foreign origin, in particular his French porcelain, the bulk of the collection reflected his interest in English history and antiquities, and especially in portraits.

He had a particular liking for portraiture as a genre. He placed it above both landscapes and history painting, explaining his reasons for this at some length to his friend John Pinkerton, the Scots antiquary and man of letters whom he befriended in his old age:

> A landscape is, we will say, an exquisite distribution of wood and water and buildings. It is excellent—we pass on, and it leaves not one trace in the memory. In historical painting there may be *sublime deception*—but it not only always falls short of the idea, but is always false; that is, has the greatest blemishes incidental to history. It is commonly false in the *costume*; generally in the portraits; always in the groupings and attitudes, which the painter, if not present, cannot possibly delineate as they really were. Call it fabulous painting, and I have no objection. But a real portrait we know is truth itself: and it calls up so many collateral ideas, as to fill an intelligent mind more than any other species.

The passage is interesting in showing that Walpole seems to have been more concerned with verisimilitude than aesthetic effect, and is abruptly dismissive of landscape painting where the aesthetic effect is paramount. In this respect, it is worth noting that most examples of this genre in his collection were pictures of specific places such as his view of Marble Hill where Lady Suffolk had lived, of Pope's villa at Twickenham, or Müntz's painting of the Vyne in Hampshire, all associated with people he had known or admired and therefore pendants, as it were, to their portraits.

Collections tended to be more diverse and less specialized in Walpole's time than they are today. An eighteenth-century 'cabinet', as they were then called, was something of a cross between an art gallery, a museum, and a junk shop, and some collectors would not hesitate to mix *objets d'art* and pictures with geological specimens and fossils. Walpole himself was limited, when buying pictures, by the space available to hang them, and as most of his rooms except for the Great Parlour, the Gallery and the Great Bedchamber were small and had low ceilings, very large pictures were out of the question, and a painter of landscapes or history paintings was more likely to use a large canvas than a portrait painter. Strawberry Hill was no Houghton; it did not have the facilities, nor was it ever intended to have, for displaying a collection of old masters. The plan of the house was conditioned by Walpole's liking for small, intimate objects, and his collecting after the completion of his building projects was restricted by the design. Criticisms of his taste have suffered in the past from some misunderstanding both as to his intentions and his methods. His collection was essentially personal, reflecting tastes and interests that were not always consistent; it was also the collection of a man of some affluence but not of great wealth. He was never in the position of his much younger contemporary William Beckford who could rival the purchasing power of kings in the sale-rooms. The predominating influence was his interest in history, especially the personal history of English monarchs and noblemen, a concern that found a parallel literary expression in his *Catalogue of Royal and Noble Authors*, a work that was inspired by his collection.

This curiosity about the past fired his taste for objects, possibly of no value in themselves, that had once belonged to historical characters or had been associated with their lives—Cardinal Wolsey's hat, Queen Mary's comb, the pipe Admiral Van Tromp had smoked during his last sea battle, objects that aroused Macaulay's amused contempt rather than his informed understanding or sympathy. Walpole was quite aware that such things, taken out of context, could easily be ridiculed. He had defined his own attitude to them quite early in his career in an essay he published in 1746, where he had written:

If the learned world could be so happy as to discover a *Roman's* old shoe (provided the Literati were agreed it were a shoe, and not a leathern casque, a drinking vessel, a balloting box, or an empress's head-attire), such shoe would immediately have the *entrée* into any collection in Europe; even though it appeared to be the shoe of the most vulgar artisan in Rome, and not to have belonged to any beau of classic memory. And the reason is plain; not that there is any intrinsic value in an old shoe, but because an old Roman shoe would be a *Unique*.

Such objects might be found anywhere, at the sale of the belongings of Mrs Kennon the midwife for instance, where, as he ruefully confessed to Conway, he was outbid for Oliver Cromwell's nightcap.

In the same spirit Walpole would accept work by friends, amateurs of some talent but not to be compared with the professional artists whose work might hang beside them. And so, among the Holbein drawings and Isaac Oliver miniatures we find sketches by Agnes and Mary Berry, a flower study painted by his mother, embroidered pictures from the tambour of Lady Ailesbury who specialized in copying old masters in silk, and Walpole's own copies of Watteau in watercolours. Presents of all kinds from friends formed another considerable part of his collection, more than 150 items fall into this category. Some of them were exceedingly fine, like the head of the Emperor Caligula that Horace Mann had given him; some of no more than average interest like the red snuff-box with enamelled top and bottom given him by his cousin Lord Hertford or the silver-gilt apostle spoon from William Cole; others were decidedly odd like the three pieces of rock made from rice, a present from Kitty Clive's brother James Raftor.

Yet to read Macaulay with his picture of Walpole bidding for works by Zinker and Petitot, cheapening fragments of tapestry or joining bits of painted glass, and those other detractors who have taken their cue from him, one would form the impression that the Gallery and Tribune contained nothing more important than some equally curious companion pieces to Raftor's eccentric offering. In fact, dispersed among the rooms of Strawberry Hill were works by, or attributed to, such considerable artists as Pompeo Batoni, Bronzino, Canaletto, Annibale Carracci, Cuyp, Cellini, Carlo Dolci, Gerard Dou, Giorgione, Hals, Nicholas Hilliard, Holbein, Kneller, Lely, Marieschi, van der Neer, Peter and Isaac Oliver, Parmigianino,

Gaspar Poussin, Sebastiano Ricci, Salvator Rosa, Steenwyck, Teniers, Vanloo, Vasari and Watteau; while among his own contemporaries Walpole had examples of the work of John Astley, Rosalba Carriera, George Dance, Ecchardt, Joseph Farington, Gavin Hamilton, H. D. Hamilton, Müntz, Paul Sandby, Allan Ramsay, George Romney, Sir Joshua Reynolds and many others. For a collection in which, as Walpole modestly claimed, 'almost everything is diminutive', it was not one to be despised.

It was, of course, extremely eclectic, as was much of Walpole's reading and scholarship as well as his taste. It also reflected his good nature. He might well have preferred to relegate Raftor's three rocks made from rice to the lumber-room or to some particularly dark corner of the house where gothic 'gloomth' could be relied upon to render them decently obscure; but this might have hurt the feelings of a man for whom he had a warm regard, and so the strange objects were found a place in his 'cabinet' with other curiosities like the Egyptian duck, the Japanese needle-case decorated with monkeys, or the gold toothpick-case given him by Lady Diana Beauclerk. These amusing objects, however, were not perhaps things by which he set much store except for their association with the donors. The three really important parts of his collection consisted of the coins and medals, the miniatures and enamels, and what he described as 'portraits of remarkable persons' of which mention has already been made.

Walpole started to collect coins in Italy on the Grand Tour when he wrote with youthful exuberance to Conway, 'I am far gone in medals, lamps, idols, prints, etc., and all the small commodities to the purchase of which I can attain; I would buy the Colosseum if I could . . .' His twenty-five most precious coins and medals were housed in a rosewood case which was kept in the glass cabinet in the library with other especially rare treasures. One medal is described as a fine gold coin of Pope Paul III 'from the collection of Baron Stosch'. This quaint and rather sinister figure, well-known at the time in Rome, is further described in Warburton's *Memoirs of Horace Walpole* as a man 'who made his antiquarian studies—for which he is deservedly famous—subservient to a profitable espionage, for which he was deservedly infamous. He took pay from the British Government to spy on the Pretender, and had similar services on his paymasters rewarded by the Jacobites.' Of the collection of miniatures and enamels, Walpole claimed that it was the largest and finest in the country. 'His Majesty has some very fine, the duke of Portland more,' he wrote in the preface to his *Description* of Strawberry Hill. 'In no other is to be seen, in any good preservation, any number of works by Isaac and Peter Oliver. The large pieces by the latter, in the royal collection, faded long ago by being exposed to the sun and air.'

He was careful that the same fate should not befall his own collection by making a set of rules governing times when people could be admitted to see it, and setting limits to the number who could view it at any one time. The fame of his house and its contents became so widespread that these rules were a necessary protection. Parties must consist of no more than four persons, and they were required to apply in advance when tickets of admission would be issued to them. If more than four people presented themselves, his housekeeper had orders not to admit them. The house was open to visitors only between twelve and three o'clock; no one was to come after dinner under any circumstances, and not at all from the first of May until the first of October. The rules ended with a firm request: 'They who have Tickets are desired not to bring Children.' The most fortunate of all, of course, were those people (and these were very often children) who had the good luck to be Walpole's personal friends, for to them belonged the privilege of being shown round by the owner himself. For them it must have been a very rewarding experience, for Walpole had some anecdote to tell, or some interesting information to impart, about almost every item they were shown. The artist Thomas Patch, when dedicating his life of Fra Bartolommeo to Walpole, called him the 'Intelligent Promoter of the Fine Arts'. At no time did he appear more agreeably in this light than when acting as cicerone to his own collection.

⋙ 4 ⋘

One thing the visitor must have noticed as he was shown round the Strawberry Hill collection was the presence, among contemporary contributions, of numerous works by Lady Diana Beauclerk. In the China Room he would be shown a set of twelve Wedgwood plates with cameos of blue and white with blue festoons of her design; in the Breakfast Room were two bas-reliefs of boys in wax modelled by her, as well as Bartolozzi's engraving of her drawing of her two daughters and a picture of the masquerade at Vauxhall showing masked and unmasked figures with 'wonderful expressions in the faces'. The Red Bedchamber displayed her water-colour drawing of gypsies telling the fortune of a country girl; two more boys modelled in wax were to be seen in the Great North Bedchamber together with two square Wedgwood flower tubs on which Lady Diana had painted antique cameos and masks in blue. There was also a two-leafed screen of Manchester velvet which she had decorated with heads of a satyr and a bacchante. Later on, as we shall see, the Beauclerk Closet was added to the house, a room especially dedicated to her work. Walpole's enthusiasm for the work of this talented lady, a daughter of the second Duke of Marlborough, was shown by the lines he composed in her honour and attached to the back of the wax bas-reliefs in the Great Bedchamber. The verses were far from being in his best manner, but they indicated the respect in which he held her work:

> Tho' taste and grace thro' all my limbs you see,
> And nature breaths her soft simplicity,
> Me nor Praxiteles nor Phidias form'd;
> 'Twas Beauclerk's art the sweet creation warm'd,
> From Marlborough sprung—We in one heaven-born race
> Th'attemper'd rays of the same genius trace;
> As big with meteors from one cloud depart
> Majestic thunder and keen lightning's dart.

As usual in the case of a close acquaintance, Walpole allowed his gift for hyperbole to run away with him when he praised the work of Lady Diana, or 'Lady Di' as her friends usually called her. In the introduction to the fourth volume of his *Anecdotes of Painting*, he wrote:

Has any painter ever executed a scene, a character of Shakespeare, that approached to the prototype so near as Shakespeare himself attained to nature? Yet there is a pencil in a living hand as capable of pronouncing the passions as our unequalled poet; a pencil not only inspired by his insight into nature, but by the graces and taste of Grecian artists—but it is not fair to excite the curiosity of the public, when both the rank and bashful merit of the possessor, and a too rare exertion of superior talents, confine the proofs to a narrow circle. Whoever has seen the drawings and bas-reliefs designed and executed by Lady Diana Beauclerk, is sensible that these imperfect encomiums are far short of the excellence of her work.

Such extravagant encomiums in fact have more the effect of taking one's breath away by their sheer audacity than of disposing one to take a charitable view of Lady Diana's work. In fact, however, Walpole was by no means alone in admiring her art. Sir Joshua Reynolds himself was known to have declared that her drawings might be studied as models, and Josiah Wedgwood made use of her designs (in addition to the examples of his ware in the Strawberry Hill collection) for a jasper bowl in 1783, a cup, saucer and bowl in 1785, and three bas-reliefs announced in his catalogue for 1785. Sir William Hamilton, the British envoy at Naples, a noted connoisseur and arbiter of taste, was another enthusiast. When his friend Lord Herbert, later eleventh Earl of Pembroke and grandson of the 'architect earl' who had designed Marble Hill, sent him a print of Bartolozzi's engraving of Lady Diana's portrait of her two daughters in December 1780, he wrote in reply:

> I always thought Lady Di had more true taste than any creature living and I defy any artist in Europe to compose two figures with more grace and elegant simplicity than these two delightful little girls. Do kiss the hand that produced them (as my proxy) the first opportunity and tell her Ladyship that I can never cease being her admirer . . .

Lord Herbert shared his view. 'If you was to see six pieces of Lady Di's from a story of Ossian,' he replied, 'you would fall down and worship her more than ever.' Perhaps it should be added that the artist was Lord Herbert's aunt and that he was later to marry her daughter Elizabeth, but this would not happen for another six years and can hardly have influenced his judgement at this time on such a matter of taste.

In fact Lady Diana's talent was a limited but by no means insignificant one. Her gift lay particularly in her studies of children, scenes of innocent bacchanals with plump *putti* decorously draped in vines, infant Pans, nymphs and cherubs. She also produced some quite charming portrait studies of children, but her more dramatic pieces, in which Walpole saw an affinity to Shakespeare, suffer from a sense of flatness, a lack of depth and perspective, with a certain stiffness in the figures that suggests a want of anatomical knowledge. Her place in art might be put high among amateurs of talent but must suffer when judged by comparison with professionals. Her sense of humour only appears in some of her informal sketches, as in the brilliant caricature of Edward Gibbon, cherubic and laurel-wreathed, like a fat little Roman emperor. Walpole overpraised her in the same way that he overpraised Anne Damer; his admiration for her artistic abilities was coloured by his affection for her as a person and also, with his genuine concern for the unfortunate, by the rather sad circumstances of her life.

She was born Lady Diana Spencer on 24 March 1732, daughter of Charles, fifth Earl of Sunderland, who succeeded in 1733 to the dukedom of Marlborough on the death of the first duke's daughter, Henrietta Countess of Godolphin, Duchess of Marlborough in her own right. Diana was the eldest daughter and was brought up in the splendid surroundings of Blenheim Palace. At the age of twenty-three she married Frederick St John, second Viscount Bolingbroke, but the marriage was unhappy. The couple soon found themselves to be incompatible, and in addition Lady Di had to submit to a husband who showed himself to be violent, drunken and unfaithful. In January 1766, after nine years of marriage, it was clear that they had reached breaking-point. Lady Sarah Lennox, writing to her friend Lady Susan O'Brien, gave it as her belief that both parties in this unhappy union were mad:

> But, seriously speaking, I believe Lord B is much the same as mad when he is drunk, and that is generally. Lady B's reason for parting is that she cannot live with him with safety to her health ... Everybody that don't love her pities him, but as I had heard he had got a woman in the house already, I can't say I do, for if he was unhappy at the thought of having used her so cruelly as he has done, surely a man that had any feeling would not recover his spirits so easily!

Lady Di had another reason for wishing to part from her husband as well as the threatened danger to her health; she herself was in love with another man. This was Topham Beauclerk, now chiefly remembered because he was a close friend of Samuel Johnson's who liked and admired him for his amusing conversation, his cultivated mind and the fact that he was a great-grandson of Charles II and Nell Gwyn. Johnson loved him uncritically and indiscriminately tolerated his faults in a way he did with few others except for Bennet Langton, who was Beauclerk's closest friend. Others were not always so enthusiastic in their opinions of him. Lady Louisa Stuart described him as being 'what the French call *cynique* in his personal habits beyond what one would have thought possible in anyone but a beggar or a gypsey'. Boswell complained of his acid manner in conversation, a fault that even Johnson acknowledged when he said that Beauclerk never opened his mouth but with the intention to give pain, and though he achieved fame as a wit and a dandy it was equalled by his reputation for dissipation. Among his more solid qualitites was a genuine love for literature. He collected an immense library said to contain some 30,000 books, an achievement that received Walpole's approval who otherwise does not seem to have liked him very much. 'Mr. Beauclerk has built a library in Great Russell Street that reaches halfway to Highgate,' he told Lady Ossory. 'Everybody goes to see it; it has put the Museum's nose quite out of joint.'

It was for this man of uncertain temper and character that Lady Diana was divorced from Lord Bolingbroke in 1768. Divorce at that period was a costly, complicated and protracted business and was only in the reach of the very rich. There was first an action for damages in Westminster Hall; this was followed by proceedings in the ecclesiastical court for separation 'from bed and board', and finally a private Act of Parliament dissolved the union and allowed the parties to remarry. As a matter of principle, the bishops felt obliged to move an amendment prohibiting any second marriage, but the clause in question was restored by the House of Commons and the bishops then gracefully gave way when the bill returned to the House of Lords and passed into law. The Bolingbroke divorce act received the royal assent on 10 August. Two days later Lady Diana and Topham Beauclerk were married. Society generally accepted the new arrangement with equanimity; only Dr Johnson thundered his disapproval, though his stern denunciation was directed at Lady Diana and not at her new husband who might be presumed to be equally at fault. When Boswell attempted to take her side the Doctor would not be appeased and swept his arguments aside. 'My dear Sir,' he growled, 'never accustom your mind to mingle virtue and vice.

The woman's a whore, and there's an end on't.' There are moments when Walpole's dislike of Johnson is easy to understand.

It is to be hoped that Lady Diana was happy in the early years of her second marriage, for Topham Beauclerk, who was five years younger than his wife, was a difficult man, self-centred and self-indulgent. As time went on, like many an ageing beau, his much famed cheerfulness and good humour were reserved more and more for his friends and for social occasions such as Johnson's Club; at home he could be disagreeable and bad-tempered. 'In the latter part of Beauclerk's life,' Lady Louisa Stuart observed, 'the man of pleasure grew morose and savage, and Lady Di had much to suffer from his temper; so had his children, to whom he was a selfish tyrant, without indulgence or affection.' In neither of her marriages did Lady Diana achieve the security and solicitude that she had the right to expect, but she seems to have accepted her situation without complaint. When Beauclerk became an invalid in his last years (he died in 1780 at the early age of forty-one) she nursed him devotedly, a fact that Dr Johnson acknowledged, making some amends for his earlier churlish comments at her expense. 'Poor Beauclerk is so ill, that his life is thought to be in danger,' he wrote to Boswell in January 1775. 'Lady Di nurses him with very great assiduity.'

Life with Topham Beauclerk was not, indeed, without its hazards. One of the problems of the eighteenth century with which we are fortunately now less familiar was the pervasion of fleas; travellers were often plagued by the unwelcome presence of these irritating parasites, but they were also liable to be encountered in some less expected places. Walpole himself had made their acquaintance on more than one occasion. Writing to Chute from an inn at Amiens where he and his dog Rosette were staying in July 1771, he complained: 'Here are old fleas and bugs talking of Louis Quatorze like tattered refugees in the Park, and they make poor Rosette attend to them whether she will or not.' Beauclerk, however, was unique among Walpole's friends in that he carried his own supply, and was quite brazen about it when detected.

We are indebted again to Lady Louisa Stuart for an account of the embarrassment caused by this unpleasant infestation:

He and Lady Di made part of a Christmas party at Blenheim, where soon after the company were all met, they all found themselves as strangely annoyed as the Court of Pharaoh were of old by visitants—'*in all their quarters*'—it was in the days of powder and pomatum, when stiff frizzling and curling, with hot irons and black pins, made the entrance of combs extremely difficult—in short, the distress became unspeakable. Its origin being clearly traced to Mr. Beauclerk, one of the gentlemen undertook to remonstrate with him, and began delicately hinting how much the ladies were inconvenienced—'What!' said Beauclerk, 'Are they so nice as that comes to? Why, I have enough to stock a parish!'

The Beauclerk fleas became something of a byword in Walpole's circle as a letter he wrote to George Selwyn in October 1779 demonstrates:

I heard last night that an ancient maiden Trevor, sister of Lord Hampden, has left some fortune to Lady Di's two girls. I most cordially hope it is true, that they may have bread to eat—if they are not eaten first, of which there is some danger, for as modern Conjurers are not greater adepts than the Pharaohs, and as that potent Sovereign's magicians had no power over lice, I doubt the visitation is inveterate.

After Beauclerk's death, Lady Di came to live at Little Marble Hill just to the east of the house where Walpole had visited Lady Suffolk in earlier years. He was delighted with his new neighbour and greatly admired the scheme of decoration she had devised for one of her rooms, 'small pictures of peasants and children, in rounds and squares, that are chained together by wreaths of natural flowers that exceed her lilies, and all flowers that ever were painted'. But his admiration for her work had reached its zenith some five years before when he had written on 27 December 1775 to Lady Ossory:

Just at present I suppose I am the vainest creature in the universe. Lady Di has drawn three scenes of my tragedy, which if the subject were a quarter as good as the drawings, would make me a greater genius than Shakespeare, as she is superior to Guido and Salvator Rosa. Such figures! such dignity! such simplicity! Then there is a cedar hanging over the castle, that is more romantic than when it grew in Lebanon!

He was in ecstasies over these illustrations to *The Mysterious Mother* (which were later increased to seven) and the following February was writing to William Mason: 'Oh! such drawings, Guido's grace, Albano's children, Poussin's expression, Salvator's boldness in landscape, and Andrea Sacchi's simplicity of composition might perhaps have equalled them had they wrought all together very fine.' He even amazed himself by the extravagance of his praise, for he added: 'How an author's vanity can bestow bombast panegyric on his flatterers!' None the less he really believed in the high quality of the drawings, for he ends by asking Mason to judge for himself: 'Seeing is believing, miracles are not ceased. I know how prejudiced I am apt to be; some time or other you will see whether I am so in this instance.' He decided that the drawings must be housed in a special room, and sent for James Essex, a Cambridge architect, to build him a turret between the Tribune and the Round Tower. He described it to Lady Ossory in October 1776: 'It is one of those tall thin Flemish towers that are crowned with a roof like an extinguisher.' It was to be called the Beauclerk Tower and the drawings were to be kept in a room on the same floor as the Gallery and the Round Room, being approached from the corridor that connected them. 'Lady Di's drawings . . . are hung on Indian blue damask,' he told Mason, 'the ceiling, door, and surbase are gilt, and in the window are two brave *fleur de lis* and the lion of England, all royally crowned and painted on glass, which as Queen Catherine never did happen to write a *billet doux* in this closet, signify Beauclerk, the denominaton of the tower.' The room was not to be shown to the profane but was to be reserved for only the most privileged friends and guests.

Shortly after his last addition was made to his 'castle' of Strawberry Hill and his collection was just about complete, Walpole had the shock of hearing of the dispersion of his father's great collection at Houghton. He had not often visited the family home in Norfolk after his father's death, but he shared Sir Robert's pride in the famous collection of works of art that had inspired his own first book *Aedes Walpolianae*, published in 1747, and had been one of the sources upon which his aesthetic taste had been founded. The reckless extravagance of his nephew the third Earl of Orford, an unstable man who was later to suffer a complete mental breakdown, was the cause of this disaster. Walpole wrote to Horace Mann on 18 December 1778:

What I have long apprehended is on the point of conclusion, the sale of the pictures at Houghton. The mad master has sent his final demand of forty-five thousand for them to the Empress of Russia, at the same time that he has been what he calls improving the outside of the house; *basta*! Thus end all my visions about Houghton, which I will never *see*, though I must go thither at last; nor, if I can help it, think of more.

His distress was mingled with indignation at this insult (as he felt it to be) to his father's memory, whose shade he believed to have been affronted by the present Earl's shabby dealings. To Lady Ossory he sadly confessed that the sale was the most signal mortification to his idolatry for his father's memory that it could receive: 'It is stripping the temple of his glory and his affection.' That the pictures had been bought by Catherine II of Russia and the collection would remain intact, displayed on the walls of the 'Hermitage' in the Winter Palace at St Petersburg, was no consolation to him; indeed he had a poor opinion of the Semiramis of the North. To him she was no more than 'a devil in a diadem'. Collections of great works of art, he knew only too well, could not survive for ever, and Houghton itself could not have boasted its fine masterpieces if the private galleries of Italy had not been despoiled for its benefit. But the departure across the North Sea of the collection of which he had written in his youth that 'there are not a great many Collections left in Italy more worth seeing than this at Houghton' was a sobering reflection to a man who was himself a lifelong connoisseur, and it must have made him ponder wistfully on the ultimate fate of his own treasures at Strawberry Hill.

VIII
Lady Ossory,
Mary and Agnes Berry:
The Last Years

⇛ 1 ⇚

Like anyone with a strong historical sense, Walpole was acutely conscious of the passage of time, and this awareness became sharper as he grew older and his memories seemed to go back ever farther into the past. In February 1782, he wrote to Mann:

> As I was an infant when my father became Minister, I came into the world at five years old; knew half the remaining courts of King William and Queen Anne, or heard them talked of as fresh; and being the youngest and favourite child, was carried to almost the first operas, kissed the hand of George the First, and am now hearing the frolics of his great-great-grandson—no, all this cannot have happened in one life!

The disappearance from the scene of certain old friends, while inflicting a sharp reminder of the inevitability of earthly extinction, at the same time emphasized his own capacity for survival. Chute had died in 1776; in 1780 Madame du Deffand made her exit from life at the age of eighty-three. William Cole's quiet existence came to an end after a brief illness in 1782, and Kitty Clive's boisterous laugh was silenced for ever in 1785. Sir Horace Mann, with whom Walpole had exchanged more than 1,700 letters over a period of forty-five years without ever seeing him again after their last meeting in Florence in 1741, was to die at his post as British minister to the Grand Duke of Tuscany, ending his long epistolary friendship with a note of 5 September 1786 concluding with the words: 'Adieu, my Dear Sir, I am quite exhausted'. He died two months later. He was over eighty and had held his post at Florence for a longer time than any other envoy in the history of British diplomacy.

In February 1785 Walpole recovered from yet another severe attack of gout largely by relying upon what he termed his own 'Herculean weakness' and, as he put it to Lady Ossory, by contriving that his doctor 'suffered me to prescribe to him what he should prescribe to me'. As he approached his seventieth birthday, his interest in humanity and its follies showed no sign of decline. He was always glad to meet new people and showed a special regard for the younger generation with whom he soon established an easy rapport. In one of the last letters he was to write to Horace Mann, he gave an instance of his continuing curiosity about the changing world and its fashions. Discussing the latest modes of female attire, he wrote:

Don't however imagine that I am disposed to be a censor of modes, as most old folks are, who seem to think that they came into the world at the critical moment when everything was in perfection, and ought to suffer no farther innovation. On the contrary, I always maintain that the ordinances of the young are right. Who ought to invent fashions? Surely not the ancient. I tell my veteran contemporaries that if they will have patience for three months, the reigning evil, whatever it is, will be cured—whereas, if they fret, till things are just as they should be, they may vex themselves to the day of doom. I carry this way of thinking still farther, and extend it to almost all reformations. Could one cure the world of being foolish, it were something—but to cure it of any one folly, is only making room for some other, which one is sure will succeed to the vacant place.

It was this philosophy that helped him to understand the minds of younger people, and made them glad to enjoy the benefits of his friendship, looking on him not merely as an interesting survival from an earlier period, but as someone whose views, whose anecdotes and whose air of cultivated and urbane distinction made his company both a pleasure and an education. One of these younger friends we have already encountered, the minor poet, Edward Jerningham, whom Mrs Damer had used as an ambassador in her attempts to sort out the social difficulties arising from the Countess of Albany's proposed visit to Park Place in July 1791. He became a close friend of Walpole's as well as of the Conway family, and some six years before the episode of Madame d'Albany and the *comédienne*, had been with Walpole to see the bridge at Henley which was a joint enterprise of the family at Park Place, the General designing the arch and Mrs Damer sculpting the keystones with heads of the river-gods. On 10 August, 1785, Walpole told Lady Ossory:

> We saw the new bridge at Henley which is complete on one side, and is most beautiful; the bend of the arch was regulated by General Conway himself, on three centres, and for grace does not veil the bonnet of the Ponte di Trinità at Florence. His daughter's head of the Thame is placed, and has a charming effect. The Isis is fixed too, but not yet uncovered.

Jerningham was born in 1737 and came, like Walpole, from a Norfolk family, but being brought up a Roman Catholic he had received most of his education at the English college at Douai in France and then at the Sorbonne. His religious background had given him a taste for theological speculation and he was to publish an essay on pulpit eloquence as well as a translation of Bossuet's *Oraisons Funèbres*. The eloquence of the Eagle of Meaux seems to have been counter-productive in his case, however, for shortly after returning to England about the year 1761, he announced his conversion to Anglicanism, in which faith he was to remain until his death. Jerningham was a person of graceful manners, 'the charming man' as Walpole always called him, but was also something of a *petit maître*, a butterfly who hovered round beautiful and elegant young women without showing much sign of settling, becoming famous for his transitory love affairs. One of his social accomplishments was to sing to his own accompaniment on the harp. 'He seems a mighty delicate gentleman,' Fanny Burney confided in her journal, 'looks to be painted, and is all daintification in manner, speech, and dress', and she recorded that Lord Mulgrave called him the pink and white poet 'for not only his cheeks but his coat is pink'. But in spite of his 'affected delicacy' he was a good-natured man and was popular in society.

As a poet Jerningham's reputation flourished mainly within the confines of certain fashionable drawing-rooms and did not penetrate very far beyond them, though he did once have a tragedy produced at the Covent Garden theatre. He admired Gray's poetry to the point of plagiarism but does not seem ever to have met the poet, though he was on familiar terms with Gray's friend Norton Nicholls. His admiration even extended to Nordic themes. 'Mr. Jerningham has just published a new poem on the doctrines of the Scandinavian Bards . . .' Walpole wrote to Gray's biographer William Mason in February 1784. 'He seems to have kept the *Descent of Odin* in his eye, though he had not the art of conjuring up the most forceful feelings, as Gray has done, in a subject in which there is so much of the terrible.' Walpole was under no illusion as to his friend's poetical talent, and was concerned on his behalf when people overpraised his efforts (a fault he so often indulged in himself). When Jerningham published a poem on the grand theme of *Peace, Ignominy and Destruction* in 1791, which Edmund Burke had praised extravagantly, Walpole wrote to Mary Berry:

> I said nothing on 'the Charming man's' poem. I fear I said too much to him myself. He said, others liked it; and showed me a note from Mr. Burke that was hyperbole itself. I wish him so well, that I am sorry he should be so flattered, when, in truth, he has no genius. There is no novelty, no plan, and no suite in his poetry; though many of his lines are pretty.

Walpole showed his affection for Jerningham in the light, bantering style of his letters to him, as when, urging him to remain overnight at Strawberry Hill, he warned him that if he returned home before morning he would be in danger of 'a body of 200 footpads between this place and Isleworth, three regiments of Housebreakers at Brentford, between three and four thousand Highwaymen encamped at Turnham Green, and a whole army of Nabobs at Knightsbridge, who plunder and murder without any treachery', whereas the next day he could send him home safely by an air-balloon. Such flights of fancy (or of air-balloons for that matter) give a pleasant impression of his relations with 'the charming man' with whom he seems to have been on easy, familiar terms, as another letter written in July 1789 suggests, with its irreverent reference to the pious Hannah More's poem *Bonner's Ghost* which had just been issued from the Strawberry Hill press by Walpole's printer Thomas Kirgate:

> I am sorry that your Muse is not pregnant, for my Apollo is so old . . . that I fear he will not be able to impregnate her. However, I

have some hopes of your finding Lady Ailesbury and Mr. Conway here; and he is still so vigorous a Poet, that who knows but he may do your Madame Clio's business? I can at worst be your accoucheur; or my assistant Kirgate shall, who has just delivered the Virgin Hannah of a Divine Babe, of which she fell in labour on fancying she saw a ghost.

Such lively exchanges were altogether too light-hearted to suit another much younger man whom Walpole first met in 1784 when he applied through the bookseller and publisher James Dodsley to dedicate a book on medals to him. Walpole declined the honour of the dedication. He had by then, he told Dodsley, given away or exchanged several of his Greek and Roman coins, but would be glad to show what remained and 'any other baubles here that can amuse him' to the author. So it was that John Pinkerton, later to establish his reputation as a historian and antiquary, first came to Strawberry Hill. He had arrived in London from his native Edinburgh in 1780 and was now about twenty-six years old and determined to make his name as a writer. He quickly followed up his first visit with the presentation of a volume of his verse and Walpole wrote to thank him and bestow some advice: 'You have talents that will succeed in whatever you pursue, and industry to neglect nothing that will improve them. Despise petty critics, and confute them by making your works as perfect as you can.' On this solemn note their friendship began.

Pinkerton has been accused of acting the toady to Walpole and extracting long letters from him on literary subjects with the object of using them later on for his own purposes; but there is nothing to suggest that Walpole found his company other than pleasant or the letters he wrote him in any way irksome, and we are indebted to him for preserving many of Walpole's views and opinions that might otherwise have been lost.

It was to Pinkerton that Walpole wrote his eloquent tribute to Madame de Sévigné, showing how she shone both in grief and gaiety, declaring that when her mind was full of any great event, 'she interests you with the warmth of a dramatic writer, not with the chilling impartiality of an historian.' He admired Voltaire (though with some qualifications, especially on the subject of Shakespeare) and Helvétius, but Rousseau he could never like: 'Take much affectation, and a little spice of frenzy, and you compose his personal character.' His view of Gibbon was cautious; he considered that the first volume of his history was 'so highly finished, that it resembled a rich piece of painting in enamel', but the second and third were inferior and the last volumes only 'medium, between the first and the two next'. He held Addison to be the master of grace, a quality he admired even above style, for style 'regards *expression, grace* . . . belongs to *manner*', and propounded the bizarre opinion that from his command of grace, especially in humour, Addison excelled all men that ever lived except for Shakespeare. On the subject of drama he compared Sheridan favourably to Congreve. 'Mr Sheridan,' he told Pinkerton, 'is one of the most perfect comic writers I know, and unites the most uncommon qualities—his plots are sufficiently deep, without the clumsy intanglement, the muddy profundity of Congreve—characters strictly in nature—wit without affectation.' His admiration for him was unstinting. 'What talents!' he concluded. 'The complete orator in the senate, or in Westminster Hall—and the excellent dramatist in the most difficult province of the drama.'

Walpole did not wish, in commending 'grace' to Pinkerton as a quality in the art of literary composition, to erect it into a capital ingredient of writing as though he were a disciple of Lord Chesterfield; it must be looked upon rather as a 'perfume that will preserve from putrefaction'. It was, in short, what might be termed the good manners of prose. His insistence upon this quality in writing was in line with his similar search for 'taste' in preference to mere pedantry where antiquarian studies were concerned. He had laboured this point with Cole, using his dispute with the Society of Antiquaries as a case in point. He was impatient with what he considered to be no more than arid research pursued for its own sake and not with some utilitarian motive in view, as though a gothic chantry or tomb had no value except as an inspiration for some contemporary design or artifact. 'The Antiquaries will be as ridiculous as they used to be,' he had assured Cole in 1778,

and, since it is impossible to infuse taste into them, they will be as dry and dull as their predecessors. One may revive what perished, but it will perish again, if more life is not breathed into it than it enjoyed originally. Facts, dates, and names will never please the multitude, unless there is some style and manner to recommend them, and unless some novelty is struck out from their appearance.

It was certainly not a theory to recommend itself to the abstract scholar, but at least Walpole could claim that his ideas on the subject were exemplified in almost every room at Strawberry Hill.

In the Biographical Sketch he prefaced to his two volumes of *Walpoliana*, John Pinkerton gives an engaging picture of Walpole's daily routine as he approached old age. He would rise about nine o'clock in the morning, his appearance in the breakfast room being heralded by the entrance of Tonton, the dog he had inherited from Madame du Deffand, by this time 'so fat that it could hardly move'. Here he would drink two or three cups of tea, sharing his bread-and-butter with the obese Tonton and the squirrels who would pop in through the open windows, quite tame and apparently in no awe of the presence of the lap-dog which was probably too lethargic to contest their portion of the spoils. His tea was drunk from 'rare and precious ancient porcelain of Japan, of a fine white embossed with large leaves'. The breakfast room was his 'constant and chosen apartment, with fine vistos towards the Thames'.

In it, among a mass of other pictures and prints, many having some reference to his various visits to France, hung portraits of some of his favourite women friends, in particular Carmantel's conversation-piece of Madame du Deffand and the Duchesse de Choiseul, one of the Countess of Ossory by 'Crayon' Hamilton, as well as of Lady Hervey, the old friend to whom he had dedicated the first volume of his *Anecdotes of Painting*. There was a Romney of Lady Craven, the vivacious authoress of *The Silver Tankard* and other plays, who was one of his younger friends, and there was a print of Diana Beauclerk's portrait-drawing of Georgiana, Duchess of Devonshire whom Walpole had proclaimed the empress of fashion. In this gallery of beauty and talent, one face from Walpole's distant past was lacking, the beautiful Marchesa Grifoni whom he had known and loved as a very young man in Florence. But Strawberry Hill, which found room for pictures of nearly all his friends, had not excluded her likeness from a place on its walls. It hung in Walpole's bedroom, a picture he had brought back with him from Italy, noted simply in the *Description* of his villa as 'a Florentine beauty'. It shared a place with portraits of his mother, his dog Patapan (that other companion of his time in Italy) and the two men who had chiefly influenced him in his early years, Conyers Middleton and John Chute.

At dinner, Pinkerton tells us, Walpole was a very moderate eater, taking a little chicken, pheasant or other light food. His drink was water, a decanter of which was placed near him under the table in a pail of ice. Wine was served to his guests, but Pinkerton saw Walpole drink it on one occasion only, when he took two glasses of white wine. This abstemiousness was lifelong but was now made necessary by his gout, which crippled him so much that when he went downstairs to dinner he had to be supported by his valet. Some years later, when well advanced into his seventies, Lord Glenbervie noted how he had grown so lame that he had to be carried in and out of the room 'but when seated was particularly cheerful and, as usual, full of anecdotes'.

After dinner, which at that time was served in the early afternoon, Walpole retired again to his sofa in the breakfast room or to the Gallery, where coffee was served. Here, Pinkerton recalled, he 'would sit till two o-clock in the morning, in marvellous chit-chat, full of singular anecdotes, strokes of wit, and acute observations, occasionally sending for books, or curiosities, or passing to the library, as any reference happened to arise in conversation.' If the weather was fine and a walk in the grounds was suggested, it was still his custom, as Cole had observed in earlier years, to go out in thin shoes even after a heavy dew, and without a hat. According to Pinkerton, this last habit derived from his first visit to Paris, presumably when on his Grand Tour. He had then been ashamed to see 'even little meagre Frenchmen, whom even he could have thrown down with a breath, walking without a hat', a custom he decided to follow. 'The first trial', we are told, 'cost him a slight fever, but he got over it, and never caught a cold afterwards.' He was, in fact, something of an enthusiast for fresh air, liking to have windows thrown open, and was quite impervious to the discomforts of draughts of cold air and damp rooms, a taste not always shared or appreciated by his guests. It must have seemed, however, a small price to pay for other more agreeable aspects of his company, especially those 'engaging manners, and the gentle, endearing affability to his friends' which Pinkerton declared, exceeded all praise. He was completely unconscious of rank and had the gift of dissipating any feelings of constraint in the company: 'his wit never gave the smallest wound even to the grossest ignorance of the world, or the most morbid hyperchondriac bashfulness'. This was Pinker-

ton's considered verdict, to which he added feelingly the Latin tag
experto crede: 'Believe me, I know.'

⤛ 2 ⤜

Though it was pleasant to receive the homage of intelligent and
talented young writers and poets, and even some who were not
noticeably talented but who made up for their lack of poetic
inspiration by their charm of manner and agreeable companionship, it was really more the company of women, rather than bright
young men, that Walpole most enjoyed and that most stimulated
his gifts as a letter-writer and raconteur. He had always sought out
the sympathetic female ear. As a young man he had pursued his
dowagers, those ageing women of the world, often former beauties,
whose fund of reminiscences he found an ample compensation for
their fading charms. Now, ageing himself and full of the stored
recollections of former days, there was nothing that delighted him
more than to discover some congenial young woman whom he could
regale with the accumulated memories of half a century and more.

The first in time and, until the last decade of his life, in affection of
these younger women to occupy a special place in his life was Anne
Liddell, who has already appeared many times in these pages under
the name by which she was known after her second marriage, as
Countess of Ossory. She was a contemporary of Edward Jerningham, being born in 1738, the only daughter of the first Lord
Ravensworth, and so was about twenty years Walpole's junior. Her
first marriage had been brilliant, but was doomed to failure almost
from the start. When only eighteen, she had become the wife of
Augustus Henry, third Duke of Grafton, who was a nephew by
marriage to Walpole's cousin Lord Hertford. Like many a *mariage
de convenance* (but by no means all) it was flawed from the beginning
by an almost total lack of compatibility. Walpole described the
duchess as being 'a woman of commanding figure though no regular
beauty, graceful, full of dignity and of art too, fond of admiration,
unbending to the Duke's temper', and the duke as a weak and
passionate man. He was reputed, at the time of his marriage, to be
already the father of some sixteen illegitimate children; and it was not
very long after it that he started the habit, humiliating to his wife's
pride, of appearing regularly in public with his mistress.

After only five years, the marriage was already nearing collapse. In May 1761, in an attempt to patch things up, the couple went on a trip to Italy. Walpole, who had long known the duke through political association as well as family connection, was by this time on very friendly terms with the duchess. Her disagreeable position as the neglected wife of an acknowledged rake naturally appealed to one who had once confessed to John Chute his partiality for the afflicted, the disgraced and the oppressed, but in this case his feelings for the duchess went somewhat deeper; in fact, it is not impossible to think that he was just a little in love with her. When the couple were about to visit Florence, he wrote to Mann announcing their arrival. The duchess he described as 'a passion of mine', she was 'one of the finest women you ever saw . . . she is one of our great ladies'. As for the duke, though a man of strict honour who wanted neither sense nor good breeding, he was 'not particularly familiar, not particularly good-humoured, nor at all particularly generous'. The Italian tour was only partially successful as a means of restoring matrimonial harmony; the duchess presented her husband in due course with another son but this did not prevent him from returning to his mistress when they were back in England again. In 1765, husband and wife agreed to separate, the duke, according to Walpole, having 'desired his relations and friends to treat her with the same respect as before, declaring he had no complaint against her but the disagreement of their tempers'.

They might have continued to live apart on fairly amicable terms more or less indefinitely had not the duchess herself fallen in love. When Walpole had paid his first visit to Madame du Deffand in September 1765, one of the other Englishmen he met at her house was the young Earl of Upper Ossory. He met him again there on more than one occasion, considering him the man he liked best in Paris, 'one of the most sensible young men I ever saw'. Back in England, he introduced the Duchess of Grafton to him, telling her that he would wonder much if she did not like him. Like him she certainly did, more, perhaps than Walpole had expected, for the earl was eight years her junior. After a while they became lovers, and the duchess some three years after her separation from the duke found herself in much the same predicament as Lady Diana Beauclerk, with a husband she despised and a lover whose child she was about to bring into the world.

When the duke heard of his wife's pregnancy, he began proceedings for divorce despite the fact that he was to be seen regularly at the opera with his current mistress Mrs Horton, otherwise known as Nancy Parsons, whose adventurous career Walpole later summed up when he dismissed her as 'the Duke of Grafton's Mrs. Horton, the Duke of Dorset's Mrs. Horton, everybody's Mrs. Horton'. The duke's flagrant conduct—he was the King's chief minister at the time—did nothing to save his wife from a good deal of criticism, however, and when the news of her situation became common knowledge in the summer of 1768 Lady Mary Coke, forgetting for a moment that her own marriage had been a total disaster, ending in separation, wrote censoriously in her journal of the unfortunate duchess: 'Tho' I never thought her Amiable, her pride, I fancy'd, wou'd have saved her from this disgrace, and tho' I saw she had the silly vanity of liking to be followed, I thought it nothing more than that, and not proceeding from a bad inclination; but it seems I was mistaken.' Lady Mary's view, so hard upon the wife and so oblivious of the conduct of the husband, was no doubt typical of what many gossiping tongues were saying, for at that time it was quite permissible for a man to have sixteen illegitimate children but fatal for a woman even to have one.

As the Duchess of Grafton, Anne Liddell had been accustomed to move in the highest reaches of the social and political life of the capital, even though her interests had not been deep, for her time was passed largely in minor gallantries and fairly heavy gambling. After her marriage to Lord Ossory, which took place three days after her divorce, all this came to an end. It was not so much a voluntary choice as an unavoidable consequence of her new situation. As a divorced woman she was banished from attendance at Court, and though the Court of King George III and Queen Charlotte was not the most scintillating place in the world, it was still the centre of social life. To be 'in society', it was necessary to appear from time to time in the royal drawing-room, especially on occasions like the sovereigns' birthdays. Even Horace Walpole would sometimes put on his Court dress and sword and hobble to St James's or the Queen's House to make his bow. Lady Ossory was too spirited a woman to wish to carry on a sort of second-class existence on the fringe of society having once so conspicuously occupied the centre of the stage, and decided, except for rare visits to London, to retire to her husband's estate at Ampthill, persuading Lord Ossory to abandon his political and military interests and share her exile. It was a brave decision, and the prospect of a pastoral life in Bedfordshire after all the glitter and excitement of London must have been daunting. The Duke of Queensberry, after visiting the couple at Ampthill, remarked to George Selwyn that they lived a dull life and there must be a great deal of love on both sides if they were not to tire of it.

It was to alleviate the tedium of this self-imposed exile that Walpole began to write bulletins of social gossip to his friend, depicting for her the scenes she was no longer able to frequent, keeping her up to date with all the latest intrigues, the balls people went to, the books they read and the plays they applauded as well as the scandals they whispered and the secrets they failed to keep. He presented her with a complete picture of the whole world of fashion as he saw it or as it was reported to him by his friends. The letters started in the autumn of 1769 and continued until his death, over 400 in all. They are among the most brilliant that he ever wrote, so much so, indeed, that they have gained for him the unmerited reputation of being, in Lytton Strachey's phrase, 'the most rapacious gossip who ever lived', a reputation that does little justice to his work when considered as a whole, as though there had been only a Lady Ossory to write to and no letters had ever been sent to Horace Mann, to General Conway, to William Mason, to Cole or to Gray; as though he had no opinions worth mentioning upon art or politics, upon literature or history, but was concerned only with 'a marriage or two, as many deaths, a housebreaking, and a murder—if they be novelties', as he once chronicled all that was 'new' in a letter to his secluded correspondent at Ampthill.

As a record of social life in London during the second half of the eighteenth century in the circles in which Walpole and his friends moved, the letters are incomparable. They do, of course, contain a great amount of gossip; they would not only be a good deal duller without it but, when all is said and done, gossip has a major part to play in the day-to-day affairs of any community, and the gossip of history is not the least interesting or the least significant part of it. But these letters also deal, with a much lighter and more delicate touch than in Walpole's *Memoirs*, with the stratagems of politicians and the rise and fall of British fortunes in the American War of Independence, though these issues never obtrude as a major theme but exist only as the background against which the comedy of life is played. More important as a subject of this correspondence, designed as it was to relieve the ennui of Lady Ossory's rustic retirement, are the brilliant little character sketches that enliven the pages, brief but telling portraits dashed off with vivid highlights of the people whom Lady Ossory had known in the days of her social splendour, or of new faces that made their first appearance on the scene after her retirement.

Thus, writing from Paris in August 1775, he describes the young Marie Antoinette, telling Lady Ossory 'it is impossible to see anything but the Queen! Hebes and Floras, and Helens and Graces, are street-walkers to her. She is a statue of beauty, when standing or sitting; grace itself when she moves . . . They say she does not dance in time, but then it is wrong to dance in time.' In July 1781, he gives her a glimpse of a Polish nobleman who has just visited London: 'Did your Ladyship hear of a Prince Sulkowski, who was lately in England? He was a competitor with the present King for the crown of Poland, is hideous, and covered with brilliants. George Selwyn said he had never before seen a monster set in diamonds.' Seeing Mrs Siddons act in November 1782, he records that 'she is a good figure, handsome enough, though neither nose nor chin according to the Greek standard, beyond which both advance a good deal. Her hair is either red, or she has no objection to its being thought so, and uses red powder.' Her acting, though 'proper', lacked in his estimation what he really wanted, which was 'originality, which announces genius, and without which I am never intrinsically pleased.' Sometimes a few words seem to give a complete picture, as in the case of Sir Blundel Carlton, 'as great a fool as the outset of his Christian name seemed to promise', or Dr Burney and his daughter Fanny who visited him at Strawberry Hill in September 1785: 'He is lively and agreeable; she half-and-half sense and modesty, which possesses her so entirely, that not a cranny is left for affectation or pretension.' Of Lady Juliana Penn, once mistress of an income of £36,000 a year and now reduced to a mere six hundred, he assures Lady Ossory 'her mind is so reconciled to her fortune that she is still very handsome'.

To these miniature sketches can be contrasted the much longer account that reached Ampthill in the autumn of 1788, describing two young ladies, sisters aged respectively twenty-four and twenty-five, who had recently made Walpole's acquaintance. As she read the glowing details, Lady Ossory must have realized that this was no ordinary encounter, but that her old friend had indeed just made a 'precious acquisition'. On 11 October he wrote from Strawberry Hill:

> It is the acquaintance of two young ladies of the name of Berry, whom I first saw last winter, and who accidentally took a house here with their father for this season. Their story is singular enough to entertain you. The grandfather, a Scot, had a large estate in his own country, £5000 a-year it is said; and a circumstance I shall tell you makes it probable. The eldest son married for love a woman with no fortune. The old man was enraged and would not see him. The wife died and left these two young ladies. Their grandfather wished for an heir male, and pressed the widower to remarry but could not prevail; the son declaring he would consecrate himself to his daughters and their education. The old man did not break with him again, but much worse, totally disinherited him and left all to his second son, who very handsomely gave up £800 a-year to his elder brother. Mr. Berry has since carried his two daughters for two or three years to France and Italy, and they are returned the best informed and the most perfect creatures I ever saw at their age. They are exceedingly sensible, entirely natural and unaffected, frank, and, being qualified to talk on any subject, nothing is so easy and agreeable as their conversation—nor more apposite than their answers and observations.

The letter continued with a long catalogue of the sisters' varied accomplishments. Mary, who even at this early stage in their relationship with Walpole emerges as his favourite, was 'a perfect Frenchwoman' in her language and also understood Latin. The other sister was a promising artist and had proved her worth by copying Lady Di Beauclerk's picture of gypsies which he had lent her, though it was the first time she had attempted colours. And their personal appearance? (which was surely what Lady Ossory wanted to know most of all):

> They are of pleasing figures, Mary, the eldest, sweet, with fine dark eyes, that are very lively when she speaks, with a symmetry of face that is the more interesting from being pale; Agnes, the younger,

has an agreeable sensible countenance, hardly to be called handsome, but almost. She is less animated than Mary, but seems out of deference to her sister to speak seldomer, for they doat on each other, and Mary is always praising her sister's talents.

It must have been more than clear to Lady Ossory that Walpole had been carried away by the charms of the Berry sisters for whom he could hardly find sufficient words of praise. 'In short,' he summed up, 'good sense, information, simplicity, and ease, characterise the Berrys; and this is not particularly mine, who am apt to be prejudiced, but the universal voice of all who know them.' They were, he finally assured Lady Ossory, 'two pearls that I found in my path'.

Not everyone, it should be pointed out, shared Walpole's opinion of the Berry sisters in quite so unreserved a spirit. Some people were to find the elder sister had grown a shade formidable a few years after her meeting with him. Lord Glenbervie would recall in his diary 'the eldest with her eagle eyes and manner—if not to *threaten* to *command*; Agnes more mild if less beautiful', and the first Earl of Dudley was to make the unkind comment that Mary 'has a loud, harsh voice, and is unacquainted with grammar', though this latter criticism is hardly borne out by her published writings. No one, however, denied that Mary was a woman of strong character and striking personality, and that Agnes, if always in her elder sister's shadow, was possessed of an equally admirable disposition. For Walpole, whatever others might say or think, they were perfection, and when they came to visit his printing press they were greeted with a set of complimentary verses that concluded its rehearsal of their virtues with the lines

> Still would his press their fame record,
> So amiable the pair is!
> But, ah! how vain to think *his* word
> Can add a straw to Berrys!

Walpole could not resist sending his little poetic offering to Ampthill for Lady Ossory to admire, but something of his old caution overtook him as he did so, for he begged her that it would go no further 'for trifles that *égayent* a little private society are

ridiculous if they get abroad, especially from a septuagenary
rhymer'.

❧❧ 3 ❦❦

The historian Edward Gibbon once acknowledged that he had drawn
a high prize in the lottery of life. If Walpole ever made a similar
reflection he must have admitted how singularly lucky he had been in
meeting the Berry sisters at just that particular point in his life when
their paths first crossed. He was growing old; an ageing bachelor, he
had neither wife, children nor grandchildren to comfort his declining
years. He was beginning to outlive his old friends and contemporaries, and in time would survive most of them except for Gilly
Williams and Lady Ailesbury. Though he had some close relatives of
a younger generation who were attached to him, in particular Mrs
Damer and the Duchess of Gloucester, daughter of his brother
Edward, their busy lives left them only with occasional moments to
devote to his company or concerns. How very fortunate, then, that
he should have met with these two young women who not only
appealed at once to his affections, but themselves delighted in his
society, were captivated by his anecdotes, and were entranced by
Strawberry Hill and all its multifarious contents.

It was perhaps also fortunate for Walpole with his morbid fear of
ridicule, that there were two sisters and not one, for as long as he
lavished his affectionate phrases upon both of them in equal shares he
was less likely to appear in the slightly absurd character of an elderly
swain dancing attendance upon a girl young enough to be his
daughter or indeed his granddaughter. It was in this dual way that he
concluded the first of his letters to them that has survived, dated
2 February 1789:

> I am afraid of protesting how much I delight in your society, lest I
> should seem to effect being gallant; but if two negatives make an
> affirmative, why may not two ridicules compose one piece of
> sense? and therefore, as I am in love with you both, I trust it is a
> proof of the good sense of your devoted H. Walpole.

Soon caution was thrown to the winds and he was calling them his
twin wives, happily writing that he was no less in love with his wife
Rachel than his wife Leah, and was amused rather than aghast when

the poem that his press had addressed to the two girls was unkindly
parodied in the lines:

> To sound your praise I dare not try.
>   My pen so prone to err is;
> I tremble while I write, lest I
>   Should add a goose to Berries.

The friendship continued to ripen during the winter of 1788 and
into the new year of 1789, bringing to Walpole a happiness he had not
known for many years. His conversations with the sisters carried his
mind back to the old days of Lady Suffolk and the vanished Court of
George II, and he began to compose his *Reminiscences written for the
Amusement of Miss Mary and Miss Agnes Berry*, based on the stories
he had told them during the long winter evenings. They were
introduced to General Conway and Lady Ailesbury; and Mrs
Damer, as has already been noted, found the fascinating Mary's
attractions quite as alluring as Walpole did, and would soon be
sending letters to her filled with warm declarations of affection: 'I
have not, it is true, been accustomed to the charm of real friendship,
but my own heart has taught me its value. Rest assured that, could
you know to what degree you contribute to the comfort, even the
repose of my mind, your utmost good nature would be more than
satisfied.' The two sisters seemed to have arrived in Twickenham like
the coming of spring, breaking hearts in all directions. And yet how
nearly had Walpole missed the chance of meeting them, for when
they first came to London, as he admitted in his letter to Lady
Ossory, he heard them praised so much that he 'concluded they
would be all pretension' and avoided an introduction. It was only on
the second occasion when they were at the same gathering and he
found himself sitting next to Mary that he discovered her to be 'an
angel both inside and out'. It was an opinion that he was never to
change.

In the summer of 1789 the Berry family went to Yorkshire to visit
friends and their absence brought home to Walpole just how much
their presence meant to him. 'How dismal was *Sunday* evening,
compared to those of last autumn!' he wrote to them when they had
gone, and returned again to the theme of his 'twin wives'. 'For my
part,' he assured them, 'I know that my affection has done nothing
but increase; though were there but one of you, I should be ashamed

of being so strongly attached at my age; being in love with both, I glory in my passion, and think it a proof of my sense.' Did it occur to him as his infatuation for the sisters, and in particular his love for Mary, continued to grow, that at the time he met them he was just the age that Madame du Deffand had been when she first met him? For now, in his seventies, he too was caught in the net of love; there was an irony in the situation that would have appealed to that cynical old heart in Paris had the future been disclosed to her.

In the autumn they were back, and Walpole settled down to enjoy their company again. While they were on their northern journey he had found a house for them at Teddington which they could take for the winter so that the agreeable evenings at Strawberry Hill could be resumed. 'I jumped for joy,' he had written, 'that is, my heart did, which is all the remain of me that is in statu jumpante, at the receipt of your letter this morning, which tells me you approve of the house at Teddington.' The next few months offered a prospect of complete content with no clouds on the horizon but those cast by occasional spasms of gout and the increasingly ominous news that reached England from across the Channel. It had been one of the topics of his letters to the Berrys while they had been in Yorkshire. 'All accounts agree,' he had written, 'in the violence of the mob against the inoffensive as well as against the objects of their resentment; and in the provinces, where even women are not safe in their houses.' After their return worse news was to be heard. 'Monsr. d'Olan, a worthy man, and nephew of my dear friend Mad. du Deffand, has been taken out of his bed, to which he was confined by the gout, at Avignon, and hanged by the mob!' he wrote to them on 25 July 1790. 'I have said for this year that I am happy she is dead; and now how much that reflection is fortified.' They were at Lymington when this letter reached them. How safe it seemed in comparison to the turmoils in France! 'Pray return . . . with blooming countenances: you must sit for your pictures before your long journey,' he told them.

The 'long journey' to which he referred was a new worry for him, made all the more acute by the troubled condition of Europe. Mr Berry, who seemed to have had an unshakeable belief in the educative propensity of foreign travel, be the state of the world what it may, had decided to take his daughters abroad again. It is true that his objective was Italy, at that moment still comparatively unaffected by the revolutionary virus, but in order to reach their destination they were to pass through France, and the prospect filled Walpole with horror. Not for nothing had he referred to the possible dangers that faced women even in the provinces; but his warnings and his perturbation were of no avail. On 11 October 1790, father and daughters set sail for Dieppe leaving their old friend in a state of high anxiety for their safety. 'In happy days I smiled and called you *my dear wives*,' he wrote the very day they left London, '*now*, I can only think of you as *darling children*, of whom I am bereaved!' Not until they were safely in Turin, he wrote sadly, would his anxiety subside and settle into a steady selfish sorrow.

Their journey to Italy, which lasted just over a year, was a heavy trial for him. In the happiness of their company he had had no need, as he now reflected in their absence, to remind himself that he was past seventy-three. His anxiety for their safety and hopes for their speedy return were mixed with some feelings of self-pity as he recorded his gratitude to them, his pride that they should have 'condescended' to spend so many hours with a very old man, while now 'these graces are lost to me, alas!, when I have no time to lose!' He looked forward eagerly to receiving their letters, trembled when they were delayed or failed to reach him on the expected date, conjuring up pictures of every imaginable disaster. At the beginning of November, he wrote from Park Place where he was staying with the Conways:

> No letter from Pougues! I think you can guess how uneasy I am! It is not the fault of the wind, which has blown from every quarter . . . What can have occasioned my receiving no letter from Lyons, when on the 18th of last month you were within twelve posts of it? I am now sorry I came hither, lest by my change of place a letter may have shuttlecocked about, and not have known where to find me.

Every detail of their health and welfare concerned him. 'You say nothing of your health,' he wrote to them in Florence, 'how are Miss Agnes's teeth? Don't omit such essential articles.'

When, in March, 1791, Mary Berry had a fall near Pisa and damaged her nose, he was again thrown into a state of panic:

> 'Oh! what a shocking accident! Oh! how I detest your going abroad more than I have done yet in my crossest mood! You

escaped the storm of the 10th October that gave me such an alarm; you passed unhurt thro' the cannibals of France and their republic of *larrons* and *poissardes*, who terrified me sufficiently; but I never expected that you would dash yourself to pieces at Pisa!

Mrs Damer, who had been in Portugal vying with Walpole in writing long letters to Mary Berry from Lisbon, heard the news on her way home at Paris, and also expressed her concern. 'I tried to persuade myself that I was less alarmed about your fall,' she told her friend, 'because I so plainly saw the care and pains you took to prevent my anxiety; but your image, pale and bleeding, has been continually before my eyes.' With Walpole fussing at Strawberry Hill and the sculptress all agitation in Paris there must have been moments when Mary Berry wished that she had kept the news of her little accident to herself.

Walpole could at least comfort himself with the thought that when they returned to England they would be living as near to him as possible. Little Strawberry Hill, or 'Cliveden' as he had called it when Kitty Clive had lived there, would become their home. He wrote eagerly during the summer to tell them that it would be ready in October, proposing that they should make their way to Twickenham directly they got back:

> your best way will be not to stop a moment in London, but to drive directly hither and stay all three with me till you can settle yourselves in Cliveden. This will not only be the most convenient to yourselves, but you are sure the most agreeable to me; and thus you will have time to unpack and arrange yourselves, without being broken in upon for some days by visits, nor expected to make them.

The idea that his dear Berrys would soon be his neighbours was his sole consolation when he learnt with renewed horror that their journey home would not only be delayed a month but would again take them through France, by the autumn of 1791 even more dangerous a place than it had been when they began their tour, and that they would be once more at the mercy of the republic of thieves and fishwives. They returned, however, unscathed, much to his relief and delight, eventually reaching London on 11 November; and it was there, and not at Strawberry Hill as he had at first suggested, that the long-awaited reunion took place.

The pleasure Walpole felt at the return of his young friends was sadly overshadowed in December 1791 by the death of the third Earl of Orford. Walpole's sadness was not so much at the thought of his nephew's death, for he had been a constant source of anxiety to him for many years and for the last period of his life had been insane, but rather at the prospect of succeeding himself to a title he had no wish to hold and to estates that had been depleted by long years of extravagance and mismanagement. Houghton, which had been the symbol of his father's power and magnificence, had become a neglected shell, despoiled of its great collection of pictures and allowed to fall into disrepair. Walpole could do no more than close down the great house, which he felt too old and dispirited even to visit, using such resources as remained in attempting to maintain what was left of the estate. As to being himself Earl of Orford, as he now became, it was a distinction at his time of life that appeared almost meaningless to him. 'My mistership, I believe, would have been very well if I could have preserved it,' he told Lady Ossory, 'but the Lordship and its train of troubles have half killed me,' and to John Pinkerton he wrote: 'Surely no man of seventy-four, unless superannuated, can have the smallest pleasure in sitting at home in his own room, as I almost always do, and being called by a new name.' To Mary Berry he dismissed his new honours in eight lines of verse:

An estate and an earldom at seventy-four!
Had I sought them or wish'd them, 'twould add one fear more,
That of making a countess when almost four-score.
But fortune, who scatters her gifts out of season,
Though unkind to my limbs, has still left me my reason;
And whether she lowers or lifts me, I'll try
In the plain simple style I have liv'd in, to die;
For ambition too humble, for meanness too high.

The way that Walpole could joke with Mary Berry on the subject of making a countess is surely the answer to those gossips who liked to whisper, after the Berrys had settled down at Little Strawberry Hill, that he had proposed marriage not only to Mary, but on her declining his offer, to Agnes as well. Everything we know about his attitude to love and marriage makes the notion absurd; but at least his niece, the Duchess of Gloucester, was sufficiently curious to ask him point blank whether he intended to marry Mary Berry or not—or so the diarist Charles Greville recorded many years after the event. Walpole was said to have replied, 'That is as Miss Berry herself pleases', a tactful enough answer; but from another entry in Greville's diaries it seems fairly certain that Walpole never made any matrimonial offer. Writing about Mary Berry after her death in 1852 in her ninetieth year, Greville recorded: 'I gathered from what she said that she never was herself quite sure whether he wished to marry her, but inclined to believe that she might have been his wife had she chosen it.' Furthermore, Mary herself, writing to a friend in 1793, showed that she had no wish to marry him and clearly had not been asked:

> And why should he? when, without ridicule or the trouble of a marriage, he enjoys almost as much of my society, and every comfort from it, that he could in the nearest connection? As the willing offering of a grateful and affectionate heart, the time and attentions I bestow upon him have hitherto given me pleasure. Were they to become a duty, and a duty to which the world would attribute interested motives, they would become irksome.

Mary Berry did, in fact, become engaged to be married in these years, but not to Horace Walpole. In the autumn of 1795, she met again a military officer whom she had known briefly in her earlier travels, and who was a friend and protégé of Field-Marshal Conway's. This was General Charles O'Hara, a bluff, red-faced Irishman who had recently been released after a period as a prisoner of war. They became engaged shortly before he went abroad again to take up his appointment as Governor of Gibraltar, but the whole business was kept a close secret, chiefly because Mary Berry had no wish to upset her father and sister who both relied upon her almost as much as Walpole did. Only Anne Damer was in the secret, nobly encouraging her friend and at the same time assuring her that the 'sympathizing bosom of some kindred being' was always within reach should the need arise. Walpole, who knew and liked O'Hara, was also kept in ignorance, though it appears from a note made by Mary Berry in 1807, long after the affair had floundered, that she did at one point gently hint to her old friend that she might in a few months be leaving him 'for a still dearer friend and a nearer connection'. How Walpole took this news, which must have disturbed him profoundly, is not recorded. Shortly afterwards various unhappy circumstances caused the engagement to be broken off. General O'Hara consoled himself with two mistresses, raising a family simultaneously by both of them, and the peace of Walpole's last years was not interrupted. Only Mary Berry was left with a wound from which she was never, to the end of her very long life, completely to recover.

✥ 4 ✥

In 1795 Walpole sat for his portrait for the last time. He was now in his seventy-eighth year and it was forty years since the young Swiss Johann Heinrich Müntz had drawn him, a slim and elegant figure, sitting by the window of his gothic library. Once again he had chosen a promising young artist, the twenty-six year-old Thomas Lawrence, who was later to be the most celebrated portrait painter of his generation. The drawing, which is little more than a sketch, portrays delicate, sensitive features, the eyebrows raised ironically, the hint of a smile on the lips. Though there is the faintest suggestion of world-weariness in the eyes it is, considering the age of the subject, a face still alert and vital that looks out at us with an amused curiosity, as though carefully assessing the posterity for whom he had always written and who would be the final judges of his work. After his death, Mary Berry gave a print of the drawing to Lord Glenbervie. It was, he wrote, 'a head, a mere outline, but the most striking likeness I ever saw, for the features and expression'.

Though age and illness were beginning to take an even heavier toll on his strength and energy, he still managed to keep in touch with his younger friends as well as those few who yet remained of his earlier circle. His sense of humour did not desert him. When Hannah More, whom he liked and admired even though he could not help occasionally mocking her more excessive moments of piety, sent him a book of her poems, he wrote saying that her kindness merited canonization. 'How I admire the activity of your zeal and perseverance,' he told her. 'Should a new church be built, I hope in a side chapel there will be an altar dedicated to St. Hannah, Virgin and Martyr; and that your pen, worn to the bone, will be enclosed in a golden reliquaire, and preserved on the shrine.' He showed his appreciation in more tangible form by sending her a copy of the Bible in three splendid morocco-bound volumes with a fulsome dedication acknowledging the comfort and relief her work had brought to 'numberless afflicted and distressed individuals'. But he was himself still too deeply rooted in the deistic principles he had learnt half a century before from Conyers Middleton to be moved by her evangelical zeal, nor would he have done more than smile gently at the thought she had expressed to her sister when describing his generous gift: 'Oh! that he would himself study that blessed book.'

Strawberry Hill continued to attract curious visitors, and in the early summer of 1795 he received a visit there from Queen Charlotte. The septuagenarian owner, conscious as he always was that he was one of the last representatives of *la vieille cour*, tottered out on his gouty feet to hand the queen out of her carriage only to discover, much to his mortification, that he had forgotten to put on his gloves. The queen showed a tactful disregard for this minor lapse of etiquette, if indeed she noticed it at all and, as Walpole wrote in one of his last letters to his cousin Henry Conway, 'She honoured me with her hand to lead her up the stairs'. Mrs Damer was fortunately there to share the burden with him, for he was kept on his feet for three whole hours while the royal party looked at his house and collection, but the visit was clearly a success. The queen was 'uncommonly condescending and gracious', and drank to his health before she left, leaving her host so overcome that he forgot his gloves again when he led her back to her coach as she took her leave.

As time went on and Walpole became less active, Strawberry Hill began to show signs of neglect. Margaret Young, his housekeeper for many years, had retired; his Swiss valet Philip was growing old and grumpy. Walpole was often confined to his room or very restricted in his movements. 'I am pinned to my couch,' he informed Lady Ossory in September 1796, 'and only move from one side of my room to the other, like a coat of arms, by two supporters.' He had all his life been such a frugal eater that he did not always remember that other people had larger appetites, and a greedy clergyman complained after dining with him that he had only been given mutton, which he detested, and had not been offered any cheese. The portraits of his friends looked down from the walls on gathering dust; outside the garden became a little desolate-looking from want of care, and the pinnacles of the roof, never very lasting constructions, showed evident signs of decay. Walpole himself was conscious that he had reached the winter of his life. 'I have very few leaves left, indeed, Madam,' he wrote to Lady Ossory, 'and feel how fast they fall.'

He was still interested in politics though it was now many years since he had taken any active part in the affairs of the country, and could write an account for Mary Berry of how the House of Commons had sat until half-past three in the morning debating the loan to the Austrian emperor in December 1796. But when Lady Ossory suggested that he should take his seat and speak in the House of Lords he refused, drawing a wry comparison between his own situation and John Singleton Copley's famous picture of the death of Chatham which had first been exhibited to the public some fifteen years before:

> You tell me it is my *duty* to go to the House and make a speech. Alas! I doubt, madam. Duty gleams but very dimly when one is on the threshold of four-score. Your other arguments strike me still more faintly: as I have none of the great abilities and renown of the late Lord Chatham, so I have none of the ambition of aping his death and tumbling down in the House of Lords, which I fear would scarce obtain for me a sixpenny print in a magazine from Mr. Copley.

His earldom had come too late in life to be much more than a slight embarrassment to him; as he had complained to Hannah More when he succeeded to the title, 'it is being called names in one's old age', and it was some time before he could bring himself even to use his new signature.

His last years were spent quietly and happily, the winter season in London, the summer at Strawberry Hill. Occasionally some irritation from the world outside his immediate circle disturbed his peace. When Kitty Clive had lived at Little Strawberry Hill, the press had not been able to resist the suggestion that they were lovers; now the similar proximity of the far from affluent Robert Berry and his two pretty daughters gave rise to snide hints that they were battening on a gullible and foolish old man. The report made Mary Berry both indignant and distressed. If a 'mean and interested world', she wrote angrily to Walpole, could put such an interpretation on their relationship, then indeed she and her family would have reason to regret 'the only circumstance in our lives that could be called fortunate'. The libel was too absurd to be entertained for long by any reasonable being and was not repeated. The proof of its falsehood, if any were needed, lay in the warm friendship that existed between Mary and Anne Damer who was known to be Walpole's most likely heir and who would have had most cause to resent the presence of the Berrys if there had been any sign of a mercenary interest in their friendship with him. Luckily no other disagreeable attacks of this sort occurred and the two households at Twickenham were left alone from any further attentions from journalists. Mary Berry was careful to keep her own private worries to herself, and the man she now looked upon as a second father remained apparently unaware of the sorrow her personal disappointments had brought on her.

As the year 1796 drew to a close, Walpole's state of health declined seriously and he made his last journey from Strawberry Hill to London. In the new year he grew worse, fever set in, and it was clear that he had not long to live. The end came early in March. Writing in his diary on 4 March, Lord Glenbervie noted:

> Lord Orford . . . died at his house in Berkeley Square the night before last. He had been from nearly the time I last saw him in a state of palsey, with a succession of imposthumes, and much pain, and a great imbecility or loss of memory, of which he was sensible, so that his condition was lamentable and his death a real relief to himself and his friends.

The 'imbecility', as Lord Glenbervie rather morbidly described Walpole's final decline, was later referred to by Mary Berry in an account she wrote of his last days:

> When not immediately suffering from pain, his mind was tranquil and cheerful. He was still capable of being amused, and of taking some part in conversation; but during the last weeks of his life, when fever was superadded to his other ills, his mind became subject to the cruel hallucination of supposing himself neglected and abandoned by the only persons to whom his memory clung, and whom he always desired to see. In vain they recalled to his recollection how recently they had left him, and how short had been their absence; it satisfied him for the moment but the same idea recurred as soon as he had lost sight of them. At last nature, sinking under the exhaustion of weakness, obliterated all ideas but

those of mere existence, which ended without a struggle on the second of March 1797.

Walpole, as fourth and last Earl of Orford, was buried in the little church in the park at Houghton, close to the shuttered and empty house. The dynasty that his father had founded came to an end in the direct line with his death. His long life had been spent almost entirely in or near London; in Norfolk he was virtually unknown except by reputation; and yet a great crowd gathered to see the funeral procession pass as the coffin made its way to join those of his father, brothers, and earlier ancestors in the family vault. He made his last journey as he would have wished, not as the celebrated dilettante, the connoisseur, the man of letters, but simply as Horace Walpole, youngest son of Sir Robert Walpole, Earl of Orford.

Three years after Walpole's death, the eighteenth century came to an end. The new century, in sharp reaction to so much that the old order had stood for, would have little time for so characteristic a representative of what Talleyrand had called *la douceur de vivre*. It could find little good to say about him. Just over twenty-five years after his death, Lord Liverpool was to write to John Wilson Croker:

> I believe Horace Walpole to have been as bad a man as ever lived; I cannot call him a violent party man, he had not virtue enough to be so; he was the most sensuous and selfish of mortals . . . I do not therefore look to any publication of any letters of his as likely to be of much service to history, and think they will rather mislead than instruct the rising generation.

Croker concurred absolutely with Lord Liverpool's view, replying:

> I entirely agree in your Lordship's opinion of Horace Walpole, there never lived a more selfish man; a more factious politician, a more calumnious writer . . . and I have no hesitation in saying that his *Memoirs* and letters, already voluminous, and of which I know that a great deal more is forthcoming, have given and will give a most false colour to the transactions and characters of his day.

Even some of those who could recall him tended to belittle his memory as the years went by. On 23 October 1842, Charles Greville wrote in his diary:

> Yesterday morning I called on Mr. Grenville, and sat with him for

an hour, while he told me many old stories of bygone times . . . He had often dined with Horace Walpole at his grandmother's in Grosvenor Square (before it was planted) and he describes him as effeminate in person, trifling in conversation, and much less amusing and piquant than might be expected from his letters.

All this was in line with the caricature that Macaulay had drawn in 1833 which had by now become the accepted point of view. As the nineteenth century advanced there seemed little to indicate that a rehabilitation would ever come about; there appeared to be no place for Strawberry Hill and all that it stood for in an age that prized above everything the quality of 'manliness' and had discovered muscular Christianity. For a while it looked as though Walpole's dream of addressing posterity from beyond the tomb might never be fulfilled, or if fulfilled that his message would be rejected as shallow and frivolous, utterly unacceptable to an age that was all earnestness and high moral purpose. What could they make of one who, as it seemed to them, was so evidently lacking in seriousness?

With the beginning of the twentieth century new and more complete editions of Walpole's correspondence began to appear and the whole sweep of his accomplishment as a letter-writer and chronicler of his age could be appreciated for the first time. The breadth of his vision, the extent of his interest and the depth of his humanity were revealed more thoroughly than ever before and a new assessment of his achievement began to take place. He was seen, if nothing else, to be one of the greatest letter-writers in the English language, indeed in any language; someone who could be spoken of in the same breath as his own revered Madame de Sévigné. Lytton Strachey wrote of his correspondence: 'the vast period of time which they cover, the immense variety of topics with which they deal, the sustained brilliancy of their execution, give these famous letters a position of pre-eminence unrivalled in English literature, and only paralleled by the letters of Voltaire in the literature of the world.' The days when Walpole's character could be dismissed as simply bad and his life's work as no more than trifling were over, Lord Liverpool's opinion of him was seen to be as absurd as Croker's, and no one would write again, as Macaulay had once written, that 'there is indeed scarcely any writer in whose works it would be possible to find so many contradictory judgments, so many sentences of extravagant nonsense.' It was at last recognized that Walpole was before all else an artist, and that his works must be judged by artistic standards. He was, Virginia Woolf declared, 'not only the wittiest of men, but the most observant and not the least kindly. And among the writers of English prose he wears forever and with a peculiar grace a coronet of his own earning.' It was a verdict which the man who so reluctantly succeeded to the earldom of Orford would have accepted gladly as his epitaph.

Bibliography

Ayling, S., *George the Third*. London, 1972.

Balderston, K. C. (ed.), *Thraliana: The Diary of Mrs Hester Lynch Thrale (later Mrs Piozzi) 1776–1809*, 2 vols. Oxford, 1942

Bettany, L., *Edward Jerningham and his Friends*. London, 1919.

Beresford, J. (ed.), *Letters of Thomas Gray*. Oxford, 1951.

Blyth, H., *Old Q, the Rake of Piccadilly*. London, 1967.

Buchan, S., *Lady Louisa Stuart, Her Memories and Portraits*. London, 1932.

Cecil, D., *Two Quiet Lives*. London, 1948.

Chute, C. W., *A History of The Vyne in Hampshire*. Winchester, 1888.

Clark, K., *The Gothic Revival*. London, 1928.

Coke, M., *The Letters and Journals of Lady Mary Coke* (ed. J. A. Home), 4 vols. Bath, 1970.

Cole, W., *The Blecheley Diary of the Rev. William Cole, 1765–67*, edited from the original MS in the British Museum by F. G. Stokes. London, 1931.

Cole, W., *A Journal of my Journey to Paris in the year 1765* (ed. F. G. Stokes). London, 1931.

Davis, T., *The Gothic Taste*. Newton Abbot, 1974.

Dobson, A., *Horace Walpole, A Memoir* (Revised and enlarged by Paget Toynbee). Oxford, 1927.

Draper, M. P. G. and Eden, W. A., *Marble Hill House and its Owners*. London, 1970.

Erskine, S., *Lady Diana Beauclerk, Her Life and Work*. London, 1903.

Evans, J., *A History of the Society of Antiquaries*. Oxford, 1956.

Farington, J., *The Farington Diaries*, 8 vols. London, 1921–7.

Fitzgerald, P., *The Life of Mrs Catherine Clive with an account of her adventures on and off the Stage*. London, 1888.

Glenbervie, Lord, *The Diaries of Sylvester Douglas, Lord Glen-bervie* (ed. F. Bickley), 2 vols. London, 1928

Gosse, E., *Gray*. London, 1882.

Gwynn, S., *The Life of Horace Walpole*. London, 1934.

Havens, M. A., *Horace Walpole and the Strawberry Hill Press, 1757–1789*. Canton, Pennsylvania, 1901.

Hawkins, L. M., *Anecdotes, Biographical Sketches and Memoirs*, vol. 1. London, 1822.

Hermann, F., *The English as Collectors: A Documentary Chresto-mathy*. London, 1972.

Hibbert, C., *The Grand Tour*. London, 1969.

Historical Manuscripts Commission: Fifteenth Report, Appendix, Part VI, *The Manuscripts of the Earl of Carlisle preserved at Castle Howard*. London, 1897.

Hodgart, M. (ed.), *Horace Walpole: Memoirs and Portraits*. London, 1963.

Hudson, D., *Sir Joshua Reynolds, A Personal Study*. London, 1958.

Hussey, C., *The Picturesque: Studies in a Point of View*. London, 1927.

Jesse, J. H., *George Selwyn and his Contemporaries*, 4 vols. London, 1882.

Johnson, S., *Lives of the English Poets*, vol. 2 (*Life of Thomas Gray*). London, 1942.

Judd, G. P., *Horace Walpole's Memoirs*. London, 1960.

Kerr, S. P., *George Selwyn and the Wits*. London, 1909.

Ketton-Cremer, R. W., *Thomas Gray, A Biography*. Cambridge, 1955.

Ketton-Cremer, R. W., *Horace Walpole, A Biography*. London, 1946.

Koven, A. de, *Horace Walpole and Madame du Deffand: An Eighteenth Century Friendship*. New York, 1929.

Lees-Milne, J., *Earls of Creation, Five Great Patrons of Eighteenth-Century Art*. London, 1962.

Lewis, L., *Connoisseurs and Secret Agents in Eighteenth Century Rome*. London, 1961.

Lewis, T., *Extracts from the Journals and Correspondence of Miss Berry*, 3 vols. London, 1865.

Lewis, W. S. *Horace Walpole*. The A. W. Mellon Lectures in the Fine Arts, 1960. London, 1961.

Lewis, W. S., *Rescuing Horace Walpole*. New Haven, 1978.

Lewis, W. S., *A Guide to the Life of Horace Walpole*. New Haven, 1973.

Lewis, W. S., *Horace Walpole's Letter from Madame de Sévigné*. Farmington, Conn., 1933.

Lewis, W. S., *Horace Walpole's Library*. The Sandars Lectures, 1957. Cambridge, 1958.

Lewis, W. S., *Collector's Progress*. London, 1952.

Lewis, W. S. (ed.) *Horace Walpole's Fugitive Verses*. Miscellaneous Antiquities, no. 5. New York/London, 1931.

Lucas, F. L., *The Art of Living: Four Eighteenth-Century Minds*. London, 1959.

Macaulay, Lord, *Literary Essays*. Oxford, 1932.

Mason, A. B., *Horace Walpole's England as his letters picture it*. London, 1930.

Melville, L., *The Berry Papers, being the Correspondence hitherto unpublished of Mary and Agnes Berry (1763–1852)*. London, 1914.

Melville, L., *Horace Walpole, a Biographical Study*. London, 1930.

Nicolson, H., *The Age of Reason (1700–1798)*. London, 1960.

Noble, P., *Anne Seymour Damer, A Woman of Art and Fashion, 1748–1828*. London, 1908.

Palmer, W. M., *William Cole of Milton*. Cambridge, 1935.

Pinkerton, J., *Walpoliana*, 2 vols. London, 1799.

Pool, B. (ed.) *The Croker Papers, 1808–1857*. London, 1967.

Praz, M., *The Romantic Agony*. Oxford, 1970.

Quennell, P., *Alexander Pope, the Education of Genius, 1688–1727*. London, 1968.

Quennell, P., *Romantic England, Writing and Painting, 1717–1851*. London, 1970.

Quennell, P., *Samuel Johnson, his Friends and Enemies*. London, 1972.

Roscoe, E. S. and Clergue, H., *George Selwyn, his Letters and his Life*. London, 1899.

Russell, C., *Three Generations of Fascinating Women and other Sketches from Family History*. London, 1904.

Sedgwick, R. (ed.), *Lord Hervey's Memoirs*. London, 1952.

Seeley, L. B., *Horace Walpole and his World*. London, 1895.

Sells, A. L., *Thomas Gray, His Life and Works*. London, 1980.

Sieveking, I. G., *The Memoir of Sir Horace Mann*. London, 1912.

Smith, W. H., *Originals Abroad, The Foreign Careers of some Eighteenth-Century Britons.* Yale, 1952.

Smith, W. H. (ed.) *Horace Walpole, Writer, Politician, and Connoisseur, Essays on the 250th Anniversary of Walpole's Birth.* Yale, 1967.

Steegman, J., *The Rule of Taste from George I to George IV.* London, 1936.

Strachey, L., *Biographical Essays.* London, 1948.

Strachey, L., *Literary Essays.* London, 1948.

Stuart, D. M., *Horace Walpole*, English Men of Letters Series. London, 1927.

Stuart, L., *Lady Louisa Stuart: Selections from her Manuscripts* (ed. J. A. Home). Edinburgh, 1899.

Stuart, L., *Notes by Lady Louisa Stuart on George Selwyn and his Contemporaries* (ed. W. S. Lewis). New York, 1928.

Toynbee, Paget, *The Correspondence of Gray, Walpole, West and Ashton (1734–1771)*, 2 vols. Oxford, 1915.

Trench, C. Chenevix, *George II*. London, 1973.

Walpole, H., *Correspondence* (various editions).

Walpole, H., *The Works of Horace Walpole, Earl of Orford*, 5 vols. London, 1798.

Warburton, E., *Memoirs of Horace Walpole and His Contemporaries*, 2 vols. London, 1851.

White, T. H., *The Age of Scandal, an Excursion through a Minor Period.* London, 1950.

Articles and Monographs

Adams, C. K., and Lewis, W. S., 'The Portraits of Horace Walpole', *Walpole Society*, vol. XLII, 1970.

Crook, J. M., 'Strawberry Hill Revisited', *Country Life*, vol. CLIV, nos. 3963–5, June, 1973.

Doyle, J., *Strawberry Hill*, Reigate, 1972.

Gooch, G. P., 'Four French Salons', *Catherine the Great and Other Studies*, pp. 109–98. London, 1954.

Honour, H., 'Horace Walpole', *Writers and their Work*, no. 92. London, 1957.

Hussey, C., 'Strawberry Hill, Middlesex', in C. Hussey (ed.), *English Country Houses, Early Georgian 1715–1760*, pp. 213–18. Rev. edn, London, 1965.

Lees-Milne, J., 'John Chute at the Vyne, Hampshire', *Connoisseur*, vol. CXLV, pp. 47–51. June, 1960.

Lewis, W. S., 'The Genesis of Strawberry Hill', *Metropolitan Museum Studies*, vol. 5, Part One, pp. 57–92. New York, 1934.

Lewis, W. S., 'Horace Walpole, Antiquary', *Essays Presented to Sir Lewis Namier*, pp. 178–203. London, 1956.

McCarthy, M., 'John Chute's Drawings for the Vyne', *The National Trust Year Book 1975–76*.

Praz, M., Introductory Essay to *Three Gothic Novels*. London, 1968.

Toynbee, P., 'Horace Walpole's Journals of Visits to Country Seats', *Walpole Society*, vol. XVI. 1928.

Varma, D. P., Introduction to *The Castle of Otranto*. London, 1976.

Index